CANADA AND KOREA
PERSPECTIVES 2000

Edited by
R.W.L. GUISSO
YOUNG-SIK YOO

Cover Photos

1. Canadian Flag and Maple Leaf
2. Korean Flag and the Rose of Sharon
3. The first known record of a Korean mentioning "Canada" in Yu Kil-chun's *Sôyukyônmun (Observations on a Journey to the Western World) (1895).* See pp. 25-26.
4. Parliament Building, Ottawa, Canada
5. The National Assembly Building, Seoul, Korea
6. Canadian missionaries with Koreans (1903), Wônsan, present-day North Korea. *Courtesy of Margaret Farrow*
7. Kim Il-whan's diary, the first Korean student who arrived at Victoria, British Columbia (1905). *Courtesy of Margaret Farrow.* See p. 29.
8. Yun Chi-ho (1934). *Courtesy of Pak So-in.* See p. 26.
9. Yun Chi-ho (1890). From: *Yun Chi-ho ilgi*
10. James Scarth Gale (1888), the first Canadian to arrive in Korea in 1888 *Courtesy of Margaret Farrow.* See pp. 10-12.
11. James Scarth Gale (1934) *Courtesy of Margaret Farrow*
12. Canadian POWs repatriated to South Korea (August 25, 1953) Len Badowich (in middle). *Courtesy of Ted Barris.*

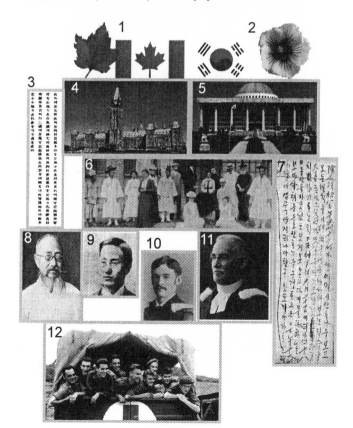

National Library of Canada Cataloguing in Publication Data
Main entry under title:
CANADA AND KOREA: PERSPECTIVES 2000

Papers originally presented at the conference "Canada and Korea:
    Into the New Millennium," held at the University of Toronto,
    May 12-13, 2000.
Includes bibliographical references.
ISBN 0-7727-7450-1

1. Canada--Relations--Korea--Congresses. 2. Korea--
Relations--Canada--Congresses. I. Guisso, R.W.L. II. Yoo, Y.S.
III. University of Toronto, Deptartment of East Asian Studies.

FC251.K67C35 2001   303.48'2710519   C2001-902588-2
F1029.5.K67C35 2001

Published by the Centre for Korean Studies, University of Toronto

Produced and distributed in Canada by:
Westward&Associates
Toronto, Ontario, Canada
Email: mikewestward@canada.com

Seoul Office:
The Association for Korea-Canada Cultural Exchange
Jinheung Building #503
104-8 Shinsol-dong Tongdaemun-gu
Seoul, Korea
Tel.: (02) 2233-4063
Fax: (02) 2235-3881
Email: koreacanada@email.com

Printed and bound in Canada by the University of Toronto Press.

ACKNOWLEDGMENTS

In May 2000, The Department of East Asian Studies in the University of Toronto hosted an international conference called "Canada and Korea: Into the New Millennium." The year 2000 was the 50th anniversary of the Korean War, and the university commemorated Canada's involvement in that "forgotten war" by hosting a month-long photo exhibition at Robarts Library, UofT. In both of these events, a great number of people, and several institutions were involved; their assistance, encouragement, generous contribution of their time, and monetary support made the events successful. With the publication of this conference volume it is our pleasure to be able to thank them publicly.

We owe a special debt to the Toronto-based Foundation for the Support of Korean Studies at the University of Toronto, which has supported the Korean Studies Programme since its inception in 1979, and the Seoul-based Korea Foundation. Both of these institutions offered generous financial support to the conference and the publication of this volume.

We would also like to thank the University of Toronto's Connaught International Symposia, which generously provided partial funding for the conference, as did the University of Toronto-York University Joint Centre for Asia Pacific Studies, Mr. Chang-Bok Lee of Pan Asia Food Co. Ltd., Dr. Chai-shin Yu of The Society for Korean and Related Studies in Toronto, and the Seoul-based Association for Korea-Canada Cultural Exchange.

A month-long photo exhibition on the 50th Anniversary of the Korean War at Robarts Library, in fact, was a result of cooperation among various devoted people and institutions. We owe a debt to Ms. Carol Moore, the University of Toronto's Chief Librarian, who kindly provided us with exhibition space in the library, and along with her staff, Mr. Gayle Garlock, Director, Development and Public Affairs, and Ms. Gabriela Bravo, Public Affairs and Patron Relations, participated in the opening reception and gave us professional support and friendly guidance throughout. A great number of artifacts, historic photographs and other war-related memorabilia were brought in for the exhibition. We owe special thanks to Mr. Moon-Ik Chang, Director, Korean Culture and Information Service at the Korean Embassy in Ottawa, whose efforts made it possible to bring a great number of photographs of the Korean War through The Korean Information Service in Korea, and for his financial support toward the publication as well.

We would also like to thank Mr. Heung-Shin Park, Minister at the Korean Embassy in Ottawa, Daniel J. Glenney, and Mike Miller of The Canadian War Museum in Ottawa, Peter Dixon of the Haida Naval Museum in Toronto, the Korean Veterans Association, the Toronto-based Advisory Council on

Democratic and Peaceful Unification of Korea, Mr. Ted Zuber who kindly loaned his own paintings of the war scene in Korea during the fifties. Mr. Bang-hyun Yoon, Mr. Byung-yuk Cho of the Council of Korean Unification Culture and Sang-oak Sim of P.G.S. International Consulting Inc. The Korean Consulate-General in Toronto was most helpful with advice and cooperation in preparing the exhibition. We thank the then-Consulate General, Dae-Won Park and Consul Hyoung-Oen Shin.

We would also like to thank Tae-Kyong Park, Ji-Il Tark, and Mike Westward who devoted their time to both the conference and the exhibition; Philip Yoo who attended to the matters of detail, as did Ms. Celia Sevilla of the East Asian Studies Department , who handled many of her arrangements on top of her routinely busy duties.

Finally, we would like to say a sincere thank you to Consul General, Sook Kim and Consul Yeon-Chul Yoo of the Korean Consulate General in Toronto whose support enabled us to cover the last mile in the publication of this volume.

R.G.
Y.Y.
September, 2001

CONTENTS

CONTENTS

INTRODUCTION

This volume is the result of a conference held at the University of Toronto on May 12-13, 2000, called "Canada and Korea: Into the New Millennium." The Conference was held in conjunction with an exhibition of historic photographs and other memorabilia which marked the fiftieth anniversary of the outbreak of the Korean War.

In that war, Canada, as part of the United Nations force, sent 26,971 military personnel to the Korean peninsula, and of the 516 who lost their lives in the conflict, 378 lie buried in the United Nations Memorial Cemetery near Pusan. Tragic though this conflict was, it brought home to Canada and Canadians the reality of Korea at a time when terms like "the Far East" and "East Asia" meant little more to Canadians than China, Hong Kong and Japan.

The war also marked Canada's entry onto the international stage, and the starting-point of what would be a growing interest in the Asia-Pacific region over the next half-century.

In spite of the Canadian contribution to the U.N. force, which on a per-capita basis, ranked among the highest, Canadian veterans of the Korean War have received scant respect from their own government in Ottawa, and the lack of public memory has inspired more than one recent historian to speak of the conflict as "Canada's Forgotten War".

In a similar vein, we might also refer to Canada's relationship with Korea as the "Forgotten Relationship".

Few Canadians today are aware that it was one of their compatriots, the Rev. James S. Gale, whose Korean-English Dictionary created the first and most essential tool for the scholarly study of Korea in the West; and whose translation of the Bible into the Korean language constituted the foundation of Korean Christianity today. Other Canadians are known to all educated Koreans. Dr. Oliver Avison, personal physician to King Kojong, is considered the founder of modern medical knowledge in Korea; and Dr. Frank Schofield, another Canadian, was so prominent in the fight for Korean independence in the early twentieth-century, that he is the only non-Korean buried in the Patriots' Plot in the Seoul National Cemetery.

How many Canadians, we wonder, are aware that in the last few years, Canada has surpassed the United States as the most-favoured destination of Korean emigrants; or that Korea and Canada rank among each others' top-ten trading partners?

The relationship between Korea and Canada seems poised to grow closer, and with it, the demand for a greater knowledge on both parts of the "Other".

In Canada, the study of Korea as a sub-field of Asian Studies, is relatively new. The first courses in Korean language, history and culture appeared in 1977 at the University of Toronto, and shortly thereafter at the University of British Columbia. Canadian Studies were virtually unknown in Korea until the 1990s when the Association for Canadian Studies was created, and the first hesitant steps were taken to inject Canadian history and culture into the curricula of some Korean universities.

In Korea, Canada is widely perceived as a safe, prosperous and multi-cultural society. It is also seen as a snowbound land, home to Banff and Niagara Falls, rich in natural resources; but a largely unknown entity, and less worthy of study than the United States or Europe.

This volume is an attempt to address perceptions.

As is the case with any conference volume, it is necessarily impression-istic, and seeks not to be comprehensive, but to reflect on some aspects of the historical relationship between Korea and Canada. It deals with the Korean War, current economic ties between Canada and the ROK, and in the Foreword and Afterword, with some thoughts by veteran observers on the future of relations between Canada and the ROK after the establishment of formal ties between Canada and the Democratic People's Republic of Korea.

Each article in the volume addresses the Korea-Canada relationship.

The Foreword, by Ms. Margaret Huber, Director-General, North Asia and Pacific Bureau Department of Foreign Affairs and International Trade, is her opening address to the Conference. In it, she emphasizes the common concerns of Canada and the ROK with regional security and with the humanitarian, commercial and economic challenges presented by the DPRK. She sees Canada's future role as a middle power as one which will enrich the current relationship with the ROK while further engaging the DPRK through a broadening of the inter-governmental dialogue.

The first article by Young-sik Yoo of the University of Toronto, reviews the "shared" history of Canada and Korea from the arrival in 1888 of the Rev. J. S. Gale and the almost 200 Canadians who arrived in subsequent years to play a role not only in spreading the Christian gospel, but in modernizing the peninsula. He tells us of the first Korean impressions of Canada ("a possession of England"), and documents the post-war shifts in perception. His article makes clear that ties between Canada and the ROK grew rapidly during the 1990s.

Hamish Ion of the Royal Military College, uses a careful case-study of a missionary station on the Manchurian border to reveal the involvement of Canadian missionaries and their Korean converts in anti-Japanese activity during the colonial period. Ion is interested in whether Korean nationalism or Christianity was more important in explaining attitudes and actions in

Lungchingtsun, and in how the missionaries attempted to walk a tightrope between Japanese imperialism and Korean nationalism. His account of this struggle shows both the strength and weakness of a missionary movement under duress.

Turning to the Korean War of 1950-1953, Ted Barris, author of *Deadlock in Korea*, puts a human face on Canadian engagement with Korea with his interviews with veterans of that conflict, and suggests reasons why he calls it the "Forgotten War". Greg Donaghy of the Department of Foreign Affairs and International Trade, places Canadian participation in the war in a wider context; that of Canadian diplomacy. He documents the gradual shift of Canada's attention from the North Atlantic to the Pacific region, and at the same time, he shows that Canada exhibited a surprisingly high degree of independence from the American view both on the conduct of the war and the disposition of the peace. Yong-pyo Hong, of Hanyang University, focuses closely on diplomacy of another sort: the efforts of Syngman Rhee to ensure that the war was prosecuted in such a way as to best serve the interests of the South, and more particularly, on his struggle after the armistice, to extract a bilateral pact from the United States which would guarantee the future security of the Republic of Korea. Hong's article portrays Rhee as a far more competent diplomat than previous studies might indicate.

Eugene Lee of Sookmyung University also writes about diplomacy, juxtaposing the Canadian policy of "constructive engagement" with the Communist regimes in China and Cuba with that of non-engagement with the DPRK. He wonders why it was, that for almost five decades, North Korea was not treated in the same way as these other two. His conclusion is hardly startling; but he makes a compelling case that economic considerations took precedence over both legal and moral consistency. What also becomes clear is that the reluctance of the DPRK to seek international recognition made the issue a very low priority for Canada.

The next two papers in the volume look in more detail at the economic relations between Canada and South Korea, and provide an interesting counterpoint to E. Lee's views. J. D. Han of the University of Western Ontario examines bilateral trade between the ROK and Canada since the early 1980s, and looks more particularly at the fluctuations in Canadian imports from Korea which have caused some dispute in recent years due to differing perspectives on the fairness of the trading relationship. Han uses statistical data both from Korea and Canada to assess the conflicting viewpoints, and concludes that both sides are partly right. He also looks at the role of NAFTA in Canada's foreign trade profile, especially as it impacts upon Korean trade.

Joung-yong Lee, of Inha University, amplifies the views of his colleague, exploring Canada-Korea trade within such contexts of the emergence of regional blocs, new forms of competition both from developing countries like China and resource-rich countries like Australia. He makes a persuasive case that both Canada and Korea would be well-advised to intensify their Research and Development spending and upgrade technology both in manufacturing and the knowledge-based sector. He also foresees a natural match between Korean manufacturing skills and Canadian technology which might well generate a leading-edge source of exports into Asian markets.

The final three papers are somewhat disparate in content but closely centered on Korean-Canadian comparisons. Moonchul Chang, of the National Police University, looks at comparative arbitration systems in settling domestic and international trade disputes, pointing out that Canada was the first country to adopt the UNCITRAL model Arbitration Law in 1986. The Republic of Korea replaced its older German-influenced system by adopting the UNCITRAL Law in 1999. Prof. Chang suggests that the Canadian experience and the body of case law developed by Canadian courts could provide useful lessons as the ROK begins to apply the law. Simon Young-suk Moon, of Kangnam University, is concerned with the question of how nations preserve cultural identity as they are faced with the onslaught of American popular culture across the globe. He focuses on Hollywood's domination of the film market in both Korea and Canada. In this instance, Canada's longer and closer experience in resisting U.S. pressures, he suggests, might offer some guidance to the lively film industry in Korea as it attempts to meet the American challenge.

The final article, by Sung-il Lee of Yonsei University, offers reflections on the universal poetic themes of time and change as they are expressed in an ancient culture like that of Korea, and in a young country like Canada. As well as presenting in his article his own elegant translations, he emphasizes the similarities in Canadian and Korean poetic visions concerned with the precariousness of human affairs, the unchanging spirit which infuses phenomenal nature, and the acceptance of mutability.

Mr. Donald S. Rickerd, a leading commentator on Asia-Pacific Affairs provides an Afterword to the volume. As an experienced observer who has visited both North and South Korea in an official capacity, he is ideally placed to reflect on the present state of the Democratic People's Republic of Korea, and on its future. In the wake of the establishment of diplomatic relations between Pyongyang and Ottawa in the spring of 2001, his reflections are worthy of note.

R.W.L.G.
Toronto
August, 2001.

Foreword
New Horizons In Canada's Relations with Korea

Margaret Huber
Director-General, North Asia and Pacific Bureau
Department Of Foreign Affairs and International Trade

We are proud that a Canadian, Dr. Oliver Avison (1860-1956), arrived with his family in Pusan in 1893 and became one of two personal physicians to the last of the Chosun Kings, King Kojong. Avison is considered by many to be the founder of modern medicine and of medical education in Korea. We are proud that another Canadian, Dr. Francis Schofield was so committed to the struggle for Korean independence in the early 20th century that he is the only foreigner honoured by burial in the Plot of Patriots in Seoul's National Cemetery. But those were simpler times. Now - as we stand at the dawn of the 21st Century - I want to share with you some of the new directions and new horizons in Canada's relations with the Koreas, both South and North.

Recent Korean Developments

This is an exciting time for those of us who are actively involved in Canada-Korea relations. The South Korean economy is firmly back on track. Last year the economy of South Korea returned to double digit growth, demonstrating that it has weathered the Asian financial crisis. From a negative growth of -5.8% in 1998, the economy registered +10.2% growth in 1999. At the onset of the financial crisis, South Korea's foreign exchange reserves were under US$4 billion. Today, they stand at US$85 billion, and are rising. The current account surplus for the past two years was US$65 billion. And Seoul has repaid all the credits which the IMF extended to it at the time of the 1997 bail-out. No one can doubt that this represents full recovery.

In 1999, South Korea attracted US$15.5 billion in foreign investment, a large chunk of which was Canadian. Its trade surplus that year was US$24 billion. At 6.3%, the unemployment rate remains high by Korean standards, but is much lower than during the recent financial crisis. Interest rates are stable. The stock market is buoyant, albeit somewhat volatile. The fully-computerized Korea Stock Exchange handles 1.6 million orders each day, and boasts an overall rate of return of 83%.

On a lighter note:

- Seoul's traffic is back to its normal congestion;
- 50,000 young Koreans visited Canada last year, according to official South Korean statistics, for language study;
- Korean credit card use overseas was up nearly 70% in the third quarter of 1999 over the same period in 1998;
- imported wine sales are up by 85% and domestic car sales are up by 133%.

Accompanying these developments, prices increased a mere 0.8% in 1999. This, indeed, is full recovery.

President Kim Dae-jung's government has been pressing ahead with economic restructuring, even though implementation is always painful and time consuming. Elections to South Korea's National Assembly elections were held last month, confirming that democratic traditions have firmly taken root and are flourishing in South Korea. Some analysts believe that the strong opposition showing could imperil the President's economic reform program. I believe, however, that such a conclusion is premature. President Kim has made clear his intention to proceed with reforms, including the promotion of foreign investment. Nevertheless, we shall surely monitor the situation and continue to reaffirm Canada's strong support for economic restructuring.

As remarkable as Korea's return to economic wellbeing are developments between Seoul and Pyongyang. I am sure you were as surprised as we were to learn of the agreement to hold a Summit meeting to be held June 12-14 in Pyongyang between the leaders of South and North Korea. This Summit is unprecedented in the stormy history of relations between the two Korean states. And it has come only one year after the navies of the two countries clashed in the Yellow Sea. And while it is important to avoid premature celebration, this historic event could, nonetheless, herald a new beginning to the long and arduous search for reconciliation on the Korean Peninsula.

The situation in North Korea, however, remains unsatisfactory in most respects. North Korea's economic experiment in central planning and self-reliance has been a failure. Particularly noteworthy is its full decade of negative growth and completely dysfunctional civilian economy. Most civilian factories are no longer operational. Those still functioning do so at a low level of efficiency because of energy and parts shortages and antiquated equipment. Only the military sectors of the economy are able to operate with any degree of normalcy. While some planners in Pyongyang may take pride in this latter point, it does not reassure the DPRK's neighbors.

80% of North Korea is mountainous, and its agricultural output has always been limited by a shortage of arable land. Productivity sharply decreased in recent years because of imprudent agricultural policies, shortages of energy and fertilizer, and floods and droughts in the middle of the 1990s. The collapse of the Soviet-bloc deprived North Korea of its traditional counter-trade markets and supplies. A humanitarian disaster of even more immense proportions has been averted in recent years only by the intervention of international relief agencies including those in the UN system (World Food Program, UNICEF) and non-governmental organizations. Nevertheless, widespread chronic famine and localized acute famine persist and food remains in short supply throughout the country.

Isolation fuels paranoia, leading to puzzling contradictions. Thus, while Pyongyang maintains a missile programme, it also fails to meet the basic nutritional needs of hundreds of thousands of its people. Isolation sustains poisonous myths and stereotypes by depriving the population of knowledge of, and contact with, the outside world. This is neither healthy nor helpful.

That having been said, we find it encouraging that the authorities in Pyongyang have - for whatever reason - initiated dialogue with various governments, which leads us to hope it will begin to emerge from its self-imposed isolation. While the steps being taken may be tentative, selective and superficial at the moment, there is hope North Korea's emergence will broaden and deepen over time. We welcome the fact that the DPRK remains engaged in dialogue with the United States and Japan, two key players in the Northeast Asian security matrix. It also has recently approached several other countries, including Australia, Italy, Spain, the Philippines and, of course, Canada, at the official level. This opening offers us a chance to help it emerge and encourage it to play a more responsible international role.

Where does this leave us in terms of the "new horizons" I mentioned earlier? Canada's security relationship with South Korea was forged during the Korean War, when 26,000 Canadian service personnel joined with others in the United Nations Command to defend South Korea. It was further nurtured during the Cold War. Now we are taking steps to update it to suit the requirements of the 21st Century.

Our approach reflects Canadian interests on the Korean Peninsula, which are multi-faceted and include elements from all three pillars of Canadian foreign policy; namely, security, prosperity and the promotion of Canadian values. Our approach was reinforced by Canadian and Korean academics and business leaders who encouraged a modern and more nuanced security relationship. It was last June at the Toronto meeting of the Canada-Korea Forum that participants urged the two governments to develop a concrete action agenda for mutual cooperation in the areas of cooperative security and human security.

And it was during President Kim's visit to Canada last July that his personal interest in Canada's human security initiative became apparent. As a result of the Forum's encouragement and the President's personal interest, we subsequently proposed that Canada and Korea begin to work jointly on various projects. I am pleased that both governments, consequently, agreed this spring to launch a programme of bilateral cooperation by jointly sponsoring a training course on Civil-Military Relations during Peace Support Operations. Experts from the 22 member governments of the ASEAN Regional Forum (ARF) will participate. The course will sensitize peacekeepers to the requirements of international humanitarian law and human rights in order to strengthen the protection of innocent civilians in areas of conflict. East Timor is a regrettable example of the challenge in this area.

Canada and South Korea's shared interest in regional security were reflected throughout the 1990s in Track II discussions between the Department of Foreign Affairs and International Trade, and the Korean Institute of Defense Analysis (KIDA). Over the past decade these regular workshops explored a variety of security challenges, including development of a model peace agreement formally to conclude the Korean War. This spring the Korean Government acknowledged the value of these Track II discussions when they proposed that they be reconstituted as formal government-to-government talks. Accordingly, I am pleased to inform you that we expect the first round of bilateral government-to-government Non-proliferation, Arms Control and Disarmament (NACD) consultations will take place this autumn.

Senior officials of our two governments hold formal Policy Consultations annually. They exchange views on the regional security situation and specific security issues. Canada and South Korea also participate in a quadrilateral forum with Japan and Australia for a broader discussion of these same issues and others. I should also note that at the annual meeting of our Special Partnership Working Group, topical bilateral issues in trade, economic relations, visas and exchange programs are reviewed by senior Canadian and Korean foreign affairs officials.

These are worthwhile endeavours which reflect the new reality of the post-Cold War world and our shared interest with South Korea in regional security.

In the past several months, however, a new issue has appeared on our policy horizon.

This is a uniquely interesting challenge.

Our interest in the issue is shared by all other countries in the North Pacific region.

This "issue" is the modest hint of a change of direction - and tentative opening - by Pyongyang, and an appropriate Canadian role. At the instruction of Minister Axworthy, and with South Korea's full support, we have embarked upon a process of broadening dialogue with North Korea. As I have mentioned, Canada is not alone in this.

What is the North Korean motivation? It has not suddenly conceded that its old policies no longer work. Nor has it turned over a new leaf. No - these explanations - however attractive - are not persuasive. In my view - and it is shared by many others - North Korea is acting out of economic desperation. It urgently needs foreign aid and investment. I consider the announcement of an inter-Korean Summit was possible only because President Kim has steadfastly pursued his engagement policy. As amplified in his recent Berlin Declaration, this policy offered Pyongyang what it really needs: unprecedented economic cooperation.

What about Canada's interests? Let us be clear: a hostile and paranoid North Korea poses a threat to the security of South Korea, our other friends in the region and potentially Canada itself. Pyongyang has the fifth largest armed forces in the world. Their guns are all aimed south. Seoul, that bustling and energetic capital of 12 million inhabitants, is within striking distance of North Korea's long-range field artillery. The rest of the country - along with Japan, Alaska and possibly parts of British Columbia - is within reach of North Korean missiles.

As well, the humanitarian disaster in the DPRK could ultimately spark large-scale human migration elsewhere on the peninsula and in neighboring countries. Our goal must be to neutralize these potential threats by helping the DPRK achieve a "soft landing". We do not minimize the magnitude of the challenge, nor do we shrink from joining our friends in dealing with it.

In doing so, however, we must never lose sight of the stark reality that Pyongyang's leaders expect to remain in power. For them, economic assistance is less important than control. Indeed, many observers believe the main goal of efforts to improve the economy is to bolster the leadership's power. Thus, while encouraging North Korea's tentative moves towards greater openness to the world, we must remain patient and moderate in our expectations. We advocate an incremental process, so that the authorities in Pyongyang will not feel threatened and abruptly revert to their old isolationism.

In practical terms, what has Canada done? First, when President Kim Dae-jung visited Ottawa last July, the Prime Minister announced Canada's firm support for his visionary "Engagement Policy" towards the North. Secondly, Prime Minister Chrétien publicly offered Canada's encouragement upon learning of the upcoming Summit meeting between the two Korean leaders. This meeting, he noted, "offers an historic opportunity for the two Korean states to work together to resolve their long-standing differences, in the interests of peace and security".

"Every journey begins with a single step." The first step in our effort to broaden dialogue with North Korea was taken last 1999 October in Ottawa when I met a delegation of visiting North Korean academics to exchange views. Then in December, my colleague Lynda Watson, Director of the division responsible for Korean affairs, visited North Korea as part of a Track II delegation led by a prominent Canadian academic from the University of British Columbia. While in Pyongyang, she had friendly and constructive discussions at the DPRK Ministry of Foreign Affairs and other ministries.

These two visits revealed an appetite on the part of the DPRK to continue to talk at the government-to-government level, despite the absence of formal diplomatic ties. This enabled us to proceed with plans for a return visit to Ottawa by a delegation of officials from the Foreign Ministry in Pyongyang.

Accordingly, in early March 2000, Mr. Ryang Thae Sik, Director of the MFA division responsible for Canada, led a group of four DPRK officials on a five day visit to Ottawa. Canada is not well known in North Korea, so it came as no surprise that the delegation had only a superficial knowledge of our country. And, quite frankly, we anticipated a degree of discomfort on their part, knowing how critical we have been - and remain - of many of their past and present policies and behaviour.

With these considerations in mind, we designed a visit program aimed at enabling the visitors to get to know Canada. We were particularly keen to build mutual trust and confidence. We realized the necessity of first establishing positive atmospherics if ever we hoped to engage the DPRK in constructive dialogue.

I believe we met our goals. We exposed the delegation to our heritage and culture, our institutions and way of life. We considered this was the best way of helping them understand our foreign policy and, in particular, our policy towards the Korean Peninsula. We escorted them on a visit to the House of Commons, where they witnessed a spirited debate among parliamentarians. They joined us for a tour of the exhibits of Canadian history and culture at the National Gallery, Museum of Civilization and Agricultural Museum. By the time we attended an NHL hockey game at the Corel Centre, they were sufficiently relaxed to cheer openly for our Ottawa Senators. And, of course, we accompanied them to business meetings at several offices around Ottawa.

In formal meetings, we outlined the main elements of Canadian foreign policy, with an emphasis on the multilateral dimension. We encouraged them to become more actively and positively involved in regional and international affairs. In particular, we repeatedly urged them to resume their interrupted dialogue with the South. There was no lecturing or finger-pointing on our part. And they reciprocated with a business-like approach.

The outcome of the visit was encouraging. The North Koreans expressed gratitude for Canada's humanitarian assistance, which now exceeds $30 million. They indicated that Pyongyang regards Canada as a valuable interlocutor, and expressed a desire to continue our exchanges at a more senior level. We are now exploring options in order to identify the most appropriate next steps.

We do not have unrealistic expectations about the results we might achieve in this dialogue. And we fully anticipate that the process will be long and arduous. Nevertheless, we are convinced that Canada, as a middle power and champion of multilateral approaches to peace and security, will be able to play a positive role on the Korean Peninsula. We will do this in concert with like-minded nations, as the final act of this Cold War drama unfolds.

Our efforts to engage North Korea and, at the same time, to enrich our security relationship with South Korea, contribute to peace and stability on the Peninsula and in the region. Equally important, they make us a more meaningful security partner for Seoul. Finally, they reinforce our credentials as a player in the security affairs of Northeast Asia, a region which remains at the intersection of Canadian interests, whether in the realm of security, prosperity or values.

CANADA AND KOREA:
A SHARED HISTORY

YOUNG-SIK YOO
UNIVERSITY OF TORONTO

I. Introduction

In April 1949, the Canadian Government recognized the Republic of Korea as the only legitimate government on the Korean peninsula. Official diplomatic relations, however, were not established until 14 January, 1963. Korea's first ambassador to Canada, Lee Soo-young (primarily assigned to the United Nations in New York), presented his credentials to the Governor General of Canada on 28 January.[1] Canada's first ambassador to Korea, Richard Bower (primarily assigned to Japan), presented his credentials to President Pak Chung-hee on 11 November, 1964. On 17 January, 1974, John Stiles (1918-2000) became Canada's first ambassador to reside in Korea. The Republic of Korea has had an ambassador in Ottawa since 23 August, 1965

---

[1] For this, see The Ministry of Foreign Affairs, *Kanada hyôn whang (Review of Canada)* (Seoul, Korea: The Ministry of Foreign Affairs, 1989), p. 117. Any works and materials other than English used in this work have been translated by the author. The customary Korean form for Korean names — the surname followed by hyphenated given names — is used in the text, notes and bibliography. However, traditional spelling used in various writings, i.e., Corea for Korea, or well-known names in the Western form are used as they originally appeared, i.e., Syngman Rhee. For more information on the history of Korean immigration to Canada, see Yoo Young-sik, "Koreans [in Canada,"] in *Encyclopaedia of Canada's People*, ed. by Paul Robert Magocsi. (University of Toronto Press, 1999), pp. 882-890; Yoo Young-sik, "Korean Culture in Canada," in *Han'guk minjok munhwa taepaekwasajôn (The Encyclopaedia of Korean Culture)*, vol. 22 (Seoul, Korea, 1993), pp. 830-31; Chung, Joseph and Yim Seong-sook, *Initiation à la société québécoise pour un immigrant* (Montréal, Québec: Communauté coréenne du Grand Montréal, 1993); Yu Chai-shin and Yoo Young-sik, "Kaenada haninûi iminsa," (Korean Immigrant History in Canada) in *Saegesokûi han'gukmunhwa (Korean Culture in the Globe)* (Seoul, Korea: The Academy of Korean Studies, 1991), pp. 211-223; Kim Ûichul, "Acculturation of Korean Immigrants to Canada." Unpublished Ph.D. thesis, Queen's University, 1988.

when Paek Sôn-yôp was installed as Korea's first Ambassador-in Residence.[2] While Canada and Korea have less than forty years of "official" diplomatic exchange, "non-officially," these two countries have shared over one hundred years of history.

This paper explores the historical relationship between Canada and Korea prior to the establishment of official diplomatic ties by investigating the roles of Canadians in Korea and Koreans in Canada.

II. Canadians in Korea

By the 1880s, Korea had begun to draw the attention of Canadians. The earliest account of Korea in a Canadian book can be found in the May 1887 issue of the *Knox College Monthly*. In his seminal article, "Our Treatment of a Great Trust," Jonathan Goforth (1859-1936), then a student of the University of Toronto's Knox College, made an earnest plea that "a missionary be sent to Corea [sic] in order to save fifteen million souls." [3] Stimulated by Goforth's plea, the University College's Young Men's Christian Association in the University of Toronto (hereafter cited as UT-YMCA) appointed James Scarth Gale (1863-1937) as their agent in this great task.[4] Gale arrived in Pusan on 12 December, 1888.

Gale was born on 19 February, 1863, in Alma, Ontario, about 80 miles northwest of Toronto. In 1884, Gale was admitted into the University of Toronto's University College; where he specialized in language and literature and graduated with a B. A. in 1888. [5] Before his graduation, the members of

---

[2] Department of Foreign Affairs, "Canada's Relations with the Republic of Korea," in *External Affairs* (Ottawa, Canada), XV (February 1963), p. 460.

[3] Jonathan Goforth, "Our Treatment of a Great Trust," in *Knox College Monthly* (hereafter cited as *KCM*) (May 1887), p. 25. For more information about the earlier Canadian missionaries to Korea, see Yoo Young-sik, *Earlier Canadian Missionaries in Korea, A Study in History, 1888-1895.* (Toronto, Ontario: Society for Korean and Related Studies, 1987). See also, Yoo Young-sik, "The Impact of Canadian Missionaries in Korea: A Historical Survey of Early Canadian Mission Work, 1888-1898". Unpublished Ph.D. dissertation, University of Toronto, 1996.

[4] "University College YMCA Minutes" (12 April, 1888), p. 220; Murray Ross, *Y.M.C.A. in Canada: The Chronicle of a Century* (Toronto, Ontario: The Ryerson Press, 1951), p. 119; See also, "Seven New Missionaries," in *KCM*, (June 1889), p. 105. For more information about Gale, see Yoo, *Earlier Canadian..,* pp. 23-36 and Yoo, "The Impact of Canadian..," pp. 137-218.

[5] This information is derived from "University of Toronto - Class and Prize Lists 1884-1888"; Ada Sale, "Life of James Scarth Gale, D.D," p. 32. Unpublished manuscript. Hereafter cited as *G-Memoir*.

UT-YMCA elected him as their representative missionary, guaranteeing him an "in-the-field" salary of $500 *per annum* for eight years. The money was to be raised by soliciting annual subscriptions from the UT-YMCA's two hundred and twenty student members.[6] Given this small fiscal base, it is not surprising that the UT-YMCA's Mission Board had serious difficulties collecting funds for Gale; the UT-YMCA's "Minutes" of 1888-89 show that only $57.65 remained in the treasury just after Gale left.[7] After about two and a half years of attempting to conduct his mission under severe financial restrictions, on 31 August, 1891, Gale transferred to the American Presbyterian Mission, North, [8] where his American counterparts earned $1,000 *per annum*. Gale married Harriet Gibson, widow of his friend John Heron, M.D. on 7 April, 1892. After marriage, Gale moved to Wônsan (present-day North Korea) in June of 1892 and established a mission center at a place called *Pongsude*, also known as "Beacon Hill." While in Wônsan, Gale completed two significant literary works: one was a translation of John Bunyan's *Pilgrim's Progress* (1895) into Korean and the other was the *Korean-English Dictionary* (1897).

Gale is regarded as "the foremost literary interpreter of the Korean mind to the Occidental world,"[9] of the missionaries working in Korea around the turn of the century; for during the forty years of his missionary career, he did far more than evangelize. He promoted the Western study of Korean history, Korean language, Korean lexicography, education, social movement and culture. Gale not only became the foremost interpreter of Korean culture for the Western world, he also emerged as the foreigner most responsible for introducing Western ideas to the Korean people, for he wrote in their own language. Gale's monumental contribution was his *Korean-English Dictionary. The Seoul Press*, then an English-language newspaper, compared Gale's study of Korea with Chamberlain's study of Japan and Giles' study of China.[10] The best-known of Gale's translations were *Pilgrim's Progress*

---

[6] "University College YMCA Mission to Corea," in *KCM* (November 1888), p. 35.

[7] "Minutes of University College Young Men's Christian Association," [18]88-[18]89, p. 244.

[8] *G-Memoir*, p. 8; "Annual Report of University of Toronto Young Men's Christian Association," (1893-94), (Toronto, Ontario: The YMCA Publication, 1894), p. 2; *Varsity* (February 16, 1892), p. 189; "Rev. James S. Gale, D.D.," in Memorial Minutes adopted by the Board of Foreign Missions of the Presbyterian Church of America, February 15, 1937; Richard Rutt, *A Biography of James Scarth Gale and A New Edition of His History of Korean People* (Seoul, Korea: Royal Asiatic Society Korea Branch, 1972), p. 21.

[9] Henry J. Morgan, ed., *The Canadian Men and Women of the Time: A Handbook of Canadian Biography of Living Characters* (Toronto, Ontario: William Briggs, 1912), p. 428.

[10] *The Seoul Press* (Korea) (September 6, 1911). Newspaper clippings. Page is unknown. Present author's possession.

(*Chôlloyôkjông*), and the *Bible* (both New and Old Testament) in 1925. Gale also translated Korean works into English, such as his 1922 translation of *Kuunmong* (*The Cloud Dreams of Nine*) by Kim Man-jung (1637-1692).[11] Gale also introduced the Ontario education system into Korean society. A Gale biographer, Richard Rutt said, "Gale produced a series of four *Korean Readers* (*Yumong ch'ônja*), owing much to the Ontario Public School Books." [12]

Gale would leave Korea permanently on 22 June, 1927, just a year before he officially retired on 31 August, 1928. Even then, his importance to Asian Studies was such that after his return to Canada, he was offered a post as an Oriental Specialist in the U.S. Library of Congress. He declined the position, choosing to spend his last years in England; he died there on 31 January, 1937, at the age of 74.

Just as the UT-YMCA was enthusiastic about sending a representative of its own to Korea in 1888, so too was the Toronto City YMCA (hereafter TO-YMCA). However, compared to the UT-YMCA, the TO-YMCA was even shorter of funds. The group's "Minutes" of July 1888 noted that, "the matter of a missionary [sent] to Corea from this Association was left in abeyance"[13] due to financial difficulties. Given this, a group of Toronto businessmen, many of them disappointed TO-YMCA members, organized an independent effort called the "Corean Union Mission" (hereafter cited as CUM) in October 1888.[14] In 1888, CUM sent Robert Harkness (1858-1938), also a graduate of University College, as "their" missionary to Korea. Prior to his commission to Korea, Harkness married Isabella Wilson of Renfrew, Ontario, "a young lady of marked piety and missionary zeal." [15] Thus, Gale, Robert and Isabella Harkness left for Korea together, landing in Pusan on 12 December, 1888. Despite their enthusiasm, the Harkness team were unable to accomplish much; Robert's health problems forced them to leave Korea less then a year after their arrival.[16]

---

[11] *Kuunmong* was published in 1689.

[12] Rutt, p. 36.

[13] Toronto City YMCA's "Minutes" (29 June, 1888), p. 288.

[14] *The Medical Missionary* (Toronto, Ontario: Missionary Board of the Toronto Medical Student YMCA, 1891), p. 4.

[15] Robert Harkness' file at the University of Toronto archives.

[16] Gale's letter to his sister, Jane, dated 22 October, 1889. Author's possession. For more information about Harkness, see Yoo, *Earlier Canadian..*, pp. 37-39; Yoo, "The Impact of Canadian..," pp. 219-221.

The fourth Canadian to arrive in Korea was Malcolm Fenwick (1865-1935) of Markham, Ontario, then a small town located northeast of Toronto. During his childhood, Fenwick laboured on the family farm. According to the *Toronto City Directory* (1887), Fenwick began to live in Toronto when he was 22 years old; he was listed as a "boarder" in his mother's home at 190 Bleeker Street, [17] in an area of Toronto's East End known today as Old Cabbage Town. While in Toronto, he worked for a short time for Risley and Kerrigan, a wholesale hardware store at 30 Front Street, and then for another hardware store, H.S. Howland Sons & Co., at 37 Front Street West; he remained with this store until leaving for Korea in 1889.[18] In regards to his lack of qualifications to become a missionary, he himself acknowledged that he had not received a college education and was not a minister, having never gone to any theological seminary; he was "only a businessman."[19] Despite his shortfalls, when it became obvious that the Harknesses would have to leave Korea, the CUM decided to send Fenwick as a non-denominational lay-missionary. Fenwick arrived in Chemulpo (present-day Inchôn) on 8 December, 1889, at the age of 24.[20] The next spring, he relocated to Songchôn, better known as Sorae in Hwanghae Province, present-day North Korea. In 1893, Fenwick went back to Canada and returned to Korea in 1896. Thereafter he settled down in Wônsan, North Korea. It was here that Fenwick, who had come to Korea with no clear denominational commitment, began promulgating his own unique creed of Christianity, a hybrid of Methodism and Presbyterianism. As the head of the "Church of Christ in Corea," he would come to oversee his flock like a Protestant "pope".

A new form of Christianity was not Fenwick's only contribution to Korean society. As detailed by Yun Chi-ho (1865-1945), a former governor of

---

[17] *Toronto City Directory* (1887), p. 463. For more information about Fenwick, see his *Church of Christ in Corea*, (New York: George H. Doren, 1911) and *Life in the Cup,* (Mesa Grande, Cal.,: Church of Christ in Corea Extension, 1917); Yoo, "The Impact of Canadian..," pp. 222-264.

[18] *Toronto City Directory* (1888), p. 903 and (1889), p. 725; Yoo, "The Impact of Canadian..," p. 223; See also Yoo, *Earlier Canadian..,* pp. 41-53.

[19] *Church of Christ in Corea*, p. 13.

[20] The present author found that there is a discrepancy in regard to the year of Fenwick's birth. By and large, the year of his birth is given either as 1861 or 1863 in Korean sources. For this, see Lee Chông-su (ed.), *Han'guk chimrye kyohoesa (History of Korean Baptist Church)* (Seoul, Korea: Chimryehoe chulpansa, 1990), pp. 43-45. See also, Kim Yong-he, *Taehan kidokkyo chimryehoesa (History of Korean Baptist Church)* (Seoul, Korea: Chimryehoe chulpansa, 1964), p. 11. However, according to the "Genealogical Table of the Fenwick Family" stored in the Markham District Historical Museum, Ontario, Fenwick was born in 1865. Fenwick's age in this paper is based on "Markham Township Census 1861" C-2, unpaginated, housed in Markham Historical Museum, Markham, Ontario. For more about the year of his birth, see Yoo, "The Impact of Canadian..," pp. 254-55.

Wŏnsan, the missionary bought a beautiful section of land soon after his arrival there. Fenwick named the site "Brookhill" [21] (*Kalmay* in Korean) and proceeded to farm it for the rest of his life.

Brookhill would serve as Fenwick's main source of income; unlike other missionaries, Fenwick received no official funding after his arrival. Fenwick planted apple trees and celery on his farm. Yun Chi-ho said that Fenwick brought apple trees from the "State of Canada in the United States of America".[22] An editorial in the missionary-published *The Korean Repository* reported that:

> His [Fenwick's] pumpkins, corns, wheat, millet and oats were the admiration of his Korean neighbours. He has grown pumpkins larger than a wash-tub, so large that it took two men to lift one onto the Korean jiggy [*jige*].[23] His celery was twenty-six inches high and seven inches [in] diameter.[24]

In 1898, Fenwick contributed an article, "Korean Farming," to *The Korean Repository*. In it, he described how Koreans were practicing primitive farming methods, and made suggestions for improvement. Fenwick noted that although the indigenous practice of mixing manure with ashes was admirable, he noted: "it should be done at the time of planting instead of continuously, as mixed continuously it loses much available ammonia which evaporates."[25] Fenwick also urged the Korean Government to introduce Western methods of farming by supporting "someone," a "Westerner" who had feelings for the Korean people, to educate Korean farmers. This suggestion, like those he made in other areas, generated little government interest or enthusiasm. However, Fenwick's expertise and successful implantation of practical techniques was such that he became known to his followers as the Triple *paksa* [Doctor]: *Nonghak paksa* (Doctor of Agriculture), *Ŭihak paksa* (Doctor of Medicine), and *Chŭkyrang paksa* (Doctor of Surveying).[26]

---

[21] Yun Chi-ho, *Yun Chi-ho ilgi (Diary of Yun Chi-ho)*, vol. 5 (September 1902) (Seoul, Korea: Kuksa p'yŏnchan wiwŏnhoe, 1973), p. 343. Hereafter cited as *Yun Chi-ho ilgi*.

[22] Kim Young-ûi, *Chawung Yun Chi-ho sŏnsaeng yakjŏn (A Brief Biography of Yun Chi-ho)* (Seoul, Korea: Kidokkyo chosŏn kamrihoe, 1934), p. 149.

[23] *Jiggy* or *Jige* is an "A" shaped frame used to carry loads on one's back.

[24] *Korean Repository*, vol. 7 (February 1898), p. 77. Hereafter cited as *KR*.

[25] Malcolm C. Fenwick, "Korean Farming," in *KR*, vol. 5, (August 1898), p. 288.

[26] Interview with Helen McRae on 8 August, 1983. Helen is a daughter of Duncan McRae who was stationed in Hamhûng, North Korea. Helen was born in Hamhûng in 1910.

Fenwick would remain in Wônsan for the rest of his life, dying there in 1935 at the age of 70. His efforts to introduce Western methods of agricultural improvements "underline the fact that the missionary impact on [Korean] society was much broader than simply the propagation of the Christian message."[27]

Shortly after Fenwick arrived in Chemulpo, Robert Hardie, M.D. (1865-1949), another Torontonian, was sent to Korea by the University of Toronto's Medical Students' Young Men's Christian Association (MS-YMCA). Hardie, his wife Margaret, and their two-year daughter, Eva, arrived in Pusan on   30 September, 1890. Their second child, Annie Elizabeth was born in Seoul on 12 December of that same year, becoming the first Canadian to be born on Korean soil.[28]

Hardie's funding organization was the same as Gale's: the UT-YMCA. Like Gale, Hardie was not provided with adequate funding. His response to this situation was to follow Gale; in May 1898, he transferred to, and acquired support from, the American Methodist Church. It was his resignation from the MS-YMCA that signalled the end of the relationship between the University of Toronto mission societies and Korea.

Hardie would spend his early Korean years, 1891 to 1896, in Wônsan. While in Wônsan, he learned Fenwick's survival techniques and was able to supplement his rather limited income by farming, raising cattle and growing fruit.[29] Like Fenwick, Hardie introduced Western fruits and vegetables, in particular apples, to Korea. This achievement would be heralded years later by *The Toronto Star*, which celebrated Hardie's contribution to Korean agriculture in 1932 under the headline: "Apple Trees from Toronto Basis of Korean Industry." The article described how Hardie had planted his first apple saplings in 1891 while he was in Wônsan with the help of his brother, E.S. Hardie, a prominent Toronto dentist. Special mention was made of the fact that the fruit from those first trees were being exported to Japan.[30] In 1935, Hardie retired after 45 years of mission work. He returned to North America, finally settling in Lansing, Michigan, where he died on 30 June, 1949, at the age of 84.

---

[27] A. Hamish Ion, *The Cross and the Rising Sun*, volume 1: *The Canadian Protestant Missionary Movement in the Japanese Empire, 1872-1932* (Waterloo, Ontario: Wilfred Laurier University Press, 1990), p. 105.

[28] James E. Fisher, *Pioneers of Modern Korea* (Seoul, Korea: Christian Literature Society of Korea, 1977), p. 110. For more information about Hardie, see Yoo, *Earlier Canadian..," pp. 57-62;* Yoo, "The Impact of Canadian..," pp. 265-303.

[29] *Yun Chi-ho ilgi*, vol. 5, (1902), p. 335; Fisher, p. 112.

[30] *The Toronto Star* (22 September, 1932), p. 4. See also "How Grandfather Created Korea's Apple Trade," in *The Toronto Star* (17 December, 1989), D5.

The next Canadian missionary appointed to Korea was William James Hall (1860-1894) of Glen Buell, Ontario.[31] In 1885, Hall had entered Medical College at Queen's University in Kingston, Ontario, and transferred two years later to New York's Bellevue Hospital Medical College. He received an M.D. from that institution in 1889. Two years later, the American Methodist Episcopal Church, North, dispatched Hall to Korea. He reached Pusan on 15 December, 1891. Upon his arrival, he immediately married Rosetta Sherwood, M.D. (1865-1951), who had been sent to Korea in 1890 by the same mission board that sponsored Hall. In 1892, the Halls became the first missionaries to settle in Pyôngyang (present-day capital city of North Korea), located about 180 miles north from Seoul. Pyôngyang's inhabitants were not immediately receptive and frequently displayed their anti-foreign sentiments by pelting the Halls with stones. On the other hand, they did receive a modest welcome from the Governor, Min Byôg-sôk,[32] who admired the Halls because of their medical expertise. This less than auspicious beginning soon turned into a positive experience. In fact, by 1894, Hall had founded *the first* mission school in Pyôngyang. *The Ninety Year History of Kwangsông School* recorded:

> The Kwangsông School opened on April 1894 by William James Hall, physician, missionary, who then worked under American Methodist Episcopal Church, North, at the West of Pyôngyang. There were thirteen students.[33]

It is generally acknowledged that Soongsil School was the first mission school founded in Pyôngyang by William M. Baird, an American Presbyterian missionary, in 1897. However, records indicate that William

---

[31] For more information on Hall, see Rosetta Hall, (ed.), *Life of Rev. William J. Hall* (New York: Young People of Canada and the United States, 1897); Yoo, "The Impact of Canadian..," pp. 304-351.

[32] Sherwood Hall, *With Stethoscope in Asia: Korea.* (McLean, Va.,: MCL Associates, 1978), p. 138. Sherwood Hall recorded that "The Governor [of the P'yôngyang] is a relative of the Queen, a powerful family here in Korea." The anonymous governor Hall mentioned here appears to be Min Byông-sôk (1858-1940), according to a Korean source. For this, see Kuksa p'yônchan wiwônhoe, *Kojong sidaesa (History of Kojong Period)*, vol. 3 (1888-1895), p. 123. Hereafter cited as *Kojong*. This work states that Min Byông-sôk was appointed as "P'yôngando kwanchalsa" (The Governor of P'yôngan Province) in November 1889, and was in P'yôngyang when Hall was there in 1894.

[33] Kwangsông kusipnyôn p'yônchan wiwônhoe, *Kwangsông kusipnyônsa (Ninety-Year History of Kwangsông School)* (Seoul, Korea: Minjung insoe kongsa, 1984), pp. 41-42. Hereafter cited as *Kwangsông*.

Hall founded his school three years before Baird's Soongsil School. Hall's letter to his wife, Rosetta, indicated that he started a school in February 1894. The letter reads: "We have started a boy's school and have an earnest Christian teacher and thirteen boys already. They study the catechism mornings and nights, and Ûnmun [a popular name of the Korean alphabet, Han'gûl]." This letter was penned February, 1894.[34]

The Hall School, renamed "Kyôkmul Hakdang" in 1903, was moved to Seoul in 1918 and rechristened the "Kwangsông School." [35] The "Kwangsông School" became William Hall's personal legacy to Pyôngyang, for he died of typhus there on 24 November, 1894, at the age of 34, after living in Korea for less than three years.

Despite his death, Hall's legacy of mission enterprise was continued by his widow, Rosetta, and their son, Sherwood Hall, M.D. (1893-1991). In 1897, Rosetta Hall built the Pyôngyang Girls' School and the Pyôngyang Blind School (Pyôngyang maeng a hakkyo), the first special education for the blind in Korea. In 1917, she relocated to Seoul and began working at Tongdaemun puin p'yôngwôn (East Gate Women's Hospital, presently Ehwa Women's University Hospital). Rosetta Hall retired in 1935, after 35 years of mission work. She passed away at Ocean Grove, New Jersey, on 5 April, 1951, at the age of 85.

The Halls' contributions to Korea were augmented by those of their son, Sherwood and his wife Marian. Born in Korea in 1893, Sherwood returned to Canada for higher education, graduating with an M.D. from the University of Toronto Faculty of Medicine in 1924. That same year, Marian—whom he had married in 1922—graduated from Philadelphia's Women's Medical College of Pennsylvania as a fully certified physician. Both Sherwood and Marian were quickly assigned to Korea as medical missionaries by the same organization (American Methodist Episcopal Church, North) that had sponsored Sherwood's parents. The couple arrived in Korea in April 1926, and for Sherwood, after sixteen years away from Korea, it was a "homecoming." Sherwood and Marian Hall began their medical work in Haeju, presently in North Korea, immediately upon their arrival. While in Haeju, Sherwood implemented a program for which he had long planned: the elimination of paebyông, tuberculosis. Paebyông had been a serious problem

---

[34] For this, see Sherwood Hall, With Stethoscope in Asia: Korea, p. 129. In regards to the foundation of the mission school in general, see, Son In-soo, Han'guk kûndae kyoyuksa, 1885-1945 (History of Modern Education in Korea, 1885-1945) (Seoul, Korea: Yônsei University Press, 1971), p. 24.

[35] Kwangsông, p. 881; Lee Man-yul, Han'guk kidokkyo munhwa undongsa (The History of the Cultural Movement in the Korean Christian Church). (Seoul, Korea: Taehan kidokkyo chulpansa, 1992), pp. 191-192.

in Korea and by the end of the 1920's; it was estimated that 15% of the Korean population was infected with tuberculosis.[36]

Sherwood's efforts resulted with the establishment of *Haeju kyôlhaek yoyangwôn* (Haeju Tuberculous Sanatorium) in 1929, a modern facility equipped with up-to-date X-ray machines and other equipment. Medical technology was not the only weapon used against the disease, the institute relied upon its own 25-acre farm to produce the "healthful" fruits and vegetables necessary for patient recovery. This farm also acted as a rehabilitation centre; to this end, Sherwood invited Dexter N. Lutz (in Korea 1921-1960), an American agricultural missionary then stationed in Seoul, to come and provide practical instruction on farming to the sanatorium's inmates.[37] Lutz taught healthy patients Western knowledge of soil analysis, the better use of land, the terrace-farming of fruits and vegetables, dairy farming, and animal husbandry.[38]

Sherwood insisted that "no patient would leave the model village until he was thoroughly strong physically, self-confident mentally, and had mastered whatever line of work in which he [or she] had chosen to specialize."[39] Thus, when patients left the sanatorium after treatment, they had gained knowledge of farming, poultry raising, sericulture, and even carpentry and handcrafts. In truth, Sherwood's sanatorium did function as both *chaehwalwôn* (Rehabilitation Centre) and medical facility. This "sanatorium community" was so successful that it became the first "modern farm" of the "modern farm movement" in Korea.[40] Moreover, it was this "sanatorium-*cum*-rehabilitation centre" which led to Sherwood being recognized as Korea's first institutional social worker. This was not Sherwood's only claim to fame; in connection with the expansion of his sanatorium program, he launched Korea's first Christmas Seal campaign. The first Christmas Seal, bearing the emblem of Seoul's South Gate, was issued on 3 December, 1932,[41] ostensibly on the authority of *Haeju kusae yoyangwôn* (Haeju Salvation Sanatorium). [42]

The profits from the Christmas Seal campaign helped not only the Sherwood Sanatorium, but also other sanatoriums in the country.

[36] *Yônsei taehakkyosa (History of Yônsei University)*, p. 136, cited in Min Kyông-bae. *Han'guk kidokkyo sahoe undongsa (History of Social Movements in Korean Church)* (Seoul, Korea: Taehan kidokkyo sôhoe, 1990), p. 262.

[37] Sherwood Hall, "Application of Sanatorium Methods to Korean Patients," in *The China Medical Journal*, vol. 44 (July 1930), p. 664. See also, *Sinhak saeke (The World of Theology)*, vol. 13: 6 (November 1928), p. 100.

[38] *Stethoscope*, p. 459.

[39] Ibid.

[40] *Kaegan Asan (Asan Quarterly)* (Winter 1984), p. 71.

[41] Sherwood Hall, "The Story of Korea's First Christmas Seal," in *Korea Mission Field* (May 1933), p. 93. Hereafter cited as *KMF.*

[42] *Haeju kusae yôyangwôn* is another name for *Haeju kyôlhaek p'yôngwôn* (Haeju Tuberculous Sanatorium).

Unfortunately, by the 1930s, these activities were carried out during Japan's occupation of Korea. As the decade wore on, mission work became increasingly difficult. Oppression of general Korean religious activity intensified, in particular, the Japanese heavily targeted foreign missions. The Halls were no exception and, under intense pressure from the Japanese colonial government, were finally forced to leave Korea on 9 December, 1940. Sherwood Hall went to India and continued mission work there until 1963 and resettled in Richmond, British Columbia, Canada, where he and his wife spent the rest of their lives. Sherwood died there on 4 April, 1991, at the age of 98 and Marian died a few months later on 19 September at the age of 95.

The four Halls (William, Rosetta, Sherwood and Marian) served a total of 76 years in Korea.

"Hereditary" medical service in Korea was not unique to the Halls; it is a tradition they share with the Avisons, another Canadian family of physicians. In fact, Oliver R. Avison (1860-1956) and his son Douglas (1893-1951) are credited with making the greatest contribution to the history of medicine in Korea. O.R. Avison founded Severance Hospital and Severance Medical College, the first Western general hospital and medical college in Korea. By fostering Koreans through these institutions, Avison made his monumental contribution to Korean society—the transformation of the "miraculous" and foreign medical profession into an indigenous one.

O.R. Avison was born on 30 June, 1860, in Huddersfield, Yorkshire, England. His family immigrated to Canada in 1866. He lived on Carlton and Sherbourne Streets in Toronto (present-day "Old Cabbage Town") until 1893, the year he left for Korea. Avison graduated from the Ontario College of Pharmacy (OCP; presently, The Faculty of Pharmacy, University of Toronto) in 1884 and the Toronto School of Medicine (presently, the Faculty of Medicine, University of Toronto, FMUT) in 1887 with a Bachelor of Medicine. [43] He taught at both OCP and FMUT until he left for Korea as a representative of the American Presbyterian Mission Board, North. Avison, along with his wife, Jennie, and their three children (Lawrence, Lera and

[43] The University of Toronto Faculty of Medicine started to confer the M.D. degree in 1928. In the days of Avison, they offered M.B. (Bachelor of Medicine). For this, see William R. Feasby, *University of Toronto: Faculty of Medicine 1843-1966* (Toronto, Ontario: University of Toronto, 1967), p. 24, mimeographed edition. For more information about Avison, see Yoo, *Earlier Canadian..,"* pp. 63-73; Yoo, "The Impact of Canadian..," pp. 352-394.

Gordon), arrived at Pusan, in mid-June 1893.[44] He took up his duties at the *Chaejungwôn* (Royal Hospital) on 1 November, 1893 and was soon appointed King Kojong's (r. 1864-1907) private physician. [45]

Avison began a new era in Korea's medical history by founding Severance Hospital, which opened on 23 September, 1904. The name "Severance" acknowledged the institution's gratitude to its major donor, Louis H. Severance (1838-1913) of Cleveland, Ohio; he was not, however, the project's first contributor. That distinction went to Toronto architect Henry B. Gordon (1854-1951) who drew up the blueprints of the hospital free-of-charge.[46]

In his article, "Creating a Medical School in Korea," Avison related his initial thoughts about the need for a medical school:

> As we could not expect the Mission Boards to send out enough doctors to do this [medical mission work], it became evident that it would be necessary to raise up a group of native physicians as quickly as possible.[47]

Avison's teaching experience at OCP and FMUT prepared him for establishing a medical college in Korea. In fact, he adopted the organization of his *alma mater* as the template for his new institution. Avison wrote:

> Naturally my [Avison's] idea of medical education was that of the University of Toronto. Plans for a medical school must include the preparation of not only doctors, but also of nurses, pharmacists, dentists and opticians.[48]

In addition to the difficulty of recruiting candidates, Avison admitted that the teaching of Western-style medicine in a society whose vocabulary lacked scientific terms and medical terminology was as difficult as "build[ing]

---

[44] There are discrepancies about the date Avison arrived in Pusan. In his book, *Avison of Korea,* Clark recorded that Avison arrived in Pusan on Sunday, June 16, 1893, p. 75. However, according to the calendar, June 16 fell on a Friday of that year, not on Sunday. A Canadian missionary, William Scott, claims that Avison arrived in Pusan on July 13, 1893. For this, see his *Canadians in Korea* (Toronto, Ontario: United Church of Canada, 1976), p. 25. Avison recalled in his *Memoir* (p. 104) that when he arrived at William Baird's house in Pusan, he found "a small group of foreigners gathered there for Sunday worship." Granting Avison's memory that it was a "Sunday" that he arrived in Pusan, he may have arrived on June 18, a Sunday.

[45] Oliver R. Avison, *Memoir*, (n.d.). Hereafter cited as *A-Memoir*, p. 535. See also, *Kidok sinbo* (Christian News) (March 1932), p. 249. Hereafter cited as *KS*.

[46] *A-Memoir*, p. 375.

[47] Oliver. R. Avison, "Creating a Medical School in Korea," in the *University of Toronto Monthly,* (November 1937), p. 40. Hereafter cited as *UTM*.

[48] *A-Memoir*, p. 41; *KS*, (July 20, 1932), p. 417.

Utopia." [49] To address this difficulty, Avison undertook the task to create a Korean-language Western-medical textbook; "By March, 1899 we had completed the translation of the [Henry Gray's] *Anatomy*." [50] Six years later, textbooks on all subjects relevant to medical training were available in Korean.[51] Avison was able to achieve this accomplishment in part to the assistance he received from Kim Pil-soon, one of the first medical students at Severance. Three years after the textbooks had been completed, seven people were certified as Korea's first Western-trained physicians on 8 June, 1908. Avison came to Korea as a medical missionary at the turn of the century, during what historians refer to as the *Kaehwagi* or Enlightenment Period. Avison's primary tool for enlightening Korean society was not philosophical Western dogma but the practical teaching of Western medical and technological sciences. It was Avison who transformed the "miraculous" foreign medical field into an indigenous one by teaching Korean physicians.

Oliver and Jennie Avison left Korea on 6 December, 1935, after forty-two years of service in Korea; however, they left behind their sons Douglas and Gordon to continue their work. O.R. Avison died on 28 August, 1956, and was buried next to his wife in Smith's Falls, Ontario, the town where they first met many years ago.[52] The four Avisons (Oliver, Jennie, Gordon and Douglas) served a total of 125 years in Korea.

After the Avisons, missionaries from Ontario faded from the Korean scene; missionaries from the Maritimes replaced them. This shift in regional representation started with William John McKenzie (1861-1895), of Cape Breton, Nova Scotia.

McKenzie graduated from Dalhousie University and Pine Hill Seminary, both in Halifax. Sent to Korea in 1893, he built a successful quasi-independent mission, only to die in the remote village of Sorae, Hwanghae Province, present-day North Korea, less than two years after his arrival.[53] Despite his short tenure, his work inspired both his Korean and Canadian Maritime congregations. In fact, after his death, the villagers of Sorae sent out an earnest plea, a Korean version of the Macedonian Call, to the Canadian church for another minister. In 1898, the Presbyterian Church of Canada

---

[49] *UTM*, (November 1937), p. 41.

[50] Ibid.; Paik Lak-geoon, *The History of Protestant Missions in Korea, 1832-1910* (Seoul, Korea: Yonsei University Press, 1971), p. 336. Unfortunately, the manuscript of the translation of Gray's *Anatomy* was lost in a fire during the time of Avison's furlough in Canada in 1899.

[51] *UTM* (November 1937), p. 41.

[52] See the picture of Dr. and Mrs. Avison's grave, in Yoo, *Earlier Canadian Missionaries in Korea.*, unpaginated.

[53] McKenzie arrived in Pusan on 12 December, 1893, and lived in Korea for only 559 days; 313 days in Sorae village where he met his death on 22 June, 1895. For more information on William John McKenzie, see Elizabeth A. McCully, *A Corn of Wheat or the Life of Rev. W. J. McKenzie of Korea.* (Toronto, Ontario: Westminster Press, 1903). Present author translated McCully's *Corn of Wheat* into Korean under the title, *Hanalûi mil i ttôlôjimyôn*, which was published by the Publishing Department of the Presbyterian Church in Korea in 1985.

(PCC) answered this call by sending "regular" missionaries to Korea; this began official mission work conducted by the PCC. Without McKenzie's influence, the relationship between Canada and Korea would have died out; Robert Grierson (1868-1965), one of the first PCC missionaries to go to Korea said, "Canada and Korea are linked together by William John McKenzie." [54]

In 1898, the Eastern Division of the Board of Foreign Missions formally authorized a trio of Maritimers — the Reverends Robert Grierson, M.D. (1868-1965), Duncan McRae (1868-1949) and William R. Foote (1869-1930) to serve in Korea under the PCC. Prior to their departure, Grierson and Foote married, making this group, the "Canadian Five." This cadre left Halifax on 20 July, and after 51 arduous days of travel, arrived in Seoul on 8 September. A strong inclination to set up a mission shop in Sorae was overridden by the fact the village was "not a suitable place" [55] given its small size.

After careful consideration, the Canadians established their base in the newly opened port of Wônsan, located in the northeastern section of the peninsula; they eventually spread their operations to Hamkyông Province of North Korea and Kando (Lungchengtsun, Manchuria). The workload became so heavy that the five Canadians requested additional support. By the early 1900s, nine more Canadians joined the mission field in Korea (Louise McCully, Edith Sutherland, Katherine McMillan, Luther Young, Alexander Ross, Jennie Robb, Catherine Mair, Mary Rogers and Elizabeth McCully).

In 1910, Korea became a Japanese colony. Harsh Japanese occupation caused widespread emigration, with Koreans fleeing to Manchuria and the region around Vladivostock, Russia. As a result, the area that the missionaries had to cover significantly expanded and their workload became heavier. The field missionaries requested more missionaries. By the mid-1910s, more than fifty Canadian missionaries were serving in Korea.[56]

Canadian women made at least two significant contributions to the welfare of their Korean counterparts. In 1903, Louise McCully founded the first theological institution for Korean women: The Martha Wilson Theological School in Wônsan. McCully and other Canadian missionary women

---

[54] Elizabeth A. McCully and J.O. Fraser, *Our Share in Korea*. (Toronto, Ontario: The Woman's Missionary Society, The United Church of Canada, 1932), p. 7. For more information about McKenzie, see Yoo, *Earlier Canadian..*, pp. 75-83/105-112; Yoo, "The Impact of Canadian.." pp. 395-435.

[55] William Scott, *Canadians in Korea*, (Toronto, Ontario: United Church of Canada, 1976), p. 43. See also, Yoo Young-sik, "Putting the 'C' in Corea: The Canadians who went to Korea," in *Presbyterian Record* (March 1998), p. 23.

[56] The data is based on the list of missionaries in the Archives of The United Church of Canada and Victoria University in the University of Toronto, and the list of missionaries in the office of the United Church of Canada in Toronto.

contributed to the organization of the Women's Missionary Society (WMS) in Wônsan during the early 1900s. This Wônsan WMS served as the predecessor for the formation of an All-Korean WMS in 1920 — Louise McCully served as its first president. Just as Avison took the University of Toronto medical educational system as his model for forming a medical college in Seoul, and just as Gale used Ontario textbooks when he modernized Korea's school system, the All-Korean WMS created itself in the image of the Canadian WMS.

Mission work in Korea came to a sudden halt in 1941 following Japan's declaration of war against the Allied Powers. One year after, the Japanese forced all missionaries to shut down their institutions and leave both Korea and Manchuria.[57] Although Canadian missionaries would return to Korea after the Second World War, the establishment of a Communist regime in North Korea prevented them from reopening their former missions.

When the Korean War broke out in 1950, Canadians who previously had served in North Korea and Manchuria returned to the Korean peninsula and established aid stations throughout the south. Understandably, they were especially attentive to those who had fled their homes in North Korea; they even established organizations such as the North-East Korean Christian Fellowship (*Kwanbuk kidok kyouhoe*) to specifically care for their former congregations. Canadian relief efforts were not limited to the spiritual and physical needs of the Korean people; they even extended to the rebuilding of South Korea's infrastructure. Korean refugees also found support by contacting former missionaries who had returned to Canada. These individuals actively sponsored their former students' resettlement in Canada. In the 1960s, former missionaries became a medium for Korean emigration to Canada.

While in Korea, Canadian missionaries had conducted various types of undertakings other than evangelical; these included medical, educational, agrarian and social. According to statistics compiled by the author, some 185 Canadian missionaries worked in Korea from 1888 to 1941. Their combined years of service totalled 3,073.[58]

These missionaries, however, were not the only Canadians in Korea. Other Canadians, who were decidedly not missionaries, were also active there. One of these was James Henry Morris (1871-1942). Born in Barrie, Ontario, on

---

[57] Scott, *Canadians in Korea*, p. 146.

[58] Yoo Young-sik, "Canadian Mind and Korean Heart: A History of Canadian Missions to Korea, 1898-1998," paper presented to the Conference of Celebrating the One Hundredth Anniversary of Canadian Missions to Korea, Emmanuel College, University of Toronto, October 17-18, 1998.

26 June, 1871, he immigrated to America at the age of seventeen. In 1899, Morris—by then a naturalized U.S citizen—came to Korea as part of an engineering team hired to construct Seoul's first streetcar and public water system. After the contract ended, he remained in Korea, establishing both an importing business and a travel agency. Morris was a philanthropist as well as a businessman. When the decision was made in 1924 to found the Seoul Foreign School, he donated both his money and time, serving as chairman of the building committee. In recognition of his services and generosity, the initial building was christened the "Morris Hall." Morris Hall was used as the main Seoul Foreign School building from 1924 to 1957.[59]

Two other Canadians who were active in Korea at the turn of the century made their contribution as journalists. The first, Helen F. M. Lewis visited Korea in 1899 and sent back articles on her experiences to *The Canadian Magazine*. These articles formally introduced Korea to the Canadian general public.[60] The second, Frederick A. McKenzie (1869-1931), is remembered for his two books, *The Tragedy of Korea* (1908) and *Korea's Fight for Freedom* (1920). Initially a London correspondent for *The Toronto Star*, McKenzie went to Korea in 1904 as a war correspondent for the *Daily Mail* of London. While reporting on the Russo-Japanese War, McKenzie also revealed to the world atrocities that the Japanese were committing in Korea through his dispatches. He visited Korea for a second time in 1906, and once again exposed Japan's harsh treatment of Koreans.[61] McKenzie should be seen not only as a friend of Korea, but also as a freedom fighter for the Korean people during the Japanese occupation.

The Government of Canada's first representative to visit Korea, Herbert M. Marler (1876-1940), was the Canadian Minister to the Japanese Empire. Though it is not clear how long he stayed in Korea, it is known that Marler arrived in Seoul in September 1930.[62] It was not until Korea's liberation from Japanese colonization in 1945 that the next Canadian official arrived. In 1948, the United Nations sent an eight-country delegation, known as the United Nations Temporary Commission on Korea (UNTCOK), to oversee the election of a National Assembly. The Canadian government sent George S.

---

[59] Horace H. Underwood, *Seoul Foreign School*. (Seoul, Korea: Seoul Foreign School, 1978), p. 4. See also, the picture of the Morris Hall, unpaginated.

[60] Helen F. M. Lewis, "A Visit to Corea in 1899," in *The Canadian Magazine* (April 1901), pp. 491-96.

[61] Hong Yi-sôp, review article on "Korea's Fight for Freedom, The Tragedy of Korea," in *Korea Journal* (November 1, 1970), pp. 22-28. For more information on F. A. McKenzie, see *Who was Who, 1929-1940* (in Canada), vol. III, (London: Adam and Charles Black, 1941), p. 867.

[62] "Visit of the Canadian Minister (anonymous), in *KMF*, (Oct. 1930), p. 220.

Patterson (1887-1953) as its UNTCOK representative.[63] When the Republic of Korea was established in the southern half of the peninsula in 1948, the Government of Canada recognized the Republic as the only legitimate government on the Korean peninsula in 1949.

During the Korean War (1950-1953), 26,971 Canadians fought for Korea as a part of the United Nations force; 516 would sacrifice their lives in Korea and an additional 1,256 were wounded. [64] Canada's involvement in the Korean war was so intense that even Prime Minister Louis St. Laurent visited Korea, accompanied by his daughter, Madeleine and his son, Jean-Paul, to meet with Canadian servicemen from 7 to 10 March, 1954. His stay in Korea also included a meeting with President Syngman Rhee (1875-1965).[65] As mentioned, official diplomatic relations were established in 1963; this relationship between Canada and Korea was reinforced with a "Special Partnership" Agreement in 1993. Since then, exchanges and bilateral trade have increased between Canada and Korea. Korea is Canada's largest trading partner in the Asia-Pacific region and there are nearly 150,000 Korean residents in Canada.

III. Koreans in Canada

The first known record of a Korean mentioning Canada is in Yu Kil-chun's (1856-1914) work, *Sôyu kyônmun (Observations on a Journey to the Western World)*, published in 1895. After signing the Chemulp'o Treaty with the United States in 1882, King Kojong (1852-1919, r. 1864-1907) sent Korea's first goodwill mission (in Korean, *bobingsa*) to America in 1883.[66] Yu was one of those selected to go and, like the other members, was directed to scrutinize Western civilization. The mission arrived in San Francisco on 2 September, 1883. After about 40 days in the States, during which they met President Chester A. Arthur (1830-1886) in New York, part of the group led by Min Young-ik (1860-1914) continued on to Europe, while the rest returned home in October 1883 under the leadership of Hong Young-sik (1855-1884).

---

[63] Blanche Finley, *The Structure of the United Nations General Assembly: Its Committee, Commissions and Other Organisms 1946-1973,* vol. 1. (Dobbs Ferry, New York: Oceana Publications, Inc., 1977), p. 246.

[64] Interview with Bill Allan, President of Korean Veterans Association of Canada (KVA). Toronto, 11 May, 2000. In 1997, the KVA erected Wall of Remembrance at Meadowvale Cemetery in Brampton, Ontario. For this, see "Korean War veterans honoured," in *Toronto Star* (July 27, 1997), A6, and "Memorial honors fallen soldiers," in *Toronto Star* (July 28, 1997), A6. For more information on Canadians in the Korean War, see John Melady, *Korea: Canada's Forgotten War,* (Toronto, Ontario: Macmillan of Canada, 1983); Ted Barris, *Deadlock in Korea: Canadians At War, 1950-1953,* (Toronto, Ontario: Macmillan Canada, 1999); David J. Bercuson, *Blood on the Hills,* (Toronto, Ontario: University of Toronto Press, 1999).

[65] St. Laurent file in the Public Archives of Canada. MG 25 L, vol. 410, pp. 12-13. The correspondence between Elizabeth Timlin, Political and Public Affairs Archives, Manuscript Division, Public Archives of Canada and present author, dated 20 May, 1986.

[66] *Kojong,* vol. 2. (1970), p. 497; Horace N. Allen, *Korea: Fact and Fancy,* (Seoul, Korea: Methodist Publishing House, 1904), p. 163.

Yu, however, remained behind, enrolling in Dummer Academy in Massachusetts; he attended the Academy until December of the next year.[67] He left the States for a tour of Europe, after which he returned home in December 1885. Yu then committed himself to writing about his experiences in, and his perception of the West.

In his *Sôyu kyônmun*, Yu noted, "there is a place called Canada in North America which totally belongs to England." [68] He not only mentioned "a place called Canada," but also mentioned Newfoundland, the sizes of Saskatchewan, the St. Lawrence River, and Lake Ontario.[69] However, there is no indication that he actually visited Canada himself. The first known Korean to actually touch foot on Canadian soil was Yun Chi-ho (1865-1945). He was a political refugee who had originally fled to Shanghai in 1885 and was sheltered by the Anglo-Chinese Southern Methodist Mission. After Shanghai, he managed to come to America with the help of an American missionary operating in Shanghai. Yun studied at Vanderbilt University in 1888 and at Emory University in 1890. He returned to Korea in 1893, stopping over in Chicago in the process. The Chicago World's Fair was in progress and it was there that he first encountered something Canadian. Specifically, he recorded in his diary that he had seen an enormous Canadian squash at the exhibition; he recorded that it "weighed 486 lbs-10 ft. 1 inch in circumference, 3 ft. 7 inch in height." [70]

---

[67] Lee Kwang-lin, *Han'guk kaehwa sasang yônku* (*The Study of Korean Enlightenment Thought)* (Seoul, Korea: Ilchogak, 1979), pp. 45-92. For more information on Yu and "Dummer Academy", see Lee Kwang-lin, *Han'guk kaehwasa yônku (Study of the History of Korean Enlightenment)* (Seoul, Korea: Ilchogak, 1979), pp. 273-289. In his article, "Koreans," in *Harvard Encyclopedia of American Ethnic Groups,* ed. by Stephen Therston, (Harvard University Press, 1980), p. 602, Kim Hyung-chan stated that "the first Korean student to come to the United States were three men who arrived in 1885. Two returned home but the other, a physician named Philip Jaisohn, spent most of his life in America." Three points must be made; a) These men were not the first Koreans to come to America; b) none could be considered students. The "three men" were political refugees: they were Pak Young-hyo, Sôh Kwang-bôm and Sôh Jae-pil (Philip Jaisohn); and c) The three men Kim mentioned arrived in America in 1885, while Yu Kil-chun arrived in 1883, as this present article revealed. After signing the Chemulpo Treaty with the U.S., in 1882, King Kojong had sent a good-will mission of young Koreans to America in 1883. Yu Kil-chun was a member of that group and after their mission was over, Yu remained in America and registered at Dummer Academy. Therefore, it should be Yu Kil-chun who was the first Korean student in the States, not Philip Jaisohn as Kim Hyung-chan stated. In his book, *Letters in Exile: The Life and Times of Yun Chi-ho* (Covington, Georgia: The Oxford Historical Shrine Society, 1980), p.iii, Kim again erred in claiming that "He (Yun Chi-ho) was the second Korean to attend an American university. The first was Sôh Jae-pil." Kim's statement is historically incorrect.

[68] Yu Kil-chun, *Sôyu kyônmun (Observations on a Journey to the Western World),* tr. by Che Hun. (Seoul, Korea: Taeyang sôjôk, 1978). See pages 360 and 370 of the translation and page 21 of the original. Che Hun, however, did not translate the part in which Canada is mentioned on p. 360.

[69] See translation of Ibid., pp. 61, 67, 68, 72.

[70] *Yun Chi-ho ilgi,* vol. 3, (1893) p. 184.

After a few days in Chicago, he continued on to Vancouver, his port of departure for Korea. Yun's train left Chicago on 9 October, 1893, and arrived in Vancouver "after four days of tedious ride over prairies, wild mountains, canyons, valleys of varied scenes." [71] By travelling through the broad stretch and barren prairies, Yun wondered "why anyone should set up his abode" in such "uninviting surroundings." [72] He also observed Indians for the first time; he noted that they painted their faces with different colours and wrapped themselves with coloured blankets. [73]

Despite his "tedious ride," he found Vancouver to be an attractive and quite cosmopolitan city, one whose citizenry included Cantonese, Japanese, Canadian, American, English, and Hong Kong Chinese. The next day was a Sunday and since he was a devout Methodist, he took the opportunity to worship at a Canadian Methodist Church. Later that afternoon, he visited Stanley Park where he collected "the prettiest of the kind of ferns and mosses." [74] It is because of his collection that he is considered to be not only the first Korean to arrive in Canada, but also the first to own anything uniquely Canadian. He subsequently set sail for home on the "Empress of India" on 16 October, 1893. [75]

About two years after Yun's visit to Vancouver, a Korean couple visited Ontario, accompanied by Rosetta Sherwood Hall, the widow of William James Hall. When Rosetta had planned to return to America, her medical assistant, Kim Chôm-dong (1877-1911), better known as Esther Pak, asked to go to America with her in order to study medicine. Rosetta agreed and brought Esther and her husband Pak Yu-san (?-1900) home with her to Liberty, New York, in early December of 1894. Accompanied by the Paks, Rosetta visited her husband's hometown, Glen Buell, Ontario, to meet with her late husband's parents and relatives in July 1895. Rosetta wrote:

> Mr. Pak still wore his long hair rolled up in a top-knot [*sangtu*], concealed by a bowler hat! He created almost as big a sensation in the West as the Western Barbarian had in the Far East. [76]

After their return to the States, Esther enrolled in the Women's Medical College of Baltimore (present-day Johns Hopkins). She graduated in 1900 with her medical degree, thus becoming Korea's first physician.

---

[71] For his trip from Chicago to Vancouver, see Ibid., pp. 186-190.
[72] Ibid., p. 187.
[73] Ibid., p. 188.
[74] Ibid., p. 189.
[75] Ibid. Yun stayed about 2 days in Vancouver.
[76] *Stethoscope*, p. 161.

A year after the Paks' visit to Ontario, a group of six Korean students headed for the U.S. stopped over in Vancouver on 11 April, 1896. This group included one of the leaders of the Independence Movement, Kim Hôn-sik (1869 -?).[77]

That same month, five Korean special envoys, originally sent abroad to attend the coronation of the Russian Tzar Nicholas II, also arrived in Canada. The group, headed by Min Young-whan (1861-1905), once again included Yun Chi-ho. For Yun, it was his second visit to Canada. The envoys, *en route* to Europe, landed in Victoria, British Columbia, on 28 April, 1896, reaching Vancouver the next day and continued on to New York.[78] There is record that three Korean men migrated to Montreal as early as 1898, possibly as settlers. According to a 1898 passenger list of the Halifax entry port, the three men were Loo Chun Shan (Yu Chun-san), Raw Qhak Tsou (Na Kwak-su) and On Wing Tsou (Ahn Young-su). Obviously, their names were sinologically romanized. They were traveling from Demerara, Guyana and their destination was Montreal. In the column of "country of birth", they were listed as "Corean"; in the "age and sex" column, they were listed as 42, 40, and 35 respectively and male; and in the "occupation" column, Loo was listed as "servant" and both Raw and On as "merchant". [79] The present author attempted every effort to trace down any track of their lives in the Montreal and Quebec areas but was fruitless, except in finding the name "On Wing" in the Montreal Telephone Directory in 1901-1902 and 1902-03. There were two "On Wings" in 1901-02 directory and four "On Wings" in 1902-03 directory. In both directories, all of them were operating a "Chinese laundry" shop, except one who was listed simply as "laundry" without the indication of nationality in both directories. The "On Wings" who were listed under "Chinese laundry" appeared again in the 1903-04 directory, but the name "On Wing" who was listed simply as "laundry" is not shown in the 1903-04 directory.[80] It is a stretch to assume that the very On Wing who was listed simply as "laundry" could possibly be one of the trio of Koreans who landed in Halifax in 1898 and came to Montreal and settled there by operating a laundry shop. These three men could be the first Koreans to "reside" in Canada, though sources are insignificant to prove such a claim.

---

[77] Pang Sôn-ju, *Chaemi hanin ûi tongrip undong (The History of the North American Movement for the Independence of Korea)* (Kangwôndo, Korea: Han Lim University Press, 1989), p. 305.

[78] Min Young-whan, *Haechôn chubôm (Sailing with Autumn Sea and Sky)* (Seoul, Korea: Eulyu munwhasa, 1959), pp. 17-18; Kim I. J, "The Korean Abroad," in, *KR* (1897), pp. 104-107; Allen, *Korea the Fact and Fancy,* p. 196; Chindan hakhoe p'yôn, *Han'guksa: Hyôndae p'yôn* (Seoul, Korea: Chindan hakhoe, 1968), pp. 756-7.

[79] Data is based on a Halifax passenger list (Immigration and Settlers) before 1900.

[80] Cf. Lovell's Montreal Directory, 1901-02/1902-03/1903-04/1904-05/1905-06

Existing records reveal that before 1900, fifteen Koreans passed through Canada. These visits, however, were only transitory affairs in that Canada was being used as a brief stopover prior before reaching the U.S., Europe, or as an embarkation point for home, except for the above mentioned three men who came to Halifax in 1898.

After 1900, the coming and going of people from Canada and Korea became much more frequent. In 1902, King Kojong sent a special delegation to attend to the coronation of England's King Edward VII (1841-1910, r. 1901-1910). The four delegates, headed by Lee Chae-gak (?-?), arrived in Victoria on 14 May, 1902, and travelled on to Vancouver, Winnipeg, Toronto and Montreal before setting sail for England.[81]

In 1905, Kim Il-whan (?-?) came to Canada to "study English Literature." [82] After landing in Victoria on the 8 of August, he headed for Berlin (modern-day Kitchener), Ontario, where he stayed with James Gale's sister, Jane (Gale) Cleghorn.[83] Kim was Canada's first official student. Contrary to his personal wishes, he registered at Berlin Vocational School;[84] it appears that he would have preferred to have gone straight into business. Two years later he moved to New York, where he was able to do as he desired. His letters to Jane indicated that he was engaged in business pursuits in both New York and New Jersey.[85] A later record indicates that he was involved with a Korean business group in Los Angeles in the 1920s.[86]

After Kim, 19 years old Chung In-pyo (1887-1943) arrived in Victoria, British Columbia, in 1906. Chung was a boarder who, in exchange for accommodations, helped out at "Mr. Hard's" store.   While Kim was in Victoria for about three years, he attended a local public school for two years and worked as a laborer. Chung was obviously one of the progressively-minded youth of late 19th century Korea. As most of those youths did so, Chung attended missionary-sponsored mission school in Seoul and he too was in favor of modernizing Korea with Western civilization and wished to

---

[81] Lee Jong-ung, *Sôsarok (The Record of Journey to the West)* 1902, *unpaginated.* The author of this paper, wishes to express thanks to Mr. Lee Hae-sok, who allowed me to use the unpublished travelogue. See also, *Kojong,* vol. 5 (1900-1903), p. 520; Allen, p. 224. This group went to London, England in company with H. Goffe, British Vice Consul.

[82] Kim Il-whan's diary, unpaginated. Author's possession.

[83] This information is based on Kim's diary, which is owned by the author of this paper.

[84] This information is based on the payment receipt issued by the Berlin Business College. According to the receipt, dated 16 October, 1905, Kim paid $3.05. The letter was signed by the Principal of the College, W. D. Euler. Author's possession.

[85] Kim's personal letters to Jane (Gale) Cleghorn, dated 22 December, 1908 and 9 August, 1913. Author's possession.

[86] Kim Wôn-yong, *Chaemi hanin osipnyônsa (The History of Fifty Years of Koreans in America)* (Davis, Calif., Charles Ho Kim: 1959), p. 289.

study in the West as his memoirs revealed: "I wanted to go to America to learn Western civilization and Western politics" [87]. He was acquainted with contemporary missionaries in Korea such as Horace Underwood, Oliver R. Avison and Allen Clark. Canada became a stepping-stone for Chung to go to America. In 1909, after about three years of residence in Victoria, he moved to San Francisco, then later to Chicago where he obtained his doctorate, possibly in medicine, in 1917. Chung lived in the States for about 15 years and returned to Korea in 1921. In Korea, he worked at Severance Hospital where he studied medicine for sometime when he was young under Dr. Avison.

The first Korean to have actually resided in Canada for a few years, though with non-residential status, was Pyôn Young-sil, also known as Sarah, who came to Halifax in 1913. She stayed with Edith, the wife of Duncan McRae, and her family.[88] Sarah remained with the McRaes at their home in Halifax, apparently as a baby-sitter, until 1917.

The relationship between Canada and Korea was solidified not only by Canadians doing missionary work in Korea but also by Koreans sent to Canada to be trained as missionary helpers. As mission work in Korea continued to grow, more field workers were needed. Considering the financial burden incurred when sending Canadian missionaries to work in the field, and realizing the need for trained indigenous personnel to assist in mission work, it was decided to train Koreans in the same church tradition that produced the Canadian missionaries. Prospective native leaders were sent to Canada to be educated and moulded in accordance with mission work requirements. Under this plan, group of students were sent to Canada, mainly to Halifax and Toronto, from the 1910s through the 1960s. While some of these students returned to Korea, or went on to the U.S., others remained in Canada and prepared the way for regular Korean immigration to Canada.

The first "privately-sponsored" student to come to Canada under the aforementioned "prospective leader training" programme was Cho (also spelled Jo) Hi-ryôm (1885-1950). Cho came to Halifax in 1914 with the help of the missionary sisters Elizabeth (1862-1941) and Louise McCully (1864-

---

[87] The information on Chung In-pyo is based on his unpublished memoir and interview with his son, Chung Jong-hun, Toronto. The author of the paper wishes to thank Mr. Chung Jong-hun for allowing me to use his personally owned unpublished memoirs. The author of this paper also wishes to thank Prof. Chung In-jae, Sogang University, who decoded the written memoirs.

[88] Helen F. McRae Parker Lee, comp., *A Bibliography of Korean Relations with Canadians and other Western Peoples which Includes a Checklist of Documents and Reports 1898-1975* (Occasional paper #12, School of Library Service, Dalhousie University), p. 124. Interview with Helen McRae on 23 July, 1985.

1945) and entered Dalhousie University in 1915.[89] He received his Bachelor of Divinity in 1920 and, immediately thereafter, went to Toronto, where he enrolled in Knox College in the University of Toronto. During his time in residence, an article in the *Globe and Mail* reported that he won the Orator's Gold Medal in the annual Knox College Undergraduate Association's speech contest.[90] According to the University of Toronto Registry, he obtained his Master of Arts from the University of Toronto in 1923.[91]

Kang Young-il (1898-1972) came to Halifax in 1919 through the help of a Nova Scotian missionary, Luther L. Young (1875-1950). Kang studied at Pine Hill Divinity College for a year, then suddenly departed for the States. He was not interested in studying theology. Once established in America, he studied at Boston University, Harvard University, and New York University. Kang would later write books, such as *The Grass Roof* (1931), *East Goes West: The Making of an Oriental Yankee* (1937) and many articles on Korea. He also taught Comparative Literature (East/West) at New York University and worked for the U.S. Government as an "Oriental Expert." After Korea gained independence from Japan in 1945, Kang returned to Seoul and worked for the American Military Government as Chief of Publications in the Office of Public Information. He did not stay long in Korea and returned to the States. After living for many years in Long Island, New York, he retired to Satellite Beach, Florida, dying there in 1972[92]

Although these first students came to Halifax as a result of private arrangements, beginning in the 1920s, a formal system of bursary students was established. These publicly supported students studied in Toronto.

The first was Kim Kwan-sik (1887-1948), who studied at Knox College, University of Toronto, during 1922-23. After Knox, he went to Princeton University and obtained his Master of Theology from Princeton in 1926.

After the birth of the United Church of Canada in 1925, the overseas missions that formerly operated under Presbyterian auspices now did so under the United Church of Canada. This led to a small change in procedure. Starting from the mid-1920s, missionary-related bursary students registered at Emmanuel College, University of Toronto, which is affiliated with the United Church of Canada. The first of these students was Moon Chae-rin (1896-1987), who came to Toronto in 1928, entered Emmanuel College, and obtained a

---

[89] Kim Jung-gun, "To God's Country: Canadian Missionaries in Korea and Beginning of Korean Migration to Canada." Unpublished thesis, Ed.D., Ontario Institute for Studies in Education, University of Toronto, 1982, pp. 78-87. See also, *Kidokyo tae paekkwa sajôn (The Christian Encyclopedia),* vol. 13 (Seoul, Korea: Kidok kyo munsa, 1985), p. 1245.

[90] *Globe and Mail* (Toronto) (28 February, 1923); *The Toronto Star* (1 March, 1923). Newspaper clippings. Page is unknown. Present author's possession.

[91] Information obtained from Biographical File in the University of Toronto Archives.

[92] Kim Jung-gun, pp. 87-107.

Bachelor of Divinity in 1932. Moon set up residence in Toronto (1971-81). While in Toronto, he established the Korean Senior's Association (an outgrowth of the Korean Senior Citizens Society of Toronto) in October 1973. [93]

In 1926, a medical student, Choi Young-wook (1891-1951), M.D., entered the physiology program at the University of Toronto with the help of O.R. Avison, M.D. Prof. John McCleod (1876-1935), who had shared the 1923 Nobel Prize with Frederick G. Banting for the discovery of insulin, supervised Choi's M.A. thesis. In a 1930 work entitled "Korean Students in America", Choi is listed as the first Korean to obtain a degree from the University of Toronto. [94] This is, however, historically incorrect as Choi obtained his Master of Arts in 1927 from the University of Toronto, four years after Cho Hi-ryôm obtained his M.A.

During the 1930s, only one bursary student came to Canada. Kim Jun-sông (1898-1978), also known as John Starr, registered at Emmanuel College in 1934 and three years later, obtained his Bachelor of Divinity degree. [95] He then went to Princeton University for advanced studies.

The Board of Foreign Missions' and the field missionaries' strategy of providing Koreans with short-term training to use them in the field was frustrated in that these mission-sponsored students tended to prolong their stay longer than their sponsors had suggested. Some — if not most — of these students harboured the idea of getting further advanced degrees, either in Canada or the U.S., instead of returning to Korea to become "native leaders" as the missionaries intended. Moreover, a sizeable proportion used their sponsorship as a steppingstone for U.S. immigration. Therefore, the Board's policy of sending Korean students to Canada was suspended. However, in 1947, the Board decided to try again and sent two individuals: one to specialize in academies and the other in medicine.

The first was Chung Tae-yi (1917 -), also known as David. He registered at Emmanuel College in 1947, obtained his Master of Theology in 1949, and went back to Korea. Later, he enrolled in the Department of Religion at Yale University and received his Ph.D. in 1959. Presently, Chung is residing in Canada.

In 1947, Whang Tai-yôn (1914-1999), M.D., was brought to Lamont Hospital (Lamont, Alberta) to be trained in clinical laboratory work and surgery. After his internship, Whang travelled throughout North America, practicing medicine in New York City, Quebec City, Saint John's, New Brunswick, and Ottawa, all the while searching for a place to set up residence.

---

[93] The Committee of Church History, *Toronto hanin yônhap kyohoe samsipnyônsa (The History of Thirty Years of Toronto United Church)* (Toronto, Ontario: The Committee, 1997), p. 48; Interview with Pak Jae-sôn on 20 December, 1993.

[94] Horace H. Underwood, "Korean Students in America and What They Bring Back," in *KMF*, (April 1930), p. 70; Choi, Y[oung] O[ok]'s file in the University of Toronto Archives.

[95] Kim Jung-gun, pp. 107-14.

He finally chose to live in Blind River, Ontario, practicing medicine there for twenty years from 1957 to 1977. Many local people of Blind River remember him as "Dr. Wang" and the street where Dr. Whang's office located is unofficially referred to as "Wang Street." [96] Whang relocated to Toronto in 1977 and lived there until he died in 1999. Although there is no document to prove so, Whang is widely regarded within the Korean community as the "first" permanent Korean immigrant to Canada,[97] though there are no official records available to prove this. There were some non-mission related Koreans who visited Canada in the early 1900s, among them were Hong Ôn, Pak In-dôk and Kim Hyông-soon.

One important role of Koreans living abroad during the Japanese occupation was their monetary support for groups in the Korean independence movement. Starting in 1920, Hong Ôn (1880-1951), a member of the North American-based National Independent Movement, visited Chinese communities in Western Canada, soliciting their help. [98]

Moreover, as part of the overseas' support for the independent movement, Pak In-dôk (1897-1980) visited Toronto in the early 1930s, and publicly lectured about the Japanese colonization of Korea. In his Memoir, *Avison* said:

> I was then in Korea and was much interested in learning how she [Pak In-dôk] was received at that great but somewhat conservative institution, the University of Toronto, Canada. I was much pleased to receive a letter from a friend there telling me that her meeting had been attended by large numbers of students and also by many professors and that she was numbered amongst the most convincing speakers that had ever visited the University.[99]

Another Korean-American, Kim Hyông-soon (1903-1977), a resident of California, visited Ontario for a *Kiwanis* meeting in 1932. At the meeting, he purportedly sang the Korean national anthem before a group of nine hundred for Korea was under Japanese occupation at that time.[100]

---

[96] Letter to the present author from Rhea Marcellus, Librarian, Blind River Public Library, dated 30 Septembe, 1996; Interviews with Whang Tai-yôn on 15 December, 1993 and 23 December, 1993.

[97] Pak Chan-ung, "Hangukin kanada imin che ilho-Ûisa Whang Tai-yôn sônsaengûl ch'ajasô," (The First Korean Immigrant in Canada: A Visit to Dr. Whang Tai-yôn), in *New Korea Times* (Toronto), 14 and 21 January, 1978.

[98] Pang, Sôn-ju, p. 269.

[99] *A-Memoir*, p. 464.

[100] Sonia Shinn Sunoo, *Korea Kaleidoscope, Oral Histories, Early Korean Pioneers in USA: 1903-1905* (Published by the Korean Oral History Project, Sierra Mission Area, United Presbyterian Church, USA, 1992), p. 27. Kim Hyông-soon appeared to be a business man in the Los Angeles area in the 1920s and was known as a millionaire. For this, see "Korean Millionaires in the 1920s in L.A." in *The Korea Central Daily* (Toronto) (10 April, 2000), A5.

He would be the first person to sing the Korean national anthem in Canada.

In 1948, several Korean politicians (Cho Pyông-ok, Chung Il-hyông, and Kim Jun-ku) visited Ottawa and met Canadian politicians, including Prime Minister St. Laurent and Lester B. Pearson, then a Minister of Foreign Affairs.[101] Sôh Jong-wook (1917-) acquired Canadian residency status through marriage. Sôh had met a Japanese-Canadian co-ed while studying in Japan. After marrying, they went to China and stayed there until 1945, the year Korea was liberated from Japanese occupation and returned to Korea. Sôh and his wife decided to immigrate to Canada and they arrived in Vancouver on 31 May, 1953.[102] Present author's research alluded that when Sôh came to Canada in 1953, he appears to have been the first Korean who obtained landed immigrant status to Canada because it was possible for him to have been granted landed immigrant status through his wife who was a Japanese-Canadian; this is contrary to what, as previously mentioned, has been long believed in the Korean-Canadian community: that Whang Tai-yôn is regarded as the first permanent Korean immigrant to Canada.

Whang being "the first Korean-Canadian" appeared to have been first suggested in Pak Chan-ung's article, "Hangukin kanada imin che ilho" ("The First Korean Immigrant in Canada"). Pak's article is based on his interview with Whang and was published in the *New Korea Times* in 1978.[103] In that article, however, one can find no direct mentioning of how or when Whang obtained his immigrant status to Canada, and yet Pak called him *"imin ilho"*, "the first Korean immigrant" in Canada. Pak's misinterpretation resulted in a completely distorted view of the fact by a later historian. In his doctoral thesis, "To God's Country: Canadian Missionaries in Korea and Beginning of Korean Migration to Canada" (1982), Kim Jung-gun claimed that Whang was "the first Korean-Canadian." [104] Kim obviously styled his claim after Pak's article. This is certainly a case where a fact has been stretched out too far without a solid historical base. Present author learned that because of Canada's Privacy Protection Law, any record on the personal history of an immigrant is "closed" to the public and after a certain time period, such documentation is discarded. This means that there is neither an official or unofficial document available to define who was "the first" Korean immigrant to Canada. Whang himself was silent about this matter. Whang came to Alberta in 1947, then to New York in 1950 and back to Canada in 1955. He practiced medicine in Quebec City, Saint John, New Brunswick,

---

[101] Pak Sil, *Han'guk oekyo bisa (The Unknown History in the History of Korean Diplomacy)* (Seoul, Korea: Kirinwôn, 1979), p. 31.

[102] Pak Chan-ung, "Han'gukin.."

[103] See note #97.

[104] Kim Jung-gun, p. 168.

and Ottawa until his settlement in Blind River, Ontario, possibly in 1957.[105] It appears that Whang's *wanderlust* life-style finally ended with his new job at St. Joseph's Hospital in Blind River. In fact, extant records and interviews did not prove in regard to his *imin ilho,* the first Korean immigrant.

The 1960s were an important period in the history of Korean emigration. Several hundred young Korean men and women went to West Germany as miners and nurses in 1962; the first group of 91 emigrants arrived in São Paulo, Brazil, in 1963; and the migration to the U.S. began in 1965. During this same decade, Koreans began to settle in Canada. Such an out-flow of Koreans from their native land occurred because the Government of South Korea officially encouraged emigration to the countries like the U.S., Brazil and Canada.

Koreans have always migrated in hopes of carving out a "better" life. Individual Koreans intending to establish "permanent residency" in Canada began to arrive in the early 1960s.[106] Two such individuals became particularly prominent in the history of Korean immigration to Canada. The first was the afore-mentioned Whang. Whang has reminisced about how terrifying his life was under the Communists in North Korea; where he lived until his migration to the south in 1947, he had long dreamed about bringing his family and friends to this vast land and building a village of their own.[107]

On 21 April, 1964, Whang wrote a letter about the possibility of bringing in Korean "farm workers" to Prime Minister Lester Pearson, who was from his electoral constituency (Algoma District, Ontario). Whang said that he submitted the list of names of about forty people, mainly his family members, in his letter to Pearson.[108] He had previously purchased a 156-acre parcel of land at Parkinson near Iron Bridge, Ontario, where he established a poultry farm. He also purchased another 153-acre farm, known as "My-T-Fresh Egg Farm", about seven miles west of Iron Bridge, where he set up a high-tech egg-processing plant.[109] Whang's plan to bring Korean farmers *en masse* to his farm was struck down by Canadian Immigration regulations. Eventually, in

---

[105] Dr. Whang's name is listed on the local Telephone Directory (Sault Ste. Marie, October 1958), p. 14. This indicates that he probably came to Blind River in 1957 and ordered a phone, his name should have appeared a year later in 1958.

[106] For more information on Korean immigrant history in Canada, see Yoo, "Koreans [in Canada]," pp. 882-890.

[107] Interview with Whang Tai-yôn, Toronto, Ontario, 15 December, 1993 and 23 December, 1993.

[108] Interview Ibid. See also, Pak Chan-ung's article, note #97.

[109] Interview Ibid. The data is based on Land Registry, Algoma District, Ontario. Present author visited Blind River and Iron Bridge on 18 May, 2000 and from 29 August to 1 September, 2000 and interviewed the owner of the farm.

mid-1964, the Parkinson Farm Co-op was able to sponsor dozens of immigrants, amongst them, Ro Yun-gô's family and Chang Young-man's family.[110]

There is another individual who made a significant contribution to open the door for Korean immigration to Canada. On 22 June, 1964, Chun Taik-bo (1901-1980), then President of the *Chônusa* Company Ltd., in Seoul, visited Ottawa and met with the Deputy Minister of Citizenship and Immigration, Claude Malcolm Isbister,(1914-). Prior to his visit to Canada, Chun met with George Woodall Cadbury (1907-), a Canadian who visited Korea early in 1964. Cadbury had previously worked as an economic and family planning advisor in Canada and the United Kingdom, as well as serving as an advisor to the Government of Japan, Korea, the Philippines, Indonesia, Sri Lanka, Thailand, Burma and Singapore. Furthermore, he had worked at the United Nations.[111] Cadbury introduced Chun to Isbister. Chun's meeting with Isbister was successful. Less than a month after his visit, Isbister sent a letter to Chun endorsing Korean immigration to Canada. This letter, dated 2 July, 1964, was the official document which formally opened Canada to "regular" Korean immigrants.[112]

At that time, all Republic of Korean applications for emigration to Canada were processed through the Office of the Superintendent of Canadian Immigration in Hong Kong. It was not until 1965, that a Hong Kong-based Canadian Immigrant officer visited Seoul for the first time; from 1966 and onward, an officer came to Seoul every month to process applications. Chun provided office space for this immigration official in his company's main office in downtown Seoul. Furthermore, Chun organized the *Canadian Immigration Council* in the Seoul YMCA, the *Korea-Canada Cultural Association* and held *Canada Night* in order to encourage Koreans to immigrate to Canada. The first immigrant to come to Canada as a result of Chun's efforts arrived in late 1965.[113] The late start to official Korean immigration to Canada was due to Canadian immigration policy legislated by MacKenzie King's government in 1947; this policy was used to exclude Asian immigration until the early 1960s. In 1966, Lester Pearson's Liberal government changed the original policy, which emphasized immigration as a means of supplying new citizens for Canada, to one in which the focus of

---

[110] Ibid.

[111] For more information on Cadbury see, Kieran Simpson, ed., *Canadian Who's Who 1992* (Toronto, Ontario: University of Toronto Press, 1993), p. 152.

[112] Letter was dated 2 July, 1964, and signed by C.M. Isbister, Deputy Minister of Citizenship and Immigration.

[113] Yoo, "Koreans [in Canada]," p. 884.

immigration was placed on manpower, or economic needs. It was this change that permitted more "people of colour" to immigrate to Canada. Korean immigration to Canada was the result of both Korea and Canada's internal economic policies regarding the control of human resources.The idiosyncrasy of Korean migration before and during the early 1900s was that, for the most part, it was done by solitary wanderers. Moreover, after their country lost its sovereignty to Japan, Koreans were forced to carry Japanese passports, something that exposed them to an extra measure of discrimination. During the 1950s, Koreans were looking for political stability; those who emigrated were looking primarily to escape the terror-filled atmosphere founded on the peninsula during the Cold War. However, the circumstances triggering emigration underwent a significant change in the 1960s.

In addition to those coming directly to Canada from Korea, starting in the late 1960s, Korean immigrants came to Canada from third countries like West Germany, South American countries and from Vietnam. These countries were stepping stones for them to enter Canada. Because such immigrants were the result of a "two-stage migration"(a migration after a migration), it has been difficult to gather verifiable data on them.

In 1991, *Census Canada* reported that 44,095 Koreans lived in Canada, an increase from the 27,680 Koreans accounted for in 1986. Canada's Korean population grew 59.3% in 5 years. In Ontario, the 1986 Census reported 17,200 and the 1991 Census reported 26,795 Koreans living in the province; this works out to an increase of 55.78% over 5 years. Admittedly, such growth is merely a rough estimate. Differences between Census Canada's figures and the actual head count are significant because of the following reasons: a lack of participatory consciousness on the part of new immigrants in regards to the Census, and a large number of transient immigrants forced to wander from place to place in search of work.

After analyzing business and local directories, community leaders and local newspapers have estimated the Korean population in 2001 to be as follows: 80,000 in Ontario; 50,000 in British Columbia; 3,000 in Quebec; 1,000 in Alberta; and 1,000 in Manitoba. When those living in the other provinces are included, there are nearly 150,000 Koreans residing in Canada. More than half live in Ontario, particularly in the Metropolitan Toronto area. Toronto is especially attractive because of the city's multi-lingual society, the area's weather, and the feasibility of finding a job in Toronto's Korean community.

Canada is a culturally diverse country in terms of the languages, religions and lifestyles maintained by its citizens. Canada has encouraged immigrants to retain their cultural heritages while participating in one common Canadian culture, a policy generally known as "multiculturalism." This idea became official policy when Prime Minister Pierre Elliott Trudeau (1968-1979/1980-1984) enacted the Policy of Multiculturalism in 1971. Korean immigrants have responded well to this ideal, participating in various multi-cultural activities as a way of becoming a part within the Canadian whole. Through the *Pavilion of Seoul* in Toronto's annual *Caravan* festival, *Folklorama* in Winnipeg, *Heritage Festival* in Edmonton, or the *Music Festival* in Newfoundland, Koreans have freely displayed their traditional costumes, food, native arts, and dances to Canadians.

IV. Conclusion:

Canadians initially came to know Korea through a single book during the late nineteenth century and through the Christian evangelists who travelled to Korea. James Gale, who would become the first to go to Korea in 1888, set the example of the pied piper, and as many as 185 Canadian Christian missionaries would follow Gale's footsteps and serve in Korea. This was temporarily halted in 1942 when foreigners were forced to leave Korea as Japan declared war on the U.S.

After the end of WWII, Korea was liberated from the Japanese occupation; the Republic of Korea was only established in the southern half of the peninsula in 1948; a year later, the Canadian government recognized the ROK as the only legitimate government on the Korean peninsula. When the Korean War broke out, 26,971 Canadians were sent to Korea to fight against the Communists; 516 lost their lives and 1,255 were wounded. Canada and Korea opened a new era by establishing official diplomatic relations in 1963.

How Koreans came to know Canada can be paralleled in the same manner as to how Canadians came to know Korea: through books and travellers. The first Korean who travelled to Canada was Yun Chi-ho, in 1893, five years after Gale touched Korean soil. Before 1900, it is estimated that fifteen Koreans visited Canada as sojourners on the way to the U.S. or Europe, or to embark on a ship for home. From 1900 to the mid-1940s, Koreans came to Canada mostly as students, with some exceptions such as Pyun Young-sil who stayed four years in the Maritimes.

In the 1960s, the Korean government encouraged emigration and consequently, massive migration took place. In the 60s, Canadian immigration policy changed favourably for all Asians, and in 1966, the Lester Pearson government changed immigration policy from an emphasis on racial criteria to Canada's economic needs. Beneficiaries of that policy, Koreans began to settle in Canada in the 60s.

According to Statistics Canada, 93 Koreans immigrated to Canada in 1965.[114] Until investment immigrants were allowed to enter Canada in the

---

[114] *Immigration Statistics* (Ottawa, 1965), p. 23.

1980s, emigrating Koreans were either independent or assisted by already-established relatives. In the year 2001, it is estimated that nearly 150,000 Koreans reside in Canada and over half of that population resides in Ontario, particularly in the Metropolitan Toronto area. In 1993, Canada and Korea started a significant relationship by agreeing to two things: the "Visa Exemption Agreement" and the "Special Partnership". These agreements have brought the two countries closer into mutual cooperation and constructive interaction. Increasing number of students under ESL programs and travellers have flocked to Canada in the 90s.

In recent years, universities in both countries have increased student exchange programs. For example, Yônsei University has created links with 17 institutions in Canada, including the University of Toronto. There are some cities in Canada and Korea that are in the process of establishing sister relationships: these include; Vaughn, Ontario, and the city of Namwôn; Richmond Hill, Ontario, and the city of Kuri; and Toronto and Seoul.

Considering the developments and interactions made in recent years, we should expected that Canada and Korea will continue to evolve into closer relationships in economics, industrial joint ventures, bilateral trade, cultural exchanges and international cooperation in the Asia Pacific region in the new millennium.

BIBLIOGRAPHY

English Language

Allen, Horace N. *Korea the Fact and Fancy.* Seoul, Korea: Methodist Publishing House, 1904.

Avison, Oliver R. *Memoir.* 1940?

Barris, Ted. *Deadlock in Korea: Canadians at War, 1950-1953.* Toronto, Ontario: Macmillan of Canada, 1999.

Feasby, William R. *University of Toronto: Faculty of Medicine 1843-1966.* Toronto, Ontario: University of Toronto Press, 1967.

Fenwick, Malcolm C. *Church of Christ in Corea.* New York: George H. Doran, 1911.

Finley, Blanche. *The Structure of the United Nations General Assembly: Its Committee, Commissions and Other Organizations 1946-1973.* Dobbs Ferry, New York: Oceana Publications, Inc., 1977.

Fisher, James E. *Pioneers of Modern Korea.* Seoul, Korea: Christian Literature Society of Korea, 1977.

Gale, James S. "Forty Years in Korea," unpublished manuscript.

Hall, Rosetta, ed. *Life of Rev. William J. Hall.* New York: Young People of Canada and the United States, 1897.

Hall, Sherwood. *With Stethoscope in Asia: Korea.* McLean, Virginia: MCL Associates, 1978.

Kim, Jung-gun. "To God's Country: Canadian Missionaries in Korea and Beginning of Korean Migration to Canada." Unpublished Ed.D. dissertation, Ontario Institute of Studies in Education, University of Toronto, 1982.

McCully, Elizabeth and J.O. Fraser, *Our Share in Korea.* Toronto, Ontario: The Woman's Missionary Society, The United Church of Canada, 1932.

Melady, John. *Korea: Canada's Forgotten War.* (Toronto, Ontario: Macmillan of Canada, 1983.

Paek, Lak-geoon. *The History of Protestant Missions in Korea, 1832-1910.* 2nd edition. Seoul, Korea: Yonsei University Press, 1971.

Ross, Murray. *Y.M.C.A. in Canada: The Chronicle of a Century.* Toronto, Ontario: The Ryerson Press, 1951.

Rutt, Richard. *A Biography of James Scarth Gale and A New Edition of His History of Korean People.* Seoul, Korea: Royal Asiatic Society Korea Branch, 1972.

Scott, William. *Canadians in Korea.* Toronto, Ontario: United Church of Canada, 1976.

Sunoo, Sonia Shinn. *Korea Kaleidoscope, Oral Histories, Early Korean Pioneers in USA: 1903-1905.* Korean Oral History Project, Sierra Mission Area, United Presbyterian Church, California, 1992.

Underwood, Horace H. *Seoul Foreign School.* Seoul, Korea: Seoul Foreign School, 1978.

Who was Who, 1929-1940 (in Canada), vol. III. London: Adam and Charles Black, 1941.

Who's Who (in Canada, 1992). Toronto, Ontario: University of Toronto Press, 1993.

Yoo, Young-sik. *Earlier Canadian Missionaries to Korea, A Study in History, 1888-1895.* Toronto, Ontario: Society for Korean and Related Studies, 1987.

_____. "The Impact of Canadian Missionaries in Korea: A Historical Survey of Early Canadian Mission Work, 1888-1898". Unpublished Ph.D. dissertation, University of Toronto, 1996.

Articles in English

"Annual Report of University of Toronto Young Men's Christian Association, 1893-94."

Avison, Oliver R. "Creating a Medical School in Korea," in *University of Toronto Monthly*, November 1937, pp. 39-42.

Fenwick, Malcolm C. "Korean Farming," in *Korean Repository*, August 1898, pp. 288-293.

Gale, Ada. "Life of James Scarth Gale. D.D." Unpublished manuscript, 1932.

Gale, James S. Gale's letter to University College YMCA, dated December 14, 1888; February 9, 1889.

Goforth, Jonathan. "Our Treatment of a Great Trust," in *Knox College Monthly,* (May 1887), pp. 23-28.

Hall, Sherwood. "Application of Sanatorium Methods to Korean Patients," in *The China Medical Journal,* vol. 44. July 1930, pp. 662-666.

_____. "The Story of Korea's First Christmas Seal," in *Korea Mission Field,* May 1933, pp. 92-97.

Hong, Yi-sup. "Korea's Fight for Freedom, The Tragedy of Korea," in *Korea Journal.* November 1, 1970, pp. 22-28.

Kim, Hyung-chan. "Koreans," in *Harvard Encyclopedia of American Ethnic Groups,* ed. by Stephen Therston, Harvard University Press, 1980, pp. 601-606.

Lewis, Helen F.M. "A Visit to Corea in 1899," in *The Canadian Magazine.* April 1901, pp. 491-96.

Medical Missionary, 1:1, 1891.

"Minutes of University College Young Men's Christian Association," 1888-1898

"Rev. James S. Gale, D.D." minutes adopted by the Board of Foreign Missions of the Presbyterian Church of America.

"Seven New Missionaries," in *Knox College Monthly,* June 1889, pp. 105-107.

Seoul Press, September 6, 1911.

Toronto City Directory, 1887.

Underwood, Horace H. "Korean Students in America and What They Bring Back," in *Korea Mission Field.* April 1930, pp. 67-72.

"University College YMCA Mission to Corea," in *Knox College Monthly*, November 1888, pp. 35-36.

"University of Toronto — Class and Prize Lists 1884-1888."

"University of Toronto YMCA Minutes 1888.

Varsity, February 16, 1892.

"Visit of the Canadian Minister," in *Korea Mission Field.* October 1930, pp. 220, 220.

Yoo, Young-sik. "Canada and Korea: Over one hundred years of Shared History," paper presented to tje International Conference on Korea-Canada Relations: Past and Present and Future. Yonsei University, Korea, October 22, 1999.

_____. "Canadian Mind and Korean Heart: A History of Canadian Missions to Korea, 1898-1998," paper presented to the Conference of Celebrating One Hundred Anniversary of Canadian Missions to Korea, Emmanuel College, University of Toronto, October 17-18, 1998.

_____. "Koreans [in Canada]," in *Encyclopaedia of Canada's People,* ed. by Paul Robert Magocsi. Toronto, Ontario: University of Toronto Press, 1999, pp. 882-890.

_____. "Putting 'C' in Corea: The Canadians Who Went to Korea," in *Presbyterian Record.* March 1998, pp. 23-25.

_____. "The Relationship Between Korea and Canada: A Historical Survey of Canadians in Korea and Koreans in Canada," paper presented to Canadian Asian Studies Association, University of Calgary, Calgary, Alberta, June 9-11, 1994.

_____. "The Impact of Canadian Mission Work in Korea: An Examination of Late Nineteen-century Canadian Missionaries in Korea, with Particular Emphasis on J.S. Gale, M. Fenwick, R. Hardie, O.R. Avison and W. McKenzie," paper presented to Association for Korean Studies in Europe, Humbolt University, Berlin, Germany, April 16-20, 1993.

Korean Publications

Chindan hakhoe p'yôn. *Han'guksa: Hyôndaep'yôn.* Seoul, Korea: Chindan hakhoe, 1968.

Committee of Church History. *Toronto hanin yônhap kyohoe samsipnyônsa (The History of Thirty Years of Toronto United Church).* Toronto, Ontario: The Committee, 1997.

Kim, Young-hûi. *Jwaung Yun Chi-ho sônsaeng ryakjôn.* Kyông Sông. Jwaung Yun Chi-hosônsaeng hûinyôn kinyôm wiwônhoe/ Kidokkyo Chosôn kamrihoe chongriwôn, sowha 9 nyôn. [1934]

Kim, Wôn-yong. *Chaemi hanin osipnyônsa (The History of Fifty Years of Koreans in America).* Davis, Calif., Charles Ho Kim, 1959.

Kuksa p'yônchan wiwônhoe. *Kojong sidaesa (History of Kojong Period).* Seoul, Korea: Kuksa p'yônchan wiwônhoe, 1967.

Kwangsông kusipnyôn p'yônchan wiwônhoe. *Kwangsông kusipnyônsa (Ninety-Year History of Kwangsông School).* Seoul, Korea: Minjung insoe kongsa, 1984.

Lee, Jong-ung, Sôsarok *(The Record of Journey to the West),* 1902. Unpublished manuscript.

Lee, Kwang-lin. *Han'guk kaewha sasang yônku (The Study of Korean Enlightenment Thought).* Seoul, Korea: Tamkudang, 1970.

Min, Kyông-bae. *Han'guk kidokkyo sahoe undongsa (History of Social Movements in Korean Church).* Seoul, Korea: Taehan kidokkyo sôhoe, 1990.

Min, Young-whan. *Haechôn chubôm.* Seoul, Korea: Eulyu munwhasa, 1959.

Ministry of Foreign Affairs. *Kanada hyôn hwang (Review of Canada).* Seoul, Korea: Ministry of Foreign Affairs, 1989.

Pak, Sil. *Han'guk oekyo bisa (The Unknown History in the History of Korean Diplomacy).* Seoul, Korea: Kirinwôn, 1979.

Pang, Sôn-ju. *Chaemi hanin ûi tongrip undong (The History of the North American Movement for the Independence of Korea).* Kangwôndo, Korea: Han Lim University Press, 1989.

Yu, Kil-chun. *Sôyu kyônmun (Observations on a Journey to the Western World).* tr. by Che Hun. Seoul, Korea: Taeyang sôjôk, 1978.

Yun, Chi-ho. *Yun Chi-ho Ilgi (Diary of Yun Chi-ho).* Seoul, Korea: Kuksa p'yônchan wiwônhoe, 1973.

Articles in Korean

Yoo, Young-sik. "Kanada hanin iminsa", (Korean Immigrant History in Canada), in *Saegesokûi hangukmunwha (Korean Culture in the Globe)* Seoul, Korea: The Academy of Korean Studies, 1991, pp. 211-223. Co-authored with Yu, Chai-shin. See also, *The Journal of Canadian Studies.* 1992 vol. 4, pp. 55-72.

____. "Kanada anûi uri munwha" (Korean Culture in Canada) in *Hanguk minjok munwha taepaekwasajôn (Encyclopedia of Korean Culture)* vol. 22. Seoul, Korea: Academy of Korean Studies, 1991, pp. 830-831.

ACROSS THE TUMEN AND BEYOND:
CANADIAN MISSIONARIES, KOREAN CHRISTIANS
AND THE JAPANESE ON THE MANCHURIAN BORDER, 1911-1941

A. HAMISH ION
ROYAL MILITARY COLLEGE OF CANADA

The fiftieth anniversary of the Korean War and the advent of the new millenium is a fitting time to commemorate a part of the Korean diaspora which sixty years ago was very well-known to churchgoing Canadians. This was the Manchurian borderland of Chientao (Kando) province which was, during the inter-war years, the cockpit of the anti-Japanese movement and the Korean nationalist armed struggle against the Japanese colonial regime in metropolitan Korea on the other side of the Tumen river. It was in these Manchurian marches that Kim Il Sung wove the mythology of his reputation as a guerrilla leader in the late 1930s.[1] Central to this paper, however, is Lungchingtsun (Yonjung, Dragon Well Village), a market town and administrative and educational centre in Chientao province. From 1911 to the advent of the Second World War in East Asia, Lungchingtsun was a major mission station of Canadian Presbyterian (after 1925, United Church of Canada) Korean Mission.[2] Even though the Canadian and Christian connections have

---

[1] See Bruce Cumings, *Korea's Place in the Sun: A Modern History* (New York: W. W. Norton & Company, 1997), pp. 160-162.

[2] For Canadian missionary activity in Korea under Japanese colonial rule, see the appropriate chapters in A. Hamish Ion, *The Cross and the Rising Sun: The Canadian Protestant Missionary Movement in the Japanese Empire, 1872–1931* (Waterloo: Wilfrid Laurier University Press, 1990); A. Hamish Ion, *The Cross in the Dark Valley: The Canadian Protestant Missionary Movement In the Japanese Empire 1931–45* (Waterloo: Wilfrid Laurier University Press, 1999). Of particular use for the study of early Canadian missionaries in Korea is William Scott, *Canadians in Korea: Brief Historical Sketch of Canadian Mission Work in Korea: Part One to the Time of Church Union* (Toronto: United Church of Canada Board of World Mission, 1970) and Yoo Young-sik, "The Impact of Canadian Missionaries in Korea: A Historical Survey of Early Canadian Mission Work, 1888–1898." Unpublished PhD diss. Centre for the Study of Religion, University of Toronto, 1996. Of considerable interest are reminiscences by Canadian missionaries including Robert Grierson, "Episodes on a Long, Long Trial" (ninety-one page typescript in the possession of Dr. G. H. Underwood, Seoul,

gone, Lungchingtsun still remains to the present an educational and cultural centre for the ethnic Korean community in that region of Manchuria.[3] Indeed, it has a place in Korean 20th century literary history for Lungchingtsun is where the Christian poet, Yondong Jo, is buried.[4]

This paper investigates the mission station at Lungchingtsun as a case study of Canadian-Korean-Japanese relations. It is concerned with the issue of Korean nationalism and Christianity during the Japanese colonial period in Korean history. Was nationalism more important to Korean converts than their Christian faith? Was the apparatus of church and mission school simply a convenient conduit through which to carry on the struggle against the cruel Japanese colonial overlords? Did Canadian missionaries naively become the pliant tools of Korean nationalists? Certainly, there are elements of all these questions in the history of the Lungchingtsun mission station during the halcyon days of the nineteen twenties and thirties. While it served both Korean nationalists and the Japanese military to exaggerate the extent of armed resistance to Japanese authority, Canadian missionaries sought to develop a Korean Christian community in a region where guerrilla warfare and brigandage were endemic. In hindsight, it is clear that neither Canadian missionary or Korean Christian comprehended the power of the forces unleashed in north-east Asia in the wake of the Bolshevik Revolution.

Korea); Florence J. Murray, *At the Foot of Dragon Hill* (New York: E. P. Dutton, 1975), and the fine biography of Duncan MacRae: Helen Fraser MacRae, *A Tiger on Dragon Mountain: The Life of Rev. Duncan M. MacRae, D. D.* (Ross Penner and Janice Penner, eds. Charlottetown: A. James Haslam, QC, 1993). For a standard history of Christianity in Korea see Allen D. Clark, *A History of the Church in Korea* (Seoul: Christian Literature Society, 1971). A good survey of religions in Korea is James Huntley Grayson, *Korea: A Religious History* (Oxford: Oxford University Press, 1989). For an important study dealing with the relationship between Korean Christianity and Koreans, see Wells, Kenneth M. *New God, New Nation: Protestants and Self-Reconstruction Nationalism in Korea 1896–1937.* (North Sydney, Australia: Allen and Unwin, 1990). Among Japanese language studies of Korean Christianity, and the Japanese religious policies toward Korean Christianity, the following are recommended: Han Soki, *Nihon no Chōsen Shihai to Shukyō Seisaku* (Tokyo: Matsue Sha, 1988); Ji Myon Kuwan [Chi Mekan], *Kantōku Gendai Shi to Kyōkai Shi* (Tokyo: Shinkyō Shuppansha, 1975); Kan Jeon, *Chsen Kindai Shi* (Tokyo: Heibonsha, 1986); Kan Wijo, *Nihon Toji Shita Chōsen no Shukyō to Seiji* (Tokyo: Seibunsha, 1976); Kaneta Ryuichi, *Senjika Kirisutokyō no Teiko to Zasetsu* (Tokyo: Shinkyō Shuppansha, 1985); Kankoku Kirisutokyō and Rekishi Kenkyūjo. *Kankoku Kirisutokyō Shi 1919–45* (Han Shyuki and Kuroda Masahiko, trans. Tokyo: Shinkyō Shuppansha, 1995); Min Kyong Be, *Kankoku Kirisutokyō Shi: Kankoku Minzoku Kyōkai Kisei no Katai* (Iru Chyun Kim, trans. Tokyo: Shinkyō Shuppansha, 1981); Sawa Masahiko, *Mika no Chōsen Kirisutokyō Shi* (Tokyo: Nihon Kirisutokyōdan Shuppan Kyoku, 1991). For a brief but perceptive account of the Japanese Kumiai Kyōkai work in Korea, see Matsuo, Takayoshi, "Nihon Kumiai Kirisutokyōkai no Chōsen Dendō." *Shisō* (July 1968), pp. 949–65.

[3] Takasaki Soji, *Chugoku Chōsen Zoku: Rekishi, Seikatsu, Bunka, Minzoku Kyoiku* (Tokyo: Akashi Shoten, 1996), pp. 90-100.

[4] Ibid., p. 94.

This, however, was not evident to even the most sanguine missionary after the end of the First World War. The Canadian missionary response to the atrocities committed by the Japanese in the wake of the March 1919 independence demonstrations and the indefatigable efforts of Frank Schofield to publicize Japanese wrongdoings in the world's press concretely demonstrated their concern for the plight of Korean Christians at this time. This can be conveniently interpreted as support for Korean nationalist aspirations for independence. Certainly, there were some Canadian missionaries, most especially, Schofield himself and O. R. Avison, one of the pioneer Canadian missionaries to come to Korea, who hoisted themselves with the petard of Syngman Rhee and as a result their reputations much benefited after the Korean War. However, such people as Schofield and Avison were in the minority. For most Canadian missionaries, sympathy for the plight of Koreans under Japanese colonial rule did not translate itself into support for Korean independence. While the leadership of the United Church of Canada publicly supported Chiang Kai-shek and the Chinese Nationalists in their struggle against the Japanese after 1937, they chose not to align themselves behind Syngman Rhee even during the Second World War.[5]

For those on the Manchurian border, the reality of the tumultuous situation existing there from 1919 meant that they would support those who harmed Korean Christians the least. It was those missionaries, living in the security of Seoul or P'yongyang far from the dangers of the borderlands, who tended to be the most outspoken in their criticism of Japanese rule. Initially, the Japanese and Chinese authorities harmed Korean Christians the most but this would change by the beginning of the nineteen thirties. By that time, of course, the Korean Christian movement had been eclipsed as the vanguard of Korean nationalist movement by the Communists. The safety and well-being of Korean Christians in Chientao was paramount to missionaries, and not the nationalistic aspirations of converts. Missionaries became virulent critics of the actions of Korean nationalist partisans for the same reasons that they had criticized the Japanese in past years. What does stand out about the late nineteen thirties and early nineteen forties, however, was the skill with which missionaries were able to maintain and to protect the Christian community in

---

[5] During the Pacific War, O. R. Avison championed the political cause of Syngman Rhee through a political lobby for the creation of an independent Korea named the Christian Friends of Korea. Avison pressed A. E. Armstrong, the assistant mission secretary of the United Church of Canada Missionary Society, to throw the weight of the United Church of Canada behind this organization. While Armstrong thought that Korea should be either granted independence or put under the supervision of the United Nations Association after the war, there remained a possibility until the very end of the war that Korea might remain a Japanese colony. Armstrong felt that if the United Church of Canada openly supported the political freedom of Korea, then this might prevent Canadian missionaries returning to Korea if Korea remained a Japanese colony. See A. Hamish Ion, *The Cross in the Dark Valley*, p. 319.

Lungchingtsun. When war broke out between Canada and Japan, missionaries were able to leave the Korean Presbyterian Church in Chientao and northern Korea in as strong a position as was conceivably possible. In doing this, the actions of Canadian missionaries ran against the anti-Japanese current of both Korean nationalism and the conservative fervour of many of their American Presbyterian missionary colleagues in regards to Japanese religious policies.

The picture world of Korean students, churches, pastors and Sunday School kids in Lungchingtsun that filled Church newspapers and magazines across Canada, wherever the banner of the United Church of Canada stood high, disappeared with the opening of the Pacific War and vanished forever with the onset of the Cold War in East Asia. Naturally, such a cheerful vision of school graduations, church gatherings, and smiling groups of missionaries and Korean Christians runs counter to the often heart-rending but always sombre photographs of burnt buildings, political demonstrations and bayoneted partisans that provide the visual grist showing the savagery of the Japanese over which the Korean nationalists heroically struggled and ultimately triumphed. Nevertheless, the sacrifices, struggles, and suffering of Korean Christians as well as the outpouring of Canadian treasure, the hard work and faith of Canadian missionaries seemingly were for nought. For while the Korean community in Lungchingtsun survived the Second World War, Canadian missionaries were unable to return.

I

On their arrival in Korea from Nova Scotia in 1898, the first Canadian Presbyterian missionaries were asked by the already established American Presbyterian societies to undertake work in northeastern Korea. Later, the territory assigned to the Canadians was extended into the adjacent Manchurian borderlands and beyond into Siberia. Wonsan, Sungjin, Hamheung and Hoiryung became mission centres. In 1909 significant missionary reinforcements arrived from Ontario, and plans were laid to expand mission work from North Hamkyung province across the Tumen into Chientao with Lungchingtsun serving as its mission centre. Lungchingtsun was at the heart of an agriculturally rich and extensively forested region. It was a place of considerable commercial activity as well as the administrative centre for the surrounding countryside, with government schools and hospitals. Relatively close to Hoiryung in metropolitan Korea, Lungchingtsun was important enough to warrant the permanent presence of a foreigner official of the Imperial Chinese Maritime Customs, and to possess enough Christian religious promise to serve as a centre for German Roman Catholic missionary endeavour.[6] Likewise, there was a Chinese Presbyterian church

---

[6] In 1932 the population of Lungchingtsun was given as slightly fewer than 20,000 of whom 32 were foreign residents. See Zai Kantō Nippon Sōryōjikan, *Kantō Jijō Kōgai* (n. p.: n. p.: 1932), p. 3.

there. However, Canadian missionaries were concerned with the evangelization of the Korean population[7] and not the Chinese.

From its establishment in 1911, the mission station at Lungchingtsun developed rapidly. By 1919 the mission compound served not only as the evangelistic centre of work expanded on the lines of the Nevius Method but also the educational centre boasting a higher school for both boys and girls that was fed from the network of rural Korean Christian primary schools connected to individual Korean congregations. Further, Lungchingtsun also possessed a mission hospital with a resident Canadian missionary doctor. The Christian presence in this region of Manchuria can be seen in the fact that in 1934 among Koreans registered as religious believers in the Chientao region, Christians were the most numerous, and Christian churches had an overwhelming presence as far as houses of worship were concerned.[8] This Christian development had taken place over less than a quarter century.

In 1913 William Rufus Foote, the Canadian Presbyterian missionary who was instrumental in establishing Lungchingtsun as a mission station, observed that:

> Kando [Chientao] was only a name to us three years ago and
> we never considered it an important part of our field. It was
> a largely unoccupied tract of land, capable under cultivation
> of sustaining a large population. After the Japanese rule in
> Korea became oppressive many natives moved there until
> now some estimate the Korean population at 500,000.[9]

---

[7] As early as 1907 a Korean Presbyterian church had been established in Lungchingtsun. Likewise, the Myong Dong Christian School was opened in 1908. See Han Ryu Ki, *Kankoku Kirisutokyō no Junan to Teikō: Kankoku Kirisutokyō Shi 1919-45*, translated by Kurata Masahiko (Tokyo: Shinkyō Shuppansha, 1995), p. 120. Canadian missionaries, therefore, began work where there was already an existing Korean Christian community.

[8] See Shinkyō Tetsuro Kyoku, *Kantō Chiho Gaiyō* (n. p.: n. p.: May 1934), p. 107, pp. 113-114. There were some 33,560 Korean believers belonging to various religions: 22,430 Christians, 6,518 Confucianists, 2,256 Buddhists and 1,346 Tendokyoists. There were 138 Christian churches in the Chientao region out of a total of 183 religious houses. Of Christian groups, the Canadian mission had 55 churches, the Roman Catholics 35, the Southern Methodists 20, and the Toa Kirisutokyōha (Holiness Church) 20. The German Roman Catholic missionaries with some 9,700 adherents were the only other Western missionaries in the immediate vicinity of Lungchingtsun.

[9] Quoted in William Scott, *Canadians in Korea: Brief Historical Sketch of Canadian Mission Work in Korea: Part One to the Time of Church Union* (Toronto: United Church of Canada Board of World Mission, 1970), p. 74. Foote's estimates of Korean immigrants in Chientao are perhaps too high, a more reliable estimate for the Chientao region and Siberia would be 190,000 in 1910, 500,000 in 1922, and 630,000 in 1931. See *Iwanami Kōza: Nihon Tsūshi* (Tokyo: Iwanami Shoten, 1994), dai 18 kan, kindai 3, p. 90.

In expanding their work into Manchuria, the Canadian Presbyterians were following the northward path of Korean immigration. It is clear that Foote, at least, felt that this immigration was caused by the Korean desire to get away from Japanese control. However, two of the results of the Russo-Japanese War were the colonization of Korea and the acquisition of Japanese rights in Manchuria.[10] While these rights in Manchuria are normally seen in terms of the Liaotung Peninsula and the development of the South Manchurian Railway, they also included concessions in Chientao and north-eastern Manchuria. The security importance of the region (in light of the co-operation between Koreans and Russians in this area during the Russo-Japanese War) was clearly illustrated in 1907 when the Japanese controlled Korean Residency-General opened a branch office in Lungchingtsun under the command of Lieutenant-Colonel Saito Suejiro. In October 1909 the Japanese government formalized its position by signing the Kantō (Chientao) Treaty with the Chinese government. This provided for the establishment of a Japanese Consulate in Lungchingtsun in order to supervise and control the Koreans who made up seventy-five percent of the population of the region.[11] In reality, the Koreans crossing the Tumen into Chientao were not getting away but its forests and hills made its policing difficult.[12] Indeed, it was among fire field peasants working in the remotest areas of the region that the nationalists found much of their support. Among the most active in the Korean nationalist movement in Chientao were Korean Christians. The intensity of anti-Japanese resistance increased as a result of the Siberian intervention of 1918, which Korean nationalists actively opposed. It came to a head with the independence movement demonstrations in the middle of March 1919 in the major towns of the Chientao region.[13]

Canadian missionaries in Lungchingtsun were caught unaware of the vital role that Korean Christians played in the organization of the demonstration in the town. A. H. Barker, a Canadian missionary resident in Hoiryung reported in late March 1919 that "in Yong Jung [Lungchingtsun] the Chinese troops fired on the crowd and Koreans were killed & 18 seriously wounded." [14] The Canadian missionaries found themselves in the middle of what was, in fact,

---

[10] Arima Manabu, *[Kokusaika] no Naka no Teikōku Nihon* (Tokyo: Chuokoron Shinsha, 999), p. 65.

[11] Kan Jeon, *Chōsen Kindaishi* (Tokyo: Heibonsha Sensho, 1986)), p. 187.

[12] The early development of the Korean independence movement in Chientao is described in Paul Ho bom Shin, "The Korean Colony in Chientao: A Study of Japanese Imperialism and Militant Korean Nationalism, 1905-1932," unpublished Ph.D dissertation, University of Washington, 1980.

[13] See Hara Kishi, "Kyokutō Roshia ni okeru Chōsen dokuritsu undō to Nihon," *San Sen Ri*, vol. 17 (Tokushu San Ichi Undō Rokyu Shūnen), 1979, pp. 47-53.

[14] U[nited] C[hurch] [of] C[anada] A[rchives], P[resbyterian] C[hurch] [in] C[anada] GA41 B6K, Box 4, File March 1919, A.H. Barker to R. P. MacKay, 27 March, 1919.

one of the most famous March 1919 independence demonstrations and the largest of its kind in Manchuria.[15] Although the numbers involved tend to vary up to 30,000 (larger than the entire population of the town), Dr. Stanley Martin, who was in charge of the mission hospital in Lungchingtsun and treated many of the wounded, reported to the British Consul in Mukden that some 8,000 had taken part in the demonstration in front of the Japanese Consulate in the centre of Lungchingtsun on 12 March, 1919. The crowd had been listening perfectly harmlessly to speeches and waving flags before being fired upon by Chinese soldiers. Martin believed that the Chinese were under the control of the Japanese and had fired on the crowd because they were afraid that if they had not done so Japanese troops would storm across the border.[16] Martin also thought the Japanese were convinced that the missionaries were involved in supporting the independence demonstrations.

William Scott, another Canadian missionary in Lungchingtsun, complained to the British Consul in Mukden that Japanese plainclothes policemen had trespassed into the mission compound hoping to arrest some of the Korean workers in the mission hospital.[17] What was at stake here was the fact that missionaries still enjoyed extraterritorial privileges as Lungchingtsun was in China and Japanese police had no right to enter. Scott was not about to let the Japanese into the mission compound which he regarded under extraterritoriality as British territory.[18] He also complained about the beatings Japanese police had given the Koreans whom they had interrogated. According to Scott, some unfortunate Koreans, including one of the teachers at the Canadian mission school for girls, had been held in prison for ten days without being questioned even once. As a result of this sort of treatment, Scott believed that the Koreans in Lungchingtsun had been reduced to living in a state of terror. Understandably, however, the fact that independence demonstrations continued to take place in other towns in the Chientao region in the days immediately after the demonstration in Lungchingtsun did nothing to improve Japanese and Chinese police treatment of Koreans.[19] While both Martin and Scott were insistent that Canadian missionaries in Lungchingtsun tried to keep as free from politics as

---

[15] See Paku Kyon Shiku, *Chōsen San Ichi Dokuritsu Undō* (Tokyo: Heibonsha, 1976), pp. 206-207. See also Paku Uon Shiku, *Chōsen Dokuritsu Undō no Ketsu Shi.* Translated by Kan Doku Sen. 2 volumes (Tokyo: Heibonsha, 1978), vol. 1, p. 182.

[16] Martin quoted in [United Kingdom] P[ublic] R[ecord] O[ffice], F[oreign] O[ffice] 371/3818/766/90971 P. E. O'Brien Butler to Sir J. N. Jordan, 11 April, 1919.

[17] The Japanese police believed that an independence newspaper was being printed in the mission compound on a mimeograph machine belonging to the missionaries.

[18] PRO FO 371/3818/766. W. Scott to P. E. O'Brien-Butler, 14 April, 1919.

[19] See Paku Kyon Shiku, *Chōsen San Ichi Dokuritsu Undō*, pp. 207-211.

possible, there is irrefutable evidence that Japanese suspicions of Korean Christians in the town being deeply involved in the independence movement were correct.[20]

Although the missionaries might not have been aware of the full details of the involvement, it would be highly surprising if they had no inkling of Christian activities in support of the independence movement. The Myong Dong (Meito) Christian school, for instance, was an especially important centre of independence activity where an independence newspaper was published (thus the suspicion of the Japanese police about the non-existent mission mimeograph).[21] Myong Dong students and teachers played a key role in helping to organize pupils from other schools and to plan the demonstration in Lungchingtsun. The school's headmaster, Kim Yaku-jon, who later became influential in the socialist movement, was closely watched by Japanese police. He had been a representative from the Chientao region at the All Russia Korean Peoples' Congress held in Vladivostock.[22] This meeting discussed sending representatives to France to press the case for Korean independence at the Paris Peace Conference and also began planning for independence demonstrations to coincide with the memorial services for ex-King Kojong. The proclamation issued by the All Russia Korean Peoples' Congress served as the basis for the alliance of Christians, Tendokyoists, and Confucianists for independence. Among the leading female organizers who had delivered one of the four speeches to the crowd at Lungchingtsun on March 12 was the teacher from the girls' school whom Scott had reported as being held by the Japanese.

It was the killing and mistreatment of innocent Koreans by the Japanese that appalled missionaries in Lungchingtsun and drove them to protest Japanese actions to the British Foreign Office. While Frank Schofield, the Canadian missionary attached to the Severance Union Medical College in Seoul, remains the most famous of hostile Canadian missionary critics of Japanese actions in the aftermath of the 1 March, 1919 independence demonstrations in Seoul, the reports of Martin, Scott and others in Lungchingtsun also helped to provide the Foreign Office with information from which to base their diplomatic protest against Japanese brutality.[23] The protest of missionaries in Lungchingtsun would be remembered by the Japanese and helped to precipitate a more serious clash between the Japanese and Canadian missionaries over the Chientao Punitive Expedition in 1920.

---

[20] Dr. Paul Hobom Shin has noted that the leaders of the Chientao wing of the 1 March, 1919 independence movement drafted their version of Korea's independence declaration in the basement of the Canadian mission hospital. See Paul Hobom Shin, "The Korean Colony in Chientao," p. 278. See also Paku Kyon Shiku, *Chōsen San Ichi Dokuritsu Undō,* pp. 205-207.

[21] Kan Jeon, *Chōsen Kindaishi,* p. 199.

[22] Hara Kishi, "Kyokutō Roshia ni okeru Chōsen Dokuritsu Undō to Nihon," p. 50.

[23] See PRO FO 371/3818/109885, Lord Curzon to B. Alston , 22 July 1919.

II

The independence movement in Chientao did not end with the suppression of the demonstrations in March 1919. The failure to obtain the swift independence of Korea by peaceful means led some within the independence movement to become increasingly more radical and militant. The change in the nature of the independence movement was exemplified by the power struggle between the two major factions within the provisional government of Korea that was formed in Shanghai in April 1919.[24] One faction, led by Syngman Rhee and drawing its support largely from the Korean expatriates in the United States, advocated the use of diplomatic means to achieve independence by exerting international pressure on Japan. The other faction, led by Yi Tong-hwi and supported by socialists and nationalists in Siberia and Chientao, advocated the intensification of armed struggle. By the end of 1919, Yi's faction was in control of the provisional government in Shanghai. In Chientao province, following the March demonstrations, anti-Japanese peoples' organizations had been formed. One of the most important was the Hunchun (Konshung) branch of the Great Korea Peoples' Congress. This single branch had the support of some 20,000 people in the district surrounding Hunchun (which was north-east of Lungchingtsun and closer to the Siberian border). Many Christians supported this branch. Hunchun was one of the outlaying stations of the Canadian mission and regularly visited by missionaries and Korean pastors from Lungchingtsun. By August 1920, the Hunchun branch was providing support for about 450 guerrillas. In all, about 2, 600 partisans were operating in north Chientao.[25]

These developments worried the Japanese. Although Hara Kei, the Japanese Prime Minister, dismissed the idea that the independence movement was motivated by a Korean desire for self-determination, other Japanese felt that the independence movement had a deep intellectual foundation.[26] Moreover, it was felt by some that the independence movement in Korea had acted in concert with the movements in Chientao, Vladivostock and Shanghai.[27] In this triangle outside of Korea, the nationalists in Chientao were seen to be particularly important because of the financial support that they gave to the independence movement.[28] In response to the March 1919 demon-

---

[24] Paku Kyon Shiku, *Chōsen San Ichi Dokuritsu Undō*, p. 225.

[25] Ibid., pp. 211-212.

[26] Taiheyo Senso Ge'in Chosabu, Nihon Kokusai Seiji Gakkai, *Taiheiyō Sensō e no Michi - Kaisen Gaikoshi* (Tokyo: Asahi Shimbunsha, 1963), volume 1 p. 178.

[27] Ibid., p. 178.

[28] Ibid., p. 178.

strations, the Japanese had despatched six battalions and some 450 military police across the Tumen into north Chientao to help subjugate the independence movement. However, Japanese efforts were hampered by the fact that Chinese authorities were in de jure control of this region of Manchuria. Nevertheless, the Japanese were clearly prepared to send large numbers of troops and gendarmes into Chientao, if an opportunity arose. By fully subjugating Chientao, they saw that they could indirectly deal a severe blow to the independence groups in Siberia and Shanghai. The appropriate opportunity came with the Second Hunchun Incident of October 1920.

Although the anti-Japanese activities of Korean nationalists were of primary importance in precipitating the Chientao intervention, it was against a background of serious reverses in Manchuria, north China and Siberia during 1920 that the Japanese government reached its decision to send a punitive expeditionary force into Chientao.[29] As early as April 1920 the Japanese residents in Lungchingtsun had petitioned Tanaka Giichi, the Army Minister, to ensure both their personal safety and Japanese commercial interests.[30] In the light of the Nikolaevsk Incident of May 1920 in Siberia in which a sizeable number of Japanese troops had been killed by partisans and the inability of the Chinese forces in Manchuria to deal with the anti-Japanese partisans there despite Japanese assistance, the Japanese Army was sympathetic. Indeed, during the spring and summer of 1920, Korean guerrillas led by Kim Chya Jin had been successful in a series of skirmishes with Japanese security forces on the Manchurian side of the Tumen.[31] What is important about these events was that this was the first time that Korean partisans in Chientao had gained victories over the Japanese. By August 1920 the Japanese military had begun to make preparations for an invasion.[32] The pretext for Japanese action occurred on 2 October, 1920, when some 300 mounted partisans attacked Hunchun and burnt the Japanese Consulate.[33] The Japanese responded quickly by dispatching large numbers of troops to Hunchun and commenced a general invasion of Chientao using the 19th Division garrisoned at Hoiryung.

---

[29] Also important was the deteriorating situation in Siberia where the Japanese army still remained after the Western powers had withdrawn from the Intervention. The Hunchun district was of considerable strategic importance to Japan because of its situation immediately behind Vladivostock. Coupled with this was Japanese annoyance with Chang Tso-lin, the Manchurian warlord, for upsetting Japanese designs in north China as well as his take-over of Harbin and the line of the Chinese Eastern Railway after the collapse of White Russian forces under General D. L. Horvath in October 1920. See E. Edmund Clubb, *Twentieth Century China* (New York: Columbia University Press, 1964), pp. 93-94, 102.

[30] *Gendai Shi Shiryo* (Tokyo: Misuzu Shobo, 1963), volume 26, pp. 61-64, especially p. 62.

[31] Kan Toku San, *Chōsen Dokuritsu Undō no Gunzō: Keimō Undō kara San Ichi Undō e* (Tokyo: Aoki Shoten, 1998 edition), p. 123.

[32] *Gendai Shi Shiryo*, vol. 26, pp. 116-122.

[33] This was the second attack by partisans on Hunchun in less than a month. See Kan Toku San, *Chōsen Dokuritsu Undō no Gunzo*, p. 125.

While there was some scepticism about the motives behind Japanese intervention in Chientao, the Japanese version of what had happened was generally accepted by the foreign press.[34] The presence of what the Japanese described as "bandits" could be used to justify the continued need for Japanese troops across the Tumen. Student demonstrations in Beijing against the Japanese intervention were to be expected.[35] However, what was not expected was the foreign press giving prominence to the accusations brought by Canadian Presbyterian missionaries in Lunchingtsun that Japanese troops committed widespread atrocities against Koreans in Chientao.[36]

In a letter published in the Toronto *Globe* just before Christmas 1920, William Scott, on furlough from Lungchingtsun, rebutted the Japanese version of events.[37] Scott reported that he had travelled extensively in the spring of 1920 in the area south of the Hunchun district and had seen no sign of "Chinese bandits." Indeed, Scott had seen only two small groups of armed Koreans who were extorting money from Korean farmers for the provisional government in Shanghai. He believed that Chinese military patrols prevented the formation of Korean revolutionary bands. Further, although he had no firsthand evidence about what happened in Hunchun, Scott had earlier witnessed the burning of a Japanese Consulate elsewhere in Chientao which had been perpetrated not by any Korean revolutionaries but by disgruntled Korean police attached to the Consulate guard.[38] Scott flatly contradicted the Japanese claim, which was supported by Korean nationalist groups themselves, that Chientao was seething with revolutionaries. Although both sides might have exaggerated their numbers, Scott must have been either wilfully blind or unusually insensate not to have known what was going on in his mission area.

By the end of October 1920, letters from William Rufus Foote, Emma Palethorpe and S. H. Martin had come to the attention of S. Shimazu, the Japanese Consul-General in Ottawa.[39] These letters attacked the burning of churches and schools including the Myong Dong Christian School. Further to this, the letters gave details of atrocities and murders committed by the Japanese Army during October 1920. The army could hardly deny burning churches, but the stock answer was that the buildings were used as meeting places by the independence movement. As to the killings, the excuse was always that those killed were independence activists who had offered resistance. Linguistic problems also aided the Japanese, missionaries in their

---

[34] See, for instance, Toronto *Globe*, 8 December, 1920.
[35] *The Times* (London), 20 November, 1920.
[36] Ibid., 15 December, 1920.
[37] Toronto *Globe*, 23 December, 1920. Cf. fn. 31.
[38] Ibid.
[39] See *Gendai Shi Shiryō*, volume 26, pp. 670-678.

letters referred to incidents that took place in villages with romanized Korean names. The Japanese used Chinese characters. Some incidents, therefore, could be conveniently lost in linguistic confusion. It goes without saying that Japanese records could not substantiate any of the claims of the missionaries about atrocities or murders by Japanese troops.[40]

In January 1920 in a letter published in the Toronto *Globe*, Stanley Martin, the young Newfoundlander physician at the mission hospital at Lungchingtsun, argued that the Japanese invaded Chientao "with the seeming intention of wiping out of existence, if possible, the whole Christian community, especially all young men." [41] Martin further noted that "village after village is daily being methodically burned and the young men shot, so that at present we have a ring of villages surrounding this city [Lungchingtsun] that have suffered from fire or wholesale murder, or both." [42] Martin detailed the atrocities committed by Japanese soldiers. He reported that either Koreans had been murdered or houses had been burned by the Japanese in 32 villages. In one village, he maintained that as many as 145 inhabitants had been killed. In another, 14 people had been positioned in front of a large grave and then shot, and their corpses burned.[43] There is no Japanese record (and the Japanese were sticklers for keeping records) that 145 people were killed in any one village. Moreover, it is very difficult to substantiate the charge that the Japanese were aiming to wipe out the entire Christian community. What was apparent, however, to the Japanese was that many Korean Christians were deeply involved in the independence movement. This was irrefutable. For their part, the Canadian missionaries were intent on protecting Korean Christians and church property. As to church property, there was little that the Canadians could do because the rural Christian churches and schools destroyed by the Japanese were owned by the individual Korean congregations (in keeping with the Nevius Method) rather than by the Canadian mission. Thus diplomatic pressure could not be applied for compensation under violation of extraterritorial privilege for that was only possible if the Canadian mission held the titles to the destroyed churches.

Yet the Japanese seemingly took the missionary accusations that they had committed atrocities seriously, for in November 1920 a military commission under a Colonel Mizumachi Takezō,[44] who had been military attache in Washington, was established to investigate the charges. The protests of the Canadians likely would not have attracted undue Western attention, especially

---

[40] Ibid., pp. 678-681.

[41] Toronto *Globe*, 20 January, 1921.

[42] Ibid.

[43] Ibid.

[44] For a brief biographical note on Mizumachi (1875-1961) see Hata Ikuhiko, *Nihon Rikukaigun Sōgō Jiten* (Tokyo: Tokyo Daigaku Shuppankai, 1996 edition), p. 140.

as the findings of the military commission did not substantiate their claims, had it not been for the naivete of the Japanese Army and Colonel Mizumachi in their dealings with the missionaries in Lungchingtsun. Without a doubt, William Foote, who was one of the original three Canadian Presbyterian missionaries in Korea and the possessor of a robust and strong personality, offended the Japanese officers stationed in Lungchingtsun. No diplomat, Foote spoke his mind. The upshot was that the Japanese Army accused the missionaries of fomenting revolution. On 7 December, 1920, *The Times* of London reported that a Major-General Satō of the War Department in Tokyo had stated:

> it is a curious circumstance that most of the insurgents are Christians while the mission schools are their headquarters. It is a matter of regret that some missionaries entertain the mistaken notion that the Japanese Army is persecuting Christians. We may suppose that the insurgents consider it to their own advantage to rely on foreigners in order to further their aims, flocking together under the shelter of missionaries and assuming the name of Christians with the same design. The missionaries and mission schools have exceeded the bounds of duty. Some directly encouraged the insurgents bands, the schools being training places. The missionaries, while accusing the Japanese troops of inhumanities and taking photographs to substantiate what they say, are themselves the cause of the tragedy that has befallen the insurgents.[45]

While there was some truth to the notion that Korean Christians had been active in the independence movement and particularly students in Christian schools had helped in its organization, there was absolutely no evidence that missionaries themselves had actively encouraged the movement. Major-General Satō further made the mistake of threatening the Canadians for he suggested that the Japanese might be forced to remove the missionaries because "Japan grants freedom of religious belief, but cannot allow treason that threatens to undermine the foundations of the Empire." [46] A Japanese Army officer had no right to threaten to stop the activities of Christian missionaries in a foreign land in which his own army was an unwanted aggressor. These accusations by a senior officer in the Japanese Army created a diplomatic incident, for Chientao was a sovereign part of China.

Both the Canadian and British governments took this incident very seriously. As late as July 1921, Miles Lampson, a British Foreign Office

---

[45] *The Times* (London), 7 December, 1920.
[46] Ibid.

official, noted after a meeting with Loring Christie, the technical adviser to the Canadian Prime Minister Arthur Meighen that "there was again the question of the Canadian missionaries in Chientao, that no doubt has made considerable stir in Canada but we had gone into the matter with the greatest care."[47] By that time, the British government had established what had taken place in Chientao and whether or not the accusations against the Canadian missionaries were justified. W. B. Cunningham, a British consular official who was sent from Mukden to Lungchingtsun to report on conditions in Chientao in May 1921, thought that the difficulties between the Japanese military and Canadian missionaries were "as much the result of the different personalities and character of the parties concerned as of anything else, as the somewhat rough and ready ways of the Canadian missionaries must be very liable to be misunderstood by Japanese officials with their love of formality of all kinds." [48] Although there were personality clashes between Canadians and Japanese, Cunningham could find no evidence to substantiate the Japanese charges against the missionaries. In regards to Japanese military attitudes toward Korean Christians in Chientao, he concluded that they were undoubtedly viewed with suspicion by the Japanese and, in certain instances, they had been deliberately singled out for persecution. However, he also believed that this persecution was not motivated by anti-Christian sentiments, so much as by the conviction that Korean Christians as a body were supporters of the independence movement. Cunningham noted that because of the superior education and broader outlook of many Christians, as a rule they manifested a greater interest in politics and were more patriotic than the average Korean, although he qualified this by adding that not many Christians were actually active partisans.[49]

To Cunningham, it was also clear that the Japanese had invaded Chientao with every intention of permanently occupying the region. Yet, he noted that "after about a fortnight of general burning and destruction the whole thing ceased as suddenly as it had begun, probably because the Japanese found that the news of what they were doing was finding its way to the outside world." [50]

It was the international protest that made them withdraw. In this context, the Canadian missionaries have to be given considerable credit for bringing about the cessation of destruction and saving Chientao for China, albeit only for a few years. The British Foreign Office was under no illusion that the

---

[47] PRO FO 371/6586/F2576/3/10, M. W. Lampson interview with L. Christie, 14 July, 1921.
[48] PRO FO 371/6586/230 Sir B. Alston to Lord Curzon, 17 June 1921, enclosure no. 2, W. B. Cunningham to F. E. Wilkinson, 7 June, 1921.
[49] Ibid.
[50] Ibid.

Japanese would not hesitate to take over Chientao at the next opportunity and that this would simply whet their appetite for further conquests in Manchuria.[51] This, indeed, had been the British diplomatic opinion at the time of the March 1919 demonstrations in Lungchingtsun. Japanese actions in the Chientao region presaged their eventual acquisition of Manchuria. The Canadian missionary response to the Chientao intervention is an early example of the missionaries' power to influence events in remote areas by publicizing their views in the international press and by pressing the Canadian government and British Foreign Office. Without the Canadian missionaries in Lungchingtsun, it is very unlikely that the Japanese explanation of its actions in Chientao would have been questioned. Following hard on the heels of the atrocities committed by the Japanese in the aftermath of the March 1919 demonstrations, the Chientao intervention occurred at an inopportune time, as the Japanese and British governments were negotiating the renewal of the Anglo-Japanese Alliance. What happened in far-off Chientao could have only contributed to Canadian public antipathy toward the renewal of the Alliance.

As far as Canadian missionaries themselves were concerned, Cunningham had been "very favourably impressed with the work which missionaries were doing in Chientao, and especially that of Dr. Martin. Their withdrawal from the district would be a calamity for its Korean inhabitants."[52] Without the missionary presence, the Korean Christian community would be completely defenceless. Their sense of outrage against Japanese actions drove missionaries to publicize what had happened. In this, their view of events was highly subjective and one-sided.

The Canadians portrayed the Koreans as innocent victims and by doing so denied the truth of the armed struggle against the Japanese. Both Korean nationalists and Japanese believed that the partisan activity in Chientao following the March 1919 demonstrations was important. Missionaries, however, were not diplomats or consular figures whose wider sources of information and training allowed them to take a holistic view of the crisis, what missionaries reported was simply that their converts were being beaten, tortured and killed by Japanese soldiers. Stanley Martin, in particular, was as zealous as Frank Schofield had been the year before in seeing that news of the atrocities reached the outside world. He was motivated by humanitarian feeling. In February 1921, Martin wrote that "it's pathetic to meet these poor people wandering over these cold bleak hills and plains persecuted and

---

[51] Ibid.

[52] Ibid.

beaten, wounded and slaughtered like helpless sheep."[53] In this letter, Martin wrote a short poem about the desolation of Chientao: the two concluding lines were "Mankind has a country/ Korea the grave."[54] This illustrates the depth of feeling that the suffering of the Koreans at the hands of the Japanese Army had evoked among Canadian missionaries.

The Chientao region was strategically very important both to Korean partisans and to the Japanese military. It was the fate of Canadian missionaries to be serving the Korean community in an area that was a battleground until 1945.

III

The position of Canadian missionaries in Lungchingtsun was linked to the world of international relations. Japanese actions in Chientao before 1931 were monitored by the Western diplomatic community because they served as one measuring stick by which to gauge Japanese ambitions concerning Manchuria as a whole. For their part British diplomats were much concerned with the maintenance of their extraterritorial privileges in Manchuria, which were contravened whenever Japanese police or military trespassed onto Canadian property. Furthermore, although the effective administration of Chientao was of direct concern to the Japanese colonial authorities in metropolitan Korea, it was the Japanese Foreign Ministry that conducted any negotiations over Chientao with the Chinese government. Ultimately, however, Chientao proved to be of little value in predicting Japanese intentions for Manchuria for it was the Japanese Kwantung Army officers rather than Japanese diplomats who precipitated the Manchurian crisis in September 1931. Once this had happened, diplomatic interest in Chientao quickly disappeared.

In 1930 the British consul general in Seoul admitted in his annual report on affairs in Korea that "the situation in Chientao is a curious one."[55] The Japanese claimed that their powers in Chientao came from extraterritorial rights secured by treaty with China. Chientao was often lawless and turbulent, and the Japanese consequently acted as a police force despite the dubious legality of it. One of the problems for the Japanese security forces was that

---

[53] UCCA PCC GA41 B6K Box 6, File February 1921, S. H. Martin to A. E. Armstrong, 4 February, 1921.

[54] Ibid.

[55] See Ann Trotter, ed., *British Documents on Foreign Affairs: Reports and Papers from the Foreign Office, Confidential Print*, volume 10: Japan [FFF1387/1387/23] Snow to Henderson, 22 January, 1931: Enclosure, Annual Report on Affairs in Korea during 1930, p. 100.

they could not guarantee complete security for Korean farmers. In the spring of 1930, the Chinese Communist Party called upon its Korea comrades to launch a major uprising in Chientao.[56] Christians were not always able to escape this trouble. Clearly, some Korean Christians were communist sympathizers, especially the mission school in Lungchingtsun. In January 1931, George Bruce, who taught at the boys' school, reported that he was being asked by his Sunday school pupils difficult leading questions about killing "those who are killing our national spirit."[57] It was very much a matter of trying to restrain the young students from doing anything that might have disastrous results on their futures. At the school, one had to be careful for Korean students were very sensitive to any apparent backsliding on Korean nationalism, and they had gone so far as to accuse one of their Korean Sunday school teachers (who had taught at the Kwansei Gakuin, the Christian college in Japan partly supported by the United Church of Canada) of being pro-Japanese. Bruce himself felt that the Koreans would be in for a difficult time if they did not cooperate with the Japanese. Although he believed that the Koreans were not ready to govern themselves, he also believed that the actions of the Korean communists in Chientao only reinforced similar views held by foreigners. However, Bruce was optimistic that the Japanese were moving toward granting Korea more autonomy as a result of the initiatives of the Governor General Saitō Makoto in regard to Korean local government.

The Manchurian (Mukden) incident of 18 September, 1931 and the subsequent occupation of strategic cities in Manchuria by the Japanese Kwantung Army created a storm of international protest against Japan. While those Canadian missionaries in Korea living well away from the Manchurian frontier condemned the Japanese action, it was welcomed by those in Lungchingtsun because Canadian missionary work in Chientao was made easier by Japanese intervention. In January 1932, E. O. Fraser wrote from Lungchingtsun that "Japan is suppressing the bandits all right, and Manchuria will be the better for it. The Chinese officials have been replaced by other Chinese who are favourable to the real rulers, and there are Japanese advisers with them, so things will smooth down, and trade will be much advanced in Manchuria."[58] According to Fraser, the border country was now much quieter

---

[56] For a brief description of the 30 May, 1930 revolt in Lungchingtsun and the Chientao region, see Kan Jeon, *Chōsen Kindai Shi*, pp. 284-288, especially p. 286.

[57] UCCA U[nited] C[hurch] [of] C[anada] B[oard] [of] F[oreign] M[issions] Korea Box 2 File 47, G. F. Bruce to A. E. Armstrong, 18 January 1931.

[58] UCCA UCC BFM Korea Box 2 File 54, E. O. Fraser to Burns, 16 January, 1932.

than it had been in 1930 when it had been much disturbed by Korean communists. For Canadian missionaries, it was primarily the methods that the Korean communists employed that appalled them[59] for they seemed to use the same tactics in their treatment of farmers as common criminals.

One of the negative consequences of the political upheaval, coupled with the Depression, was the large number of destitute Koreans coming into Lungchingtsun and causing a refugee problem.[60] However, on a more positive note, the Japanese had begun to survey for a new railway line that would connect Lungchingtsun to Fukjaga, a large Chinese town thirteen miles away. It was also hoped that within a year a line between Kirin and Korea would be completed on which both Lungchingtsun and Hoiryung across the border would have stations. While the new railway had its military purposes, it facilitated not only travel between the two Canadian mission centres but also brought prosperity to this agriculturally rich but underdeveloped region.

The lessening of communist disturbances augured well for Christian work. In April 1932, Fraser saw evidence of a spiritual movement in the Korean Church that he though connected to the disturbances caused by communist activities. One Korean evangelist had told him that he had been able to bring 80 new people into regular worship in his district in one month because some "see the evils of communistic teaching and wish to get their families away from its contamination. Others feel that communism is not a satisfying thing and wish to get the satisfaction they feel that Christianity can offer."[61] The hope for the rapid growth in the number of Korean Christians was short lived, though, for the political situation took a turn for the worse. The fighting between communist and Japanese security forces was brought home to missionaries in Lungchingtsun when Father Rapp, one of the German Roman Catholic missionaries, was killed outside the town. Although the Japanese military was suspected, the Japanese conveniently blamed Chinese bandits for his murder.[62] Conditions had deteriorated so much in Manchuria that the British diplomats suggested evacuation, and, indeed, the wives and children of Canadian missionaries in Lungchingtsun took the precaution of crossing over the border to the safety of the garrison town of Hoiryung.[63]

---

[59] UCCA UCC BFM Korea Box 2 File 55, Ross to Armstrong, 13 February, 1932.

[60] Ibid.

[61] UCCA UCC BFM Korea Box 2 File 54, Fraser to Burns, 18 April, 1932.

[62] UCCA UCC BFM Korea Box 2 File 55, Bruce to Friends, 28 June, 1932. See also UCCA UCC BFM Korea Box 2 File 63, Bruce to Armstrong, 17 January, 1933. The dangers to missionaries, even when they were escorted by Japanese cavalry, were further underlined in the fall of 1932 when Lloyd P. Henderson, an American Presbyterian North missionary, who worked at Sinpin in West Manchuria, was killed by bandits during an itinerant journey.

[63] UCCA UCC BFM Korea Box 2 File 55, Bruce to Friends, 28 June, 1932.

Despite the unsettled state of Chientao, the Canadian missionaries in Lungchingtsun were in no danger, because the Japanese maintained a garrison in the town. Furthermore, the Japanese controlled the main roads and the railway line into Korea. Having failed to establish solid links with local Chinese patriotic groups, the Korean communists in Chientao suffered setbacks during 1932 that led to them being forced out of the cities and towns. Desperate for food because of pressure from the Japanese military, the partisans had no alternative but to raid rural villages and homesteads for supplies. However, despite the best efforts of the Japanese military, the Korean communists continued to survive in Chientao.[64] Nevertheless, the immediate result of the sustained Japanese campaign against the communists was a marked lessening of trouble in the countryside.

Regardless of the international consequences of the Manchurian crisis for Japan and the world beyond Manchuria, the Canadian missionaries in Lungchingtsun clearly believed that the creation of a Japanese-dominated Manchukuo would benefit the Koreans. They thought that the Japanese had the best chance of any group to bring law and order and prosperity to their part of Manchuria, and a Japanese withdrawal would lead to anarchy.[65] It was bandits and communist partisans, in the opinion of missionaries in Lungchingtsun, who posed a greater threat to the well-being of Korean Christians in the Chientao region than the Japanese with their armoured cars and railways. The view of Lungchingtsun missionaries was parochial, for their concern was the safety of Korean Christians whom they served. They were virulently anticommunist at a time when many Canadians at home were sympathetic to communist ideas. Similarly, they were anticommunist when many in Korea, including some Christians, saw the very Korean partisans in Chientao, whom the Canadian missionaries so abhorred, as the vanguard of the movement to liberate Korea from Japanese colonial rule. In order to achieve their nationalistic goal, communist groups burnt crops and buildings and terrorized and slaughtered innocent farmers, including Christian ones. What Canadian missionaries saw in Chientao were the violent and destructive results of these actions. The safety and well-being of Korean Christians was far more important to them than any desire to identify themselves with the vanguard of the Korean nationalist movement.

---

[64] Kan Jeon, *Chōsen Kindai Shi*, pp. 288-292.

[65] See, for instance, UCCA UCC BFM Box 2 File 62, Bruce to Armstrong, 1 October, 1933; UCCA UCC BFM Box 2 File 61, D. Black to Armstrong, 15 October, 1933.

This put them into a difficult position. It made them open to charges of being pro-Japanese in a community that was highly sensitive to any apparent backsliding on Korean nationalism. The question of Christian attendance at ceremonies at Shinto shrines, the so-called Shrine question, offered an opportunity for missionaries and Korean Christians alike to reinforce their identification with the nationalist aspirations of Koreans. Although missionaries and Christians based their challenge to the Japanese authorities on religious principles, their resistance could also be interpreted (and was by the ever suspicious Japanese) as being politically motivated. The Shrine question was a long-standing one about which the prevalent Korean Christian point of view was that the ceremonies at state Shinto shrines were religious in nature and to coerce Christian students and teachers to attend them ran counter to their right of religious freedom.[66] After 1925 when Japanese colonial officials first began to press Koreans to attend Shrine ceremonies, the Shrine question quickly became associated with protests by students in mission schools. In November 1935 a critical crisis was created when two American Northern Presbyterian educational missionaries in P'yongyang refused to take part in the opening ceremonies of a conference of educators held at the state Shinto shrine in P'yongyang. In their stand, the two Americans had the widespread support of the Korean Presbyterian Church for Korean Christians saw participation in Shinto ceremonies as threatening the evangelistic nature of their Church.[67] This contrasted with American missionaries who saw the threat of the Shrine question in terms of mission schools, Christian education, and Shinto.

For their part, the Japanese held the position that Shrine ceremonies were not religious but a display of patriotism and loyalty on the part of students or others taking part in them. It was not a matter of freedom of religion, which was assured by the Japanese Meiji Constitution of 1889; rather, attendance at the shrine had to do with instilling reverence and respect for ancestors, and these values were "most important from the point of view of national education as the essentials of our national moral virtue."[68] Christian Churches in Japan had already come to terms with the Shrine question, and taken the government's position that the ceremonies were non-religious in nature

---

[66] Sawa Masahiko, *Mika no Chōsen Purotesutanto Shi*, pp. 232-233.

[67] Kurata Masahiko, *Tennōsei to Kankoku Kiristutokyō* (Tokyo: Shinkyō Shuppansha, 1991), p. 143.

[68] A[rchives] [of the] P[resbyterian] C[hurch] [in] C[anada], Formosa File re Shrine Question 1935-37, " 'A Warning to Dr. G. S. McCune, Principal of the Sujitsu School,' Copy of statement handed to Dr. G. S. McCune, to Mr. T. S. Soltau and to J. G. Holdcroft by H. E. T. Watanabe, Director of the Educational Bureau of the Government General of Chōsen, December 30th 1935."

at face value. As it was considered so significant by the colonial authorities, the Shrine question was not a matter over which the Japanese were prepared to compromise with Korean Christians. Moreover, the Japanese authorities were quite willing to resort to strong-arm methods to get their way. The stand of the Presbyterian Church in Korea led to widespread persecution of Christians and to then forced closure of many Christian churches. In September 1938, the Korean Presbyterian General Assembly was forced by the colonial authorities to pass a resolution declaring that shrine worship was not religious in nature and that all Christians should participate in the state Shinto ceremonies.[69]

Unlike their American Presbyterian colleagues, Canadian missionaries accepted the Japanese government's position on the Shrine question. In December 1936 William Scott argued that more harm would be done by refusing to participate in shrine ceremonies, because nonparticipation would lead to the closure of Christian schools and complete government control over education in Korea.[70] While American Presbyterian and American Methodist missionaries were prepared to close many of their schools in protest, the Canadians kept theirs open. In taking a position that was different from that of many American missionaries and also the mainstream of the Korean Presbyterian Church, the Canadian missionaries were not taking up the opportunity to curry to Korean nationalism that the Shrine question offered by resisting Japanese demands.[71] In doing so, they ran the risk of isolating themselves from the mainstream of Korean Presbyterians and losing the support of Korean Christians for not resisting the Japanese on this issue. Yet, it might also be suggested that the majority of Canadian missionaries in Chientao and Korea were more liberal in their theological views than many of the older American missionaries and the majority in the Korean Presbyterian Church. The different response of the Canadian missionaries to the Shrine question was rooted in their more liberal religious outlook as well as their practical desire to maintain mission schools as a Christian alternative to the government schools and secular private schools.

The Shrine question was compounded in Lungchingtsun because, after 1931, it was in puppet Manchukuo which was not recognized by either Britain or Canada. Dr. Donald Black, the medical doctor in charge of the Lungchingtsun mission hospital, reported in October 1936 that a missionary

---

[69] Sawa Masahiko, *Mika no Chōsen Purotesutanto Shi*, p. 266.

[70] UCCA UCC BFM Korea Box 3 File 86, Scott to Armstrong, 13 December, 1936.

[71] It has to be pointed out that Duncan MacRae, the pioneer Canadian Presbyterian missionary who retired in Baddeck, Cape Breton Island, Nova Scotia, was virulently opposed to the stand taken by his younger colleagues in Korea over the Shrine issue.

in Manchuria had been asked by a Japanese military official about whom he considered more divine Heny Pu Yi, the Emperor of Manchukuo or God. The implication was that anyone who taught that any one was superior to the Emperor was guilty of treason.[72] Although it did not effect the Korean Christian congregations, the Manchukuo authorities, taking their cue from the Japanese Shinto ceremonies, had, in early 1936, started to make Confucius worship compulsory in schools. This had led to a confrontation between the Irish Presbyterian mission school in Kirin and the Manchukuo authorities.

There was a suspicion among missionaries that the Manchukuo authorities were persecuting the Chinese Christian community who had close ties to Scottish and Irish Presbyterians as a way to pressure the British government to recognize the state of Manchukuo.[73] It was also understood that although the Manchukuo government was ostensibly in power "the real power is the Japanese army, anti-foreign and anti-Christian." [74] The army also remained highly suspicious of Koreans in Chientao, all but a few of whom they considered anti-Japanese.[75] For its part, the British government realized that the predominant official feeling in Manchukuo, especially in the Japanese Kwantung Army, would be pleased to see the departure of foreign missionaries.[76] The missionaries in Lungchingtsun were in a delicate situation.

The beginning of the Sino-Japanese War in the summer of 1937 only exacerbated this. The Japanese authorities, eager to ensure the loyalty of Koreans, placed increased demands on missionaries to make changes in their educational work. Korean language was dropped from school curriculum, and all schools were raised to the same standing as schools in Japan with similar privileges for their graduates.[77] Missionary educators were faced with the need to cope with new regulations designed, amongst other things, to eliminate foreign influence in education. The need for extensive Japanese language instruction in schools geared to teach in Korean was difficult enough. However, there were also organizational changes at the institutional level for the two mission schools in Lungchingtsun as well as those in metropolitan Korea for they were required (as their counterparts in Japan were also doing) to form a zaidan hōjin (a jurisdical foundation) which would take the school out of the direct control of missionaries. The missionaries

---

[72] UCCA UCC BFM Korea Box 3 File 83, D. Black to Armstrong, 24 October, 1936.

[73] APCC Formosa File re Shrine Question 1935-37, "Religious Liberty under Japanese Rule."

[74] Ibid.

[75] Bruce Cumings, Korea's Place in the Sun, p. 161.

[76] British Documents on Foreign Affairs, vol. 15 Japan [F1051/1051/10] Knatchbull-Hugessen to Eden, 6 January 1937. Enclosure, Annual Report on Manchukuo for 1936, p. 316.

[77] UCCA UCC BFM Korea Box 4 File 90, Scott to Armstrong, 23 June, 1938.

were able to insist, however, that the constitution of the zaidan hōjin provided safeguards for the Christian nature of the school board (by a combination of missionary and Korean Christian members) and stipulated that the head teacher be a Christian. In order to create a zaidan hōjin, money was needed for the regulations required a school endowment. George Bruce, the missionary principal of the Canadian middle school for boys' in Lungchingtsun, expressed the deepest concern in October 1938 about the support of the United Church of Canada for educational work as the Mission Board in Toronto was extremely slow in granting permission to form zaidan hōjin for the schools in Manchukuo and Korea.[78] The feeling that the Church in Canada had little interest in maintaining educational work among Koreans could only have added to an already nightmarish situation that confronted Canadian missionaries in Lungchingtsun.

In June 1939 Donald Black, the doctor in Lungchingtsun, argued that the mission had to form zaidan hōjin for its two schools in Lungchingtsun or close them. To do the latter would mean the virtual end of Christian education. Black thought that the schools could still maintain a Christian atmosphere under the control of a zaidan hōjin and there would also continue to be opportunity for extra-curricula Bible classes. Black and the other missionaries in Lungchingtsun felt that the only possible decision for the Church in Canada to make was to allow the schools to continue to operate under the control of zaidan hōjin.[79] In agreeing to abide by Japanese colonial regulations, Canadian missionaries showed that they had perhaps a greater understanding of Japanese colonial government than their American Presbyterian and Methodist missionary counterparts who had closed schools in Korea rather than follow Japanese regulations. Canadians understood that what the Japanese were primarily concerned about was that their authority as colonial overlords in Korea or in Chientao should not be challenged. If it was not, then the Japanese were quite prepared, as in the case with the zaidan hōjin for the two mission schools in Lungchingtsun illustrates, to allow them to continue as Christian schools.

While the zaidan hōjin protected the Christian nature of the schools, George Bruce and Francis Bonwick, the respective principals of the two schools in Lungchingtsun, were faced with increasing difficulties. This was especially true after the Canadian declaration of war against Germany in September 1939. Some of these difficulties were not new such as the

---

[78] UCCA UCC BFM Box 4 File 96, Bruce to Armstrong, 9 October, 1938.
[79] UCCA UCC BFM Korea Box 4, Black to Armstrong, 14 June, 1939.

recurrent problem of not being able to attract good teachers because salaries were too low. Others were new or had been largely dormant such as growing anti-foreign feeling among school staff and students. In November 1940 William Scott wrote that there had been trouble over the summer at the boys' school in Lungchingtsun between the head teacher and the Korean principal. Apparently, the head teacher in concert with the police and gendarmes had fostered a suspicion that the school was a centre of foreign influence and that George Bruce was a spy. This had led to a strike at the school engineered by the head teacher in which the students refused religious training and opposed the Korean principal and foreign influence.[80] The strike brought in the provincial educational authorities. Initially, the aim of the provincial authorities was to order changes in the composition of the zaidan hōjin so that authority over the school would be placed in non-Christian hands. William Scott who led the negotiations with the provincial authorities was able to conclude a satisfactory outcome for the Canadians. This was that missionaries would withdraw from the zaidan hōjin "provided that the government would allow it to continue under the supervision of a Christian board and with the privilege of carrying on Christian work - bible study and worship." [81] The missionaries persuaded Yi Tai Jun, a former schoolteacher and Christian minister who had become a successful businessman, to take over the school from them. Yi was appointed founder by the school board and was therefore in control of the school's zaidan hōjin. Even though George Bruce and Frances Bonwick left their respective schools in Lungchingtsun in early 1941 to return home, the schools in Lunchingtsun continued to operate without government interference as late as March 1942. William Scott himself taught without any obstacle put in his way at the Hamheung boys' school until 8 December, 1941.[82]

As well as the struggle to maintain the Christian atmosphere of the two schools in Lungchingtsun, there was a concern about the question of mission property in Manchukuo (where Canadian property deeds were not recognized by the puppet regime). In September 1941 three of the four missionary residences in Lungchingtsun were rented to the Japanese mayor of the town so that they could be used by military officers. As a result of doing this, the Canadians, at least, ensured that the Japanese recognized that the residences belonged to them. More immediately important than property was the

---

[80] UCCA UCC BFM Box 4 File 112, Scott to Armstrong, 29 November 1940.

[81] Ibid.

[82] UCCA UCC BFM Korea, Box 4 File 1942 Aug. [misfiled in Box 4, no file number except pencil word *food*], Report of the Interim Committee of the Korean Mission of the United Church of Canada, August 1942.

decision of Canadian mission executives in the spring of 1941 to advance payments for two years to all institutions and personnel such as Bible women, provided this money could be raised from funds already in Korea or through the sale of property not considered necessary for future Christian work.[83] What this meant was that even though war began in December 1941, the Canadians had left their Korean Christian community with sufficient funds to tide them through to the spring of 1943. Nobody could have foretold that the war in East Asia would last until 1945.

The approach taken by Canadian missionaries in Lungchingtsun and northern Korea during the nineteen thirties was not one which would endear them to Korean nationalists. The Canadians, by and large, enjoyed good relations with the Japanese as a result of which no Korean pastor (at least, until March 1942 when Scott left Korea) had been imprisoned in the Canadian mission's section of operation nor any missionary home been subject to examination or search.[84] During the nineteen thirties, Korean Christians in Chientao enjoyed for the first time in many years (and sadly also what turned out to be the last time for many years to come) peace and even perhaps prosperity. What price Salvation? Canadian missionaries had borne witness to the horrendous sufferings of Korean Christians in Chientao at the hands of the Japanese during the suppression of the 1 March, 1919 independence movement and during the following Chientao Punitive Expedition. They had seen ordinary Korean folk suffer from the handiwork of desperate Korean partisans who, for all the ideological cant that they might use to justify their armed struggle, were often indistinguishable from common robbers and thugs. What Scott, Black, Bruce and the other Canadian missionaries did with the consummate skill was to protect and to endeavour to maintain a Korean Christian community complete with churches and schools despite tremendous obstacles. They were the shield and buckler for a Korean Christian community that had few other protectors. During the nineteen thirties, Canadian missionaries stood apart from the mainstream of the foreign missionary movement and the Korean Presbyterian Church who both relished resistance to the Japanese colonial regime and were prepared to sacrifice all in defence of conservative theological views. The example of the Canadians in Lungchingtsun reveals that political activism is not necessarily a part of Christian missionary work. Similarly, it reveals that the identification between Christianity and Korean nationalism was, by chance, rather than design.

---

[83] Ibid.
[84] Ibid.

In 1942, Emma Palethorpe, who had served in Lungchingtsun for over twenty years before her evacuation back to Canada in 1941, wrote:

> No one who has had fellowship with the humble, faithful Korean Christians, scattered through the mountain valleys of Korea and Manchuria can doubt that the Korean Church will survive the present wave of suppression and oppression. These Christians have come into vital, personal contact with the Living Christ and would die rather than deny Him. They carry in their hearts a treasure which even a totalitarian government cannot deprive them. Surely this makes the work of the past worth while and insures at least a remnant, for the future.[85]

Palethorpe's words convey the tremendous depth of attachment and genuine affection that many Canadian missionaries felt for the Korean Christians whom they had served in remote Chientao. Canadian missionaries in Lungchingtsun practised diplomacy of a person-to-person kind at a crucial time in the modern history of the Korean people. However, there would be no happy return to Lungchingtsun for Canadian missionaries after the war. Whatever the future might hold for the Korean community across the Tumen in Chientao, its past shows that it once held a special place in the history of Canada's relations with Koreans.

---

[85] UCCA UCC BFM General 1942, Box 16 File 322, Conference on "Mission Policy as Affected by the War," 2 April, 1942. "The Future of the Korean Church," conference paper by Emma Palethorpe.

THE WAR THAT HISTORY FORGOT

TED BARRIS
JOURNALISM DEPARTMENT, CENTENNIAL COLLEGE, TORONTO

Let me begin with an excerpt from my book, Deadlock in Korea; in fact, the segment comes from the final chapter entitled "The War That History Forgot".

It was just over a month after the armistice in Korea - August 30, 1953 - when eleven former inmates of Communist Chinese prison camps stepped off the airplane that had brought them home to Canada. Canadian Press reporter Joe MacSween was in Vancouver to meet them. He posed questions to a few of the men and just noted the behaviour of others. He described Pte. Bernard Jewer as "outwardly laconic." He watched as Lt. Gordon Owen "gathered his family into his arms." And he noted that returning with the men was war correspondent Bill Boss, who said the soldiers shied away from publicity because "their Communist captors had photographed them at intervals for propaganda purposes, leaving an unpleasant association with the men."

In contrast to the subdued demeanor of some, former POWs Pte. Donald Orson and Pte. Ronald Watson kibitzed with other soldiers, reporters and family members as they milled about the lawn in front of the Sea Island airport reception building.

"Did it happen?" said Orson, repeating MacSween's question about his Korean experience. He didn't answer. He just raised his arm and swept it over the gathering, referring to the gaiety of the occasion.

"No, it never happened," said Butch Watson. "Let's forget it ever happened." [1]

Just that. They forgot, or in many cases never even acknowledged the Korean War had taken place.

---

[1] Joe MacSween, "Lost Weight in Red Prison Camps, Freed Canadians Decline to Talk" *Canadian Press*, August 30, 1953, p. 7.

Prophetic words, because without being encouraged, most Canadians did. That excerpt epitomizes the pathetic welcome many Canadians, returning from the Korean War, received. At the opening ceremonies of this conference I alluded to the fact that although the United Nations forces and those of Communist forces of North Korea and China signed an armistice on July 27, 1953, the war did not end.

In fact, the battle for recognition was just beginning for some 25,000 to 30,000 Canadians returning from the Far East. They had to battle to wear the medals they had earned including: The U.S. Presidential Distinguished Unit Citation (won by the Princess Patricia's Canadian Light Infantry at Kap'yong); the Syngman Rhee volunteer medal (earned by all Canadians who volunteered); and the Canadian government volunteer medal (not awarded until 1992, a year after Canadian veterans from the Persian Gulf War received theirs).

Canadian veterans of the Korean War had to battle to build their own national war monument - the 200-foot-long granite wall created by, paid for and erected courtesy of the Korea Veterans Association of Canada - at Brampton, Ontario, in 1997. They had to battle so that their service on the Korean peninsula could be called "a war," because technically, politicians and diplomats had always referred to the mission as "the Korean conflict" or "a police action." [2] The returning Canadian servicemen had to battle in Canada for their veteran status, that is their right to pensions, their right to housing, education and even medical assistance.[3] They had to battle to get their stories told by historians, the media and the public. They even had to battle for acknowledgment from their comrades-in-arms. To illustrate, another excerpt from my book:

Bill Jackson arrived home on the prairies nine months before the Panmunjom armistice. By October, 1952, he had served his voluntary tour of a year with the Princess Patricia's Canadian Light Infantry and had witnessed his share of warfare and war zones. On the way in, his troop train north from Pusan killed dozens of civilians on the track in Taegu. His first night on the Jamestown Line he had to bury dead Chinese soldiers near his slit trench. During Operation Pepperpot north of the Imjin, one of his friends was blown to pieces by a mortar bomb. And many nights in his bunker "I'd wake up with the nose of a rat inches from my face."

---

[2] Louis St. Laurent, Debates, House of Commons, 1950, IV, p. 4, 253.

[3] "DDT used in Korea": Handbook of Army Health, 1950, and included in "16 Korean Veterans' Mortality and Health Study Research Papers" prepared by Col. Allan E. Limburg, CVO, (RL), 1998.

The night he came home to Brooks, Alberta, the platform was empty. He had to phone long-distance to the family farm for someone to pick him up. About a month later, Jackson attended an Armistice Day observance and then joined an evening smoker at the local Legion Hall. No women. Just forty or fifty veterans sitting, drinking and telling war stories. At one point, a friend of the Jackson family rose to address the gathering. He and Jackson's father had served in the First World War together.

"Hold it. Hold it," the veteran said.

The chatter in the room quieted down.

"We've got a guy just back from the trenches in Korea," he said. "And we'd like to welcome him..."

Bill Jackson felt a little embarrassed.

"Go ahead," encouraged Jackson's father. "Stand up and say something."

Jackson slowly got to his feet. But before he could utter a word, a voice boomed from the back of the Legion hall, "Sit down, you asshole. So you were in Korea. So what?" [4]

So what, indeed. There was ample reason for historians, the media and the public to acknowledge and remember the role played by Canadian servicemen and women in the Korean War. Among other things, the Korean War was the first ever military action ordered in defence of the United Nations peace charter (signed in 1945). It was the first ever military clash between armed forces of the Communist East and those of the Western Democracies.

The war in Korea was also the first time there was a real threat that nuclear arms might be used since the bombing of Hiroshima and Nagasaki in the Second World War; indeed in November of 1950 Gen. Douglas MacArthur strongly suggested the use of atomic weapons to create a "radioactive no-man's-land" [5] in Manchuria (China). This clash on the Korean peninsula was also the first indication that the Cold War (now several years brewing in Europe) could escalate to become the Third World War. In contrast, dispatching a Special Force to Korea was also Canada's first foray into peace-making and peacekeeping, a role that would one day move Canada closer to the significant decision-making circle of the U.N. Security Council.

The participation of Canadian troops in the Korean War also added an important component to Canada's long and illustrious military tradition of participating in what the country (or at least its Parliament) believed was a just cause - preservation of sovereignty and democracy. Still, despite there

---

[4] Interview, Bill Jackson, Saskatoon, SK., August 2, 1997.

[5] Bruce Cumings, *Korea's Place in the Sun: A Modern History* (New York: W.W. Norton, 1997), p. 291.

being testaments to the determination and bravery of Canadians, Korean War battlefields have never achieved the cache of such locations as Vimy Ridge (in the First World War) or Ortona, Normandy and the Scheldt Estuary (in the Second World War).

The public consciousness of Canada's military legacy should include Kap'yong, where for three days in April 1951, 300 members of the Princess Patricia's Canadian Light Infantry blocked the advance of some 6,000 Communist Forces troops attempting to re-take Seoul.[6] It doesn't. Canadian classrooms should echo with the retelling of veterans' accounts of the offensives undertaken by the Royal Canadian Regiment at Chail-li and Mt. Kakhulbong as they advanced on the 38th Parallel in 1951.[7] They don't. Historians in this country ought to document the heroics of the Royal 22e Regiment (the Vandoos) in defence of the base of Little Gibraltar (Hill 355) in November of 1951.[8] They don't. And they should further recall the defence of that same strategic height in October of 1952, when the forward companies of the RCR withstood the onslaught of a full Chinese army battalion despite being overrun early in the battle. Finally, the people who profess to know their Canadian history should also herald the efforts of the Royal Canadian Navy at Chinnampo with the same reverence they herald the rescue of the British Expeditionary Force at Dunkirk in 1940:

When Canadian seamen returned to the Japanese port of Sasebo, in late November, they received word they would not be going home in time for Christmas. Plans to recall the three RCN Tribal Class destroyers to Canada had been reversed and Capt. Jeffry Brock (aboard Cayuga) assumed command of a new task force consisting of six destroyers and several minesweepers. They were dispatched to prowl waters and islands off the west coast of Korea, between Inch'on and the Yalu River, to search out junks and sampans that might be transporting Chinese soldiers to the Korean peninsula. At sea and in the air United Nations forces had supremacy. Not so on land. Facing upwards of 300,000 Chinese troops, UN forces were now retreating pell-mell back to the 38th parallel and beyond it. To the east, the US X Corps was falling back from the Chosin Reservoir. The ROK Army had collapsed in the centre of the front. And to the west, the Eighth US Army was in full flight back to P'yongyang. The withdrawal was known as "the Big Bug-Out."

---

[6] PPCLI War Diary, April 1951.
[7] Don Stickland, "Up the Slippery Slopes of Mount Kakhulbong" (KVA files).
[8] R22eR War Diary, November 1951.

Overnight, Capt. Brock's orders to blockade North Korean ports on the Yellow Sea were altered; he and his task force were to assist by all means in their power the evacuation of the Eighth US Army from Chinnampo, the port for the North Korean capital of P'yongyang. The UN naval squadron would now have to cover a fleet of US transport ships exiting the harbour, give gunfire support to the retreating army and make sure that the large stores of fuel and munitions in Chinnampo did not fall into Chinese hands.

The problem was that Chinnampo was about thirty kilometers up the Daido-Ko River, well beyond the range of Brock's naval guns. In addition, the Daido-Ko estuary was cluttered with a maze of low islands and shifting mudflats. The tides would be difficult to navigate. So would the floating mines left behind by the North Koreans. Complicating matters was the winter weather, which had closed in with drizzle that froze on contact - north winds effectively reduced the temperature to below zero. Late on December 4, 1950, as Brock assembled his armada, he received word that Chinnampo was bulging with soldiers, civilians and equipment and that the situation had reached "emergency" proportions.[9] The RCN captain would have to launch his Dunkirk-like mission in the dead of night.

The minesweepers led the way upriver, clearing a channel 500 yards wide and marking its edges with unlit dan-buoys. The strong current kept pulling the markers loose, necessitating the use of ASDIC radar to monitor for mines every step of the way. Meanwhile, the tide had ebbed so the flotilla advanced, Cayuga at the lead, "dead slow ahead" because at times the ships were operating in less than a meter of water. Despite all precaution, HMAS Warramunga grounded on a shoal. A half hour later HMCS Sioux grounded on a sandbar and tangled a propeller shaft on a dan-buoy wire. The two destroyers eventually freed themselves but were forced to withdraw to make repairs. The other four pushed on up the estuary.

The drizzle became a blizzard. Visibility diminished until as Capt. Brock later wrote "it was as black as the inside of a cow." [10] More lookouts were positioned in the bows and shells stockpiled on deck to reduce the number of steps should the shooting start. Below decks the watch became a nightmare for ships' navigators as they dashed from radar screens to chart tables and back. In Cayuga's plot room Lt. Andrew Collier made 132 navigational fixes that night, which Lt. Bill Davis described as "a masterful piece of work...

---

[9] Thor Thorgrimsson and E.C. Russell, *Canadian Naval Operations in Korean Waters 1950-1955* (Ottawa: Queen's Printer, Department of National Defence, 1965), p. 31.

[10] Jeffry Brock, *Memoirs of a Sailor: The Dark Broad Seas*, Volume 1 (Toronto: McClelland & Stewart, 1981).

Nobody had confidence in the unlit buoys to get us through. We'd seen one mine blow a hole in a US destroyer... Meanwhile, there were pieces of dead people in the water, so we were pretty apprehensive about the mines." On the bridge, Brock conned the ship through the darkness, so that before dawn HMCS *Athabaskan*, USS *Forest Royal*, HMAS *Bataan* and HMCS *Cayuga* were safely anchored in Chinnampo harbour.

Throughout that day, December 5, Capt. Brock, now in charge of defending the port, supervised the evacuation. Troops and material were loaded aboard the US transports. A steady stream of sampans moved refugees out of the city. Brock ordered Athabaskan downriver to scrutinize the civilian vessels for mines and other weapons. Navy demolition and fire parties were dispatched to destroy what equipment couldn't be saved. As reports of a Chinese breakthrough north of the city reached the port, the transport vessels weighed anchor, leaving the last three destroyers alone in the harbour to complete the job.

At 1735 hours, Brock ordered all guns to open fire. Within minutes, explosions were rocking the railway marshaling yards, the city's cement factory, its shipyards and gasoline storage tanks. North Korea's key port city, which had once been home to 75,000 people, was now - from its industrial district to its waterfront - an inferno. A day later, when the entire flotilla was safely clear of the Daido-Ko River channel and back at sea, Chinnampo was still ablaze.

The mission was a complete success. The Eighth US Army had been safely withdrawn from western North Korea. Any booty the advancing Chinese armies hoped to find in Chinnampo had been destroyed. And the entire naval task force under Jeffry Brock's command had returned virtually unscathed in what some call "the most important and most dangerous naval mission of the Korean War." [11] Cayuga's captain was awarded the Distinguished Service Order; its navigator, Andrew Collier, the Distinguished Service Cross; and its coxswain, D.J. Pearson, the British Empire Medal.

Similarly, Canadian history textbooks never include the Herculean achievements of the Royal Canadian Air Force in the famous "Korean Airlift." From the earliest days of the war, when No. 426 Transport Squadron operated its full compliment of transports, the RCAF mission in the Korean War was nothing less than a wartime miracle. Maintaining, fuelling and flying its 16 North Star aircraft around the clock, the members of Transport

---

[11] Edward C. Meyers, *Thunder in the Morning Calm, The Royal Canadian Navy in Korea 1950-1955* (St. Catharines: Vanwell Publishing, 1992), p. 95.

Command completed approximately 600 round trips (from North American across the Pacific and back) ferrying 3 million kilograms of freight, about 13,000 passengers and did it without the loss of one life. [12]

Nor does Canadian consciousness of the Korean War effort include the price paid by members of the 2nd Field Regiment of the Royal Canadian Horse Artillery in the fall of 1950. In November, as it hurried to transport Canadian gunners and equipment to the American staging centre on the Pacific coast in Washington, the RCHA sustained one of the toughest losses of the war. The second of two trains carrying 338 men westbound to the coast, crashed head-on with an eastbound passenger train on a remote mountain hillside near Canoe River, B.C. [13]

The crash killed 12 artillerymen and four train crew members; four more soldiers died en route to hospital, one more in hospital. In all 52 were injured in the accident. Most frustrating of all, to this day the 17 RCHA artillerymen who died have never received posthumous volunteer medals from the Canadian government. It was Canada's worst ever military train accident; for the family survivors of those killed at Canoe River, the lack of recognition is one of the country's most shameful oversights.

Additional shame must be borne for the treatment Canada officials dispensed to those who were captured and imprisoned in POW camps in North Korea. Thirty-three Canadians survived the torture, starvation, sensory depravation, solitary confinement and attempted brainwashing dispensed by their Chinese captors.[14] I offer another except from "Deadlock in Korea" that illustrates the summary treatment the former POW inmates endured upon their return to South Korea at Freedom Village and Panmunjom.

Waiting for all of the prisoners was the de-lousing process - spraying to be disinfected. Then the POWs got re-kitted with proper uniforms. Most were invited to enjoy a meal of steak and eggs, beer and ice cream or chocolate for dessert. Jim Gunn got the greatest pleasure from drinking a glass of cold milk. George Griffiths had his foot operated on again, this time in a real hospital with real anesthetic, not opium seeds. But Len Badowich remembers "being interrogated yet again, this time by our own Intelligence Officers.

"The first thing they did, was have us swear allegiance to the Queen, because the King had died while we were in prison... Then they asked, 'Why

---

[12] RCAF Number 426 Squadron Diary, quoted in Larry Milberry, *The Canadair North Star* (Toronto: CANAV Books, 1982), p. 143.

[13] Hugh A. Halliday, *Wreck! Canada's Worst Railway Accidents* (Toronto: Robin Brass, 1997), pp. 195-203.

[14] R. Bruce McIntyre, "The Forgotten Thirty-Three: An Examination of Canadian Prisoners of War of the Korean War" (thesis unpublished, Ph.D., University of Waterloo, 1994).

didn't you escape?' How the hell do you escape in Korea, where the place is full of Orientals? You're white. Where do you go? Nobody could have escaped. These assholes made us feel like we had committed a crime or deserted." [15]

Thirty-three Canadians had been POWs in Korea. Several did try to escape and had paid dearly in solitary confinement. Two prisoners - Allain and Bellefeuille - "acknowledged that they signed a Communist petition in June 1952 petitioning Lord Alexander, British defence minister, to stop the imperialist war," but no Canadian POWs wrote declarations against the United Nations Command. There is no definitive evidence of Canadians in North Korean prison camps collaborating with their captors. Indeed, there is every reason to believe the thirty-three Canadians imprisoned there resisted interrogation and indoctrination and they sabotaged Chinese "brainwashing" attempts to a man.[16]

Still, after debriefing the POWs, Canadian Intelligence officers issued them grades for their performance during internment in North Korea. A "white grade" meant undistinguished performance with satisfactory resistance. A "light gray grade" meant low resistance. And a "black grade" indicated low resistance and suspicion of collaboration with the enemy. Eleven Canadians were graded "light gray," nineteen POWs were graded "white," one got "black" and the last two were not graded. In other words, Canadian officials graded the majority of Canadian POWs' performance in Korea between satisfactory and undistinguished. None was considered better than average in the service of his country while in military prison.

Thousands of Canadian veterans have revisited Korea since 1953. They've marvelled at the metropolis that emerged from the ashes of war-ravaged Seoul. They've stood at Panmunjom on the edge of the demilitarized zone and realized most of the hills they fought for or defended now lie in either the DMZ or North Korea. They've been wined and dined by the descendants of the displaced people they felt they were defending. They've cried at the Pusan cemetery for fallen comrades. But most of them have not yet closed this chapter in their lives.

And it's not only the psychological aftermath they're coming to terms with. Far too many Korea veterans remember feeling their country sent them to the ends of the earth ill-informed and ill-equipped. Veterans of the Special Force

---

[15] Interview, Len Badowich, Petawawa, ON., May 2, 1997.
[16] Bill Boss, "Eight Canadians To Be Freed, Red Disclose" *Canadian Press*, August 24, 1953.

still resent being labeled "scruff" when the non-commissioned men in its ranks earned such battle honours as a US Presidential Citation as well as Military Medals and Mention In Dispatches.[17] The survivors of Korean battlefields - on land, sea and air - knew that the Canadian public was tired of talk of war, but that shouldn't have diminished their voluntary service for their country. The Korean War had no days that seized the nation's attention, such that people remembered where they were "the day war was declared" or "the day the Canadians landed." But its veterans don't believe their contribution should be left off community cenotaphs or out of the pages of history books. There remains a gap in public perception that from 1950 to 1953 Canadians were at war in Korea. And their experience was unique.

---

[17] G.R. Stevens, *The Royal Canadian Regiment*: volume Two 1933-1966 (London: London Printing, 1967), p. 219.

PACIFIC DIPLOMACY:
CANADIAN STATECRAFT AND THE KOREAN WAR, 1950-53

GREG DONAGHY
HISTORICAL SECTION
DEPARTMENT OF FOREIGN AFFAIRS
AND INTERNATIONAL TRADE

In 1974, the political scientist Denis Stairs published one of the first and most persuasive studies on Canada and the Korean War. In his work, *The Diplomacy of Constraint: Canada, the Korean War and the United States,* Stairs argued simply that Canadian policy-makers, worried that Washington might become bogged down in Asia and ignore the Soviet challenge in Europe, tried "to moderate and constrain" American policy in Korea.[1] But in the last decade, with the demise of active controversy over the nature of American (and Canadian) cold war diplomacy in Asia, and the collapse of Canadian nationalism, differences between Canada and the U.S. have mattered less, and younger scholars have taken Stairs to task. Drawing on unpublished sources unavailable 30 years ago, they insist that the "diplomacy of constraint" over-emphasizes the difference in outlook between Canada and the U.S., and exaggerates Ottawa's influence in Washington. In this view, the Korean War serves mainly to underline how dependent Canada was on the United States for its definition of Western policies and objectives in the Asian cold war.[2]

However, a close reading of the Canadian diplomatic record, still neglected and overlooked as a source of primary material, suggests that despite Ottawa's early support for the American effort, there were important differences in outlook that shaped Canada's response to the war from the beginning. Unlike the United States, Canada was not a Pacific nation in June 1950, but a North Atlantic one, whose economic and political interests lay in Europe, where the principal cold war threat remained the Soviet Union. Moreover, with only a limited stake in Asia, Canada thought that the job of containing Asian communism properly belonged to India and the other Asian democracies, who were able to appreciate the complexities of post-colonial

Asia better than either the United States or the colonial powers of Europe. The implications of this Canadian view of the cold war emerged sharply during the Korean conflict. On the one hand, Canada sought to moderate American policy to ensure that Washington did not lead the West into a costly war in Asia, a concern that grew stronger as the war dragged on. At the same time, Ottawa was preoccupied with India, anxious to resolve the tensions between it and the West, and hand over to New Delhi greater responsibility for halting the spread of Asian communism. While Ottawa's perspective on the Korean War and its implications was different from Washington's, more often than not, Canada carried too little weight in the American capital to make its views felt. But sometimes, as this study contends, the differences in outlook did matter, and, at the margins, Canada did make a difference.

Like their counterparts throughout the Western world, Canadian officials and politicians were surprised and dismayed by the North Korean attack on 25 June, 1950. However, Ottawa had little reason to hope that there would be any response to North Korea's attack on its southern neighbour. The United Nations had no effective forces at its command, and the United States, which had the power to act, had indicated several months earlier that Korea was "not vital to our security." [3] On the evening of 26 June, the secretary of state for external affairs, Lester B. Pearson, told the Ottawa press gallery in an off-the-record session that "the present issue would be concluded before we could do anything to help." [4]

At roughly the same time, U.S. President Harry Truman and his advisors reached a very different conclusion. Eager to meet this communist challenge to the Western position in Asia and determined to demonstrate the UN's capacity to respond to aggression, Truman decided to make American air and naval support available to South Korea. He also agreed to take a number of other steps intended to enhance the American position in Asia, including the deployment of the 7th Fleet to neutralize Formosa.[5] Informed of the American decision on the morning of 27 June, Pearson reacted cautiously. Although pleased with Truman's determination to resist communist aggression and act in accordance with the principles of collective security, he was also disturbed by Washington's desire to act before the Security Council's anticipated resolution asking UN members to assist South Korea. The American action should be brought "within the terms of the Charter."[6] On balance, however, as Pearson indicated to cabinet that afternoon, he applauded Washington's decision to pursue a restrained "middle-course [of] giving limited assistance" to Korea. "If the United States' action was effective, the result would be helpful generally in the cold war." [7]

Prime Minister Louis St. Laurent, however, was reluctant to approve even a token Canadian contribution in the face of a hostile French Canadian press that was suspicious of American motives. Before Canada would contribute anything to the defence of Korea, he insisted on 28 June, the UN aspect of the operation needed to be strengthened.[8] During the next two days, pressure for a Canadian contribution mounted steadily as the situation in South Korea deteriorated. American officials in Washington pointedly hoped "that something ... would be forthcoming promptly from Canada ... in order to make the action to restore conditions in Korea a collective action under the auspices of the United Nations." [9] Though this early sign of Washington's desire to act within a UN framework was welcomed, St. Laurent refused to sanction a Canadian contribution that was not clearly under the auspices of the international organization. On the afternoon of 29 June, 1950, Cabinet again deferred a decision on Canada's contribution. Late that evening, supported by C.D. Howe, the powerful minister of trade and commerce, and Brooke Claxton, the minister of national defence, Pearson confronted the prime minister. The resulting compromise committed the government to supply three destroyers to assist South Korea provided "that such assistance ... [was] in response to a request from the United Nations and in support of an operation authorized and sponsored by the United Nations." [10]

As it turned out, the United States was as determined as Canada to ensure that the UN's role in the defence of Korea was fully acknowledged. John Holmes, Canada's acting permanent representative to the United Nations, reported from New York that the Americans were "bending as far as possible to give this all the characteristics of a United Nations project." [11] For constitutional reasons, the United States could not, as Ottawa proposed, simply ask the UN to give General Douglas MacArthur "a mandate to organize and direct the forces now being made available by various members of the UN." [12] Instead, Washington would ask the Security Council to adopt a resolution whose operative clause "would recommend that all members providing forces under the Security Council resolutions [of 25 and 27 June 1950] should place these forces under the unified command of the United States." [13]

Pearson worried that this did not go far enough, and he tried to strengthen the UN's position by including references to "United Nations forces" and the "United Nations Commander." Both Washington and London, however, overruled him, worried lest such phrases might invoke the UN's defunct military staff machinery and hand Moscow a voice in the Korean operation. The minister was also alarmed when Washington insisted on revising the resolution at the last minute to insert language that raised the possibility that the UN might be drawn into the defence of Formosa. However, as Canada's principal objective – ensuring a face-saving role for the UN – was addressed in the resolution's key operative clauses, which remained unchanged, Pearson did not express his reservations forcefully.[14]

With the UN's role defined, attention in Ottawa shifted to the difficult question of a Canadian contribution of ground troops. As it became obvious that the Americans expected their Western allies to increase their stake in Korea, Hume Wrong, Canadian ambassador to the United States, reminded Pearson that Washington's willingness to maintain the UN character of the effort in Korea depended largely on the contributions from member states. "I think that readiness to welcome proposals from other countries will be increasingly determined by the extent of the contribution which each country is making, relative to its resources and its commitments." [15] Pearson agreed, but insisted that he needed time to allow support for the UN effort to build. He was confronted with a reluctant cabinet, whose uneasiness at Washington's initial unpreparedness had been compounded by Truman's decision to neutralize Formosa, and he urged Wrong to ensure that matters were not still further complicated by a public appeal for ground troops.[16]

Pearson was too late. Even as Wrong discussed the matter at the State Department, the secretary general of the United Nations, Trygve Lie, yielded to American pressure and issued an appeal for ground troops. In Ottawa, where ministers and officials were only too aware that Canada had no troops available, there was little inclination to meet Lie's request. Arnold Heeney, the under-secretary of state for external affairs, advised the minister not to allow his attention to be distracted from events in Europe:

> Serious as is the Korean situation, and important as it is that we should not fail in our responsibility as a member of the United Nations, it would seem, at least as yet, that Korea is but a "side-show" in the over-all struggle between the USSR and the Western world. There is no room to believe that Western Europe is not still the main theatre, and it would be unfortunate if our attention should be diverted from Europe by reason of Korea.[17]

Claxton and the Chiefs of Staff Committee were also horrified at the prospect that Canadian resources might be frittered away in Korea when the real battle was more likely to be fought in Europe, if not in North America itself.[18] When the cabinet defence committee discussed Lie's appeal on 18 July, the prime minister joined the formidable group opposed to a Canadian ground force contribution.[19] Though the pressure became almost intolerable once Britain, Australia and New Zealand agreed on 25 July to make ground forces available, cabinet deferred a decision at the end of July until Pearson could consult with the American secretary of state, Dean Acheson, on the situation in Korea and its relationship to the cold war struggle in Europe.[20]

Acheson's views were soothing. The United States was aware that the conflict in Korea was not the primary struggle, and it would quickly retreat from Asia if Moscow launched a major attack elsewhere. The American also reassured Pearson that Truman's decision to neutralize Formosa was not made in panic but reflected a careful calculation of the strategic situation that was created by the outbreak of war in June 1950 and would not lead to war with China. Pearson returned to Ottawa comforted about American intentions in Korea and the Far East, and on 7 August Cabinet agreed to recruit a new brigade for service with the UN in Korea.[21]

Canadian misgivings arose almost immediately. MacArthur's high-profile visit to Formosa in mid-August, implying that the off-shore islands too might become a UN responsibility, raised fears of a direct clash with China. The general's visit also disturbed Asian opinion and reinforced Pearson's concern that the gap between the Western alliance and the Asian bloc had been allowed to grow dangerously wide during the early phase of the war. The minister was well aware that reducing the divergence between Asia and the West over Far Eastern issues would require adjustments in American policy. In mid-August he wrote Acheson an informal letter to express his apprehension at Truman's decision to isolate Formosa and the continuing risk of a direct confrontation with China. The consequences of an American conflict with China would obviously be far-reaching:

> [T]he cooperation between Asian and non-Asian members of
> the United Nations might be seriously – even disastrously –
> affected ... at the very time when an encouraging measure of
> unity has been achieved in the decision to repel aggression in
> Korea.[22]

Despite this emerging concern over the nature of Washington's Far Eastern activities, Canada was equally disturbed by Indian policy. India's apparent reluctance to endorse the Security Council's June resolutions calling on member nations to support South Korea, its refusal to consult with its Commonwealth colleagues at the UN, and Prime Minister Jawaharlal Nehru's ill-considered offer to mediate in Korea, made Pearson uneasy. Henceforth, Canadian efforts at the UN, the cabinet decided in early September, "should be directed toward eliminating misunderstanding and bridging where possible, the gaps between the policies of the U.S. Government and Asian governments." [23]

Pearson's efforts to draw India closer to the Western cause first came to a head in October 1950 when MacArthur's landing at Inchon threw North Korea into retreat and forced the UN to consider whether its troops should cross the 38th parallel, uniting Korea by force. In New York, a resolution was quickly drafted to meet the circumstances. In addition to creating the UN Commission for the Unification and Rehabilitation of Korea (UNCURK), it anticipated and endorsed MacArthur's decision to cross the 38th parallel. With a significant UN victory in sight, Pearson was happy to support the UN's resolutions and its determination to secure a "united Korea, a free Korea." In doing so, he hoped that the West could persuade the Asian nations to assume "a major share of the responsibility for advising the Korean people upon methods of government which they should adopt and procedures which they should follow." [24]

But it was soon clear that India would refuse to accept any responsibility for a Korean settlement that united the country by force. The Indian representative to the United Nations, Sir Benegal Rau, announced that the 38th parallel should be crossed only as a last resort and only after every avenue of negotiation had been exhausted. At the very least, if the UN was determined to cross the parallel, then North Korea ought to be given a chance to surrender. In Ottawa, India's opposition to the UN resolution was greeted with dismay. St. Laurent was particularly upset and he urged his foreign minister "to go some distance toward meeting the Indian position and so preserve the united front to which we attach so much importance." [25]

Pearson went right to work, pushing India and the resolution's principal sponsor, the United States, closer together. In New York, the Canadian minister told Rau that the time had come for India, having voted for peace and security in Korea, to accept its UN responsibilities.[26] In Washington, Wrong convinced Acheson, to allow the UN to issue a statement urging the North Koreans to surrender in the brief period expected to lapse between the adoption of the resolution and the UN invasion of North Korea.[27]

With the small American concession in hand, Pearson hoped that the Indian delegation might try to build on the Western effort to meet its position. He waited in vain. India abstained when the United Nations adopted the resolution authorizing its forces to proceed into North Korea on 7 October, 1950. Though Pearson criticized the "confusion and division" in Washington that led to this result, he thought New Delhi should shoulder most of the blame:

> Following its current tendency to try to bridge the gap
> between the Stalinist and non-Stalinist worlds ... India failed
> to make any real contribution which might have brought the

majority position closer to her own, thereby giving rise to the suspicion that New Delhi is perhaps more concerned with the appearances of compromise than with finding an acceptable solution to the Korean problem. Perhaps the Indians realize that any solution in Korea can only make the best of a bad job and therefore they do not wish to soil their hands unnecessarily at this stage in the proceedings.

Pearson found "the whole episode ... a discouraging one," which left him uneasy about the differences dividing the West from its potential allies in Asia.[28]

For the moment, however, these worries were allowed to slip into the background, and for most of October 1950 Canada watched without undue concern as UN forces rolled northward towards China. However, the discovery of a small number of Chinese troops in North Korea in early November set alarm bells ringing in Ottawa, and prompted Pearson to seek assurances from Washington that MacArthur would give Peking no cause to enter the conflict. As UN troops drew closer to the Chinese border, Pearson redoubled his efforts to have Washington indicate to Peking that the UN represented no threat to China. Though assistant secretary of state for Far Eastern affairs Dean Rusk tried to mollify the Canadian minister, Pearson was not appeased. Observing American tactics at Lake Success, where the Security Council was debating a U.S. resolution calling on China to refrain from aiding North Korea, he worried that "intimidation is now being administered to such a degree that it may be difficult for [the] Chinese to discern [any] elements of reassurance." [29] In mid-November, convinced that the "present atmosphere of haste and emotion" might lead to war with China, Pearson tried unsuccessfully to persuade France and the United Kingdom to create a small demilitarized zone around the Yalu River hydro-electric facilities to calm growing Chinese fears.[30]

Canadian worries about MacArthur's precipitous advance up the Korean peninsula were well-founded. In November, over 250,000 Chinese "volunteers" were discovered hiding in North Korea, and in short order, MacArthur's forces were in full retreat. Canadian officials quickly concluded that intervention on such a large scale precluded any limited objectives. The only safe assumption was that Peking had acted "with the approval of, or more likely, at the behest of the Russians." [31] The emotional, indeed almost hysterical, reaction in Washington, where Acheson accused China of an "act of brazen aggression ... even more immoral" than North Korea's original outrage, was no less disturbing. When Truman mishandled a reporter's question and implied that the United States would use atomic weapons if required, Pearson was horrified. Suddenly, the spectre of a general war pitting China and the Soviet Union against the West seemed imminent. Escott Reid, deputy under-secretary of state for external affairs, would soon warn his minister that "Russia and China are now prepared to run grave risks of precipitating a third world war. It is possible that these two powers have by now decided to precipitate that war during the next twelve months." [32] Neither Pearson nor the prime minister had any trouble agreeing on Canada's immediate priority: "The main objective at the moment must be to get at least a de facto cease fire in order to create an atmosphere in which private negotiations might have the best chance for success." [33]

This was easier said than done but when the General Assembly agreed on 13 December to create a committee to search for a cease-fire, St. Laurent agreed that Pearson should join Rau and Nasrollah Entezam, the Iranian president of the General Assembly, in this exposed and risky venture. Canada had several objectives. First, though Pearson and his officials thought it unlikely, there was an outside chance that the committee might actually find the basis for a cease-fire. Second, and just as important, Pearson saw the exercise as an ideal opportunity to bridge the gap that had opened between the West and India over the decision to cross the 38th parallel. Should China reject a reasonable offer for a cease-fire, India would be forced to support the UN's efforts in Asia. And finally, the committee's work delayed United Nations consideration of a draft American resolution that denounced China as an aggressor, giving time for cooler heads to prevail in Washington, Peking and Moscow.

The task before the committee was daunting. Peking, which considered the threesome to have no official standing, insisted that there could be no cease-fire talks except as part of a larger discussion that would include consideration of a Korean political settlement, the withdrawal of all foreign troops from Korea, and the status of Formosa. In contrast, Washington emphasized that there could be no negotiations on these broader issues until a cease-fire had been obtained in Korea. Initially, Pearson and his colleagues hoped that the two positions might be reconciled by having the committee issue a report that linked a cease-fire with negotiations on outstanding Far Eastern questions, thereby assuring China that the UN would not overlook its interests once the military situation had stabilized. They were soon disappointed. In a series of frustrating meetings with Ernie Gross, the deputy head of the American mission at the United Nations, Pearson failed to persuade the United States to concede any ground.

In the week before Christmas, Pearson continued to press Washington to adopt a more accommodating policy. His efforts were eventually rewarded as the United States demonstrated a renewed appreciation of the need to maintain UN support for any subsequent action it wished to take against China and moderated its opposition to the committee's work. On 21 December, the American embassy in Ottawa informed the minister that if a cease-fire was arranged, Washington would acknowledge privately that while any initial talks must be confined to Korea, it "would not rule out the inclusion in the agenda of other items including Formosa." [34] Pearson was heartened at what he called an "important and welcome change in U.S. policy," and he quickly arranged for word of the American concession to be passed through New Delhi to Peking. He was not surprised, however, that China declined to respond to the shift in American policy for he shared Rau's opinion that the concession was still too vague to satisfy Peking. As a result, he renewed the pressure on Washington to be "more specific in describing the subjects which ... could be included in post cease-fire discussions." [35]

As it waited in early January for American policy to evolve in a more hopeful direction, the cease-fire committee decided to draft its own statement of principles, outlining a "basis for a political settlement of Korean and Far Eastern problems." The final, and most important, principle in the draft committed the U.S., Britain, the Soviet Union and China to hold a conference following a cease-fire to discuss the "peaceful settlement of existing issues." This was hardly an advance over the terms that the United States had offered privately, prompting Pearson to press the United States to approve a draft which promised a conference on "the peaceful settlement of Far Eastern problems, including, among others, those of Formosa and the representation of China at the United Nations." [36]

Almost immediately, Nehru, who was in London for a meeting of the Commonwealth prime ministers, rejected the draft as unlikely to meet Peking's requirements. The Indian leader wanted the statement to indicate that any discussions would proceed "in conformity with existing international obligations and the provisions of the UN charter." Again, Pearson successfully persuaded Washington not to oppose this new language. Indeed, he insisted that the United States not merely abstain, but actually vote in favour of the draft statement. At the same time, he arranged for St. Laurent to press Nehru, who remained skeptical of American intentions, to carry out his promise to co-sponsor the resolution. On 13 January, 1951, the UN adopted the committee's statement of principles, with votes from both India and the United States. In a single stroke, two important Canadian diplomatic objectives had been realized: the peace process remained on track, and India seemed firmly linked with the Western cause.

Pearson's diplomatic success was short-lived. On 17 January, the Chinese delivered their reply, which Washington denounced as a "complete rejection" of the UN's position even before "the text was completely translated." [37] Almost immediately, the U.S. tabled its resolution condemning China as an aggressor. Convinced that the ambiguous Chinese message was "open to several interpretations," Pearson sought an additional delay, while St. Laurent asked Nehru to seek clarifications from Peking. But the United States had delayed long enough, and the effort to clarify the Chinese message was abandoned in the face of Washington's "vigorous and uncompromising opposition." [38] In the UN debate over the American resolution, India distanced itself from the West, contending that Washington was closing the door on a cease-fire. Ottawa agreed but with the possibility of global war still all too real, Pearson and his cabinet colleagues realized that it was impossible to stand on the sidelines. Though he considered it "premature and unwise," (and said so publicly), Pearson supported the U.S. resolution in the interests of Western unity. Thus was the diplomacy of constraint, constrained.

Diplomatic efforts to end the war largely disappeared after the UN condemned China in February 1951 and as attention shifted to the situation on the battlefields of Korea. For a while, it seemed that diplomacy might regain its importance when the front stabilized, and armistice negotiations between the United Nations Command (UNC) and communist military authorities commenced in the summer of 1951. But there was little need for diplomacy as the talks between the two military commanders dragged on until deadlocked in May 1952 over the disposition of prisoners-of-war (POWs). Aware that many POWs would refuse to return willingly to their communist homelands, the United States insisted that the UNC not use force to compel their return, a decision reflecting both Washington's belief in individual freedom as well as its recognition that the defection of communist POWs represented a substantial propaganda victory. Not surprisingly, Chinese and North Korean negotiators insisted that all POWs be repatriated - voluntarily or otherwise – in accordance with the provisions of the 1949 Geneva Convention on POWs.

Initially, at least, Canada was not especially concerned with either the slow pace of the talks or the deadlock that developed in the spring of 1952. Indeed, Pearson was generally pleased with the efforts of the American negotiators at Panmunjom, and hopeful that a de facto armistice might emerge from the deadlock. Nevertheless, Canadian policy-makers were haunted throughout 1951 and 1952 by a lingering fear that the unpredictable, and increasingly frustrated, Americans might adjourn the talks and seek to step up UN military activities against China. As preparations for the 8th UN General Assembly got underway in August 1952, Pearson was alarmed to discover that the United States was planning to seek UN support for just that course of action.

By the summer of 1952, the Truman administration was under intense economic and political pressure to end the fighting in Korea. Convinced that a little additional pressure on China would result in a more flexible attitude among Chinese negotiators, the State Department set out in August 1952 to enlist the support of its key Western allies for a UN initiative in support of a greater UN effort against China. As a first step, it proposed that the UN adopt a resolution endorsing the UNC's current negotiating posture and urging the communist negotiators to accept its position on the repatriation of POWs. Anticipating that this resolution would be rejected by Peking, the United States suggested that the UN should then pass a second resolution urging its members to take additional sanctions against China.[39]

Ottawa was alarmed at the American scheme and warned the State Department that "public pressure has the effect of making the communists more stiff-necked and more determined to follow whatever course they have embarked upon." Moreover, repeating a familiar Canadian refrain, Pearson cautioned that the effort to isolate Peking would not receive broad support at the UN, further dividing Western and Asian members, and increasing "neutral sentiment." [40] Despite these warnings, which were echoed by Britain and France, Washington decided to proceed with its first resolution, leaving Ottawa little choice but to support the motion endorsing the UNC's position. Pearson agreed to co-sponsor the American resolution but worried that the United States still planned a second resolution calling for increased "economic, diplomatic, and possibly military pressure on the Chinese," he explicitly reserved the right to support an alternate resolution on Korea if one emerged.[41] Acheson tabled the U.S. resolution with 21 co-sponsors on 24 October.

While the UN debated the American resolution during the last week in October, Commonwealth delegations held a series of secret meetings to explore other ways the UN might advance the search for an armistice. When it became clear that India would not support the 21-power resolution, Commonwealth representatives urged the vice-chairman of the Indian delegation, V.K. Krishna Menon, to find an alternative. With considerable support from Pearson, who had been elected president of the General Assembly, and Selwyn Lloyd, the British minister of state for foreign affairs, Menon set about translating his rather vague suggestion that the UN might simply fudge the POW issue into a formal resolution.

Menon's draft was a complicated piece of work. Its preamble effectively endorsed the Communist position that the repatriation of POWs must take place in accordance with the Geneva Convention, thereby acknowledging the principle of forcible repatriation. Its operative clauses, however, asked each side not to use force to repatriate POWs. Instead, when the armistice was signed, the POWs would be turned over to a repatriation commission composed of four mutually acceptable states, with a fifth to be chosen as umpire, if necessary. After three months, the question of what to do with any unrepatriated POWs would be turned over to the post-armistice political conference on Korea's future for disposition. Precisely what would happen to them next was not clear.[42]

Although Pearson and Paul Martin, the minister of health and welfare who headed the Canadian delegation in Pearson's absence, recognized the difficulties involved for the United States in retreating from the principle of non-forcible repatriation, they cast Canada's influence strongly behind Menon's resolution. There were good reasons for doing so. Obviously, if India succeeded in overcoming the deadlock over POWs, all would enjoy the advantages of an armistice. Even if the initiative failed to achieve its ultimate objective, it still offered Canada and the West some important benefits. If the initiative floundered despite strong Western support, New Delhi would appreciate how difficult it was to negotiate with the Communists, and henceforth would be more inclined to support the Western effort in Asia. Moreover, from the Canadian perspective, an Indian initiative at the General Assembly that secured Washington's support (however reluctantly) would effectively limit any future American plans to seek UN support for greater sanctions against China.[43]

Washington was outraged. In part, its anger reflected the feeling that its closest allies had abandoned and betrayed it. In his memoirs, for instance, Acheson scathingly denounces Pearson and the other members the "Menon cabal." [44] But American objections were also substantial. The resolution provided no direction for the ultimate disposition of the hard-core POWs, who did not wish to return to their homelands except indefinite detention while the post-armistice political conference squabbled over their fate. It was, the U.S. secretary of state told Lloyd, "almost frighteningly clear where efforts like Menon's would lead us ... we had started on basis we would not use force to repatriate prisoners, we had now reached the point where if this resolution were passed we would be starting POWs on road to forced repatriation." [45]

With Truman's support, Acheson and his delegation in New York mounted a sustained campaign to convince Canada and Britain to abandon Menon and support the 21-power resolution. On 13 November, the U.S. secretary of state confronted Pearson and British foreign secretary Anthony Eden. Acheson launched a "vigorous onslaught" against India's draft resolution, denouncing it as "completely unacceptable." [46] He argued that it did not make it "sufficiently clear" that force would not be used to repatriate POWs, and did nothing to resolve the problem of "hard core" POWs. "The whole burden of the Indian draft resolution," he concluded, "was on the side of forcing the prisoner to stay in custody until he should agree to repatriation." [47] Acheson urged Pearson and Eden to return to the 21-power resolution as the basis for UN action, amending it to meet any Indian objections.

The burden of reply fell on Pearson. The Canadian emphasized the vital importance of securing an armistice and the opportunity the resolution offered for getting the Indians "off the fence." Even if the resolution retreated from the principle of non-forcible repatriation (and Pearson gamely insisted that it did not), it would free those POWs who wished to go home, reducing the whole POW problem to more manageable proportions. He insisted that the West should rally in support of the Indian resolution, adding amendments where necessary. The meeting ended at an impasse.

An Anglo-Canadian redraft of the Indian resolution brought the two sides a little closer together. Though the new draft "affirmed" in its preamble that force would not be used to repatriate POWs, it still referred the problem of hard core POWs to the post-armistice political conference. Acheson was not impressed, and on 16 November, he arranged to have Robert Lovett, the secretary of defense, and General Omar Bradley, chairman of the Joint Chiefs of Staff, visit New York to emphasize the importance Washington attached to the 21-power resolution. Steadfastly, Pearson and Lloyd held out little hope that Menon could be brought any further towards the American position.[48]

Faced with unwavering opposition from Canada and Britain, the United States finally agreed to accept the Indian resolution as the basis for UN action, as long as it indicated that the repatriation commission "shall release" all POWs still in its custody 90 days after the armistice was signed. Menon balked, but after almost 12 hours of negotiations with Pearson, Lloyd and Eden, he agreed that if the post-armistice political conference failed to resolve the POW question within 60 days, they would be transferred to the UN "for their care and maintenance until the end of their detention." Though he still refused to agree to their unconditional release, convinced that Peking would reject such terms, Menon's concession was enough to persuade Washington to proceed on the basis of the Indian resolution. After another round of negotiations, Washington and New Delhi agreed on compromise language that directed the post-armistice political conference to "transfer" hard-core POWs to the UN for "their care, maintenance and ... subsequent disposition." On 3 December, the UN adopted Menon's revised resolution by a vote of 54 to 5, with only the Soviet bloc opposed.

Although the Indian effort to advance the prospects for an armistice proved futile when Peking rejected the UN's resolution out of hand in late December, Canada was pleased with the result. India was firmly allied with the West on a Korean issue, and since the December resolution would establish the starting point for any future negotiations, Canada and its allies had a potent instrument to resist the temptation in Washington to look for an easy solution to the Korean deadlock through escalation. This provided some comfort to Canadian officials as they watched President Dwight Eisenhower's new Republican administration, with the virulently anti-communist John Foster Dulles as secretary of state, assume office in January 1953.

The final round of armistice negotiations resumed suddenly in the spring of 1953 when the communists offered to negotiate on the basis that the two sides agree to repatriate those POWs who wished to go home and send the remaining POWs to a neutral state "so as to ensure a just solution to the question of their repatriation." [49] The Canadian reaction was quick and warm. "No proposal since the Korean War began has raised such high hopes of an armistice," observed David Johnson, Canada's representative to the UN.[50] Canada, like the United States, opposed the communist suggestion that POWs be physically transferred to a neutral state, but concluded that "the principle underlying the Chinese proposal is sufficiently close to that underlying the Assembly's resolution to justify immediate resumption of the full armistice negotiations." [51]

During the first two weeks of the negotiations, which began on 26 April, UNC negotiators made it clear that they could not accept the communist proposals as they stood. As a result, China and North Korea revised their offer on 7 May. Adhering closely to the terms of Menon's resolution, the communists suggested that a repatriation commission, composed of Poland, Czechoslovakia, Switzerland, and Sweden, with India as chairman, take custody of the POWs in Korea. The commission would function on a majority basis. The POWs would be held for four months, during which time each side would be free to explain to its nationals the process of repatriation. At the end of the four months, the problem of the hard-core POWs would be sent to the post-armistice political conference.

Pearson was pleased with the communist proposals. He thought that they went "a long way to meet [UNC] objections" and considered the communist willingness to leave the POWs in Korea "an important concession." Indeed, the only difference he noted between these proposals and the Indian resolution adopted by the General Assembly was that the communists did not refer the hard-core POWs back to the UN if the post-armistice political conference failed to deal with them. As neither North Korea nor China was a member of the United Nations this was neither surprising nor disturbing. Canada's foreign minister optimistically concluded that "the way was now open for the conclusion of an armistice." [52]

American negotiators, who seemed anxious to demonstrate the new administration's determination to stand up to global communism, were less impressed. The UNC's counter-proposals rejected the idea of allowing Polish or Czech troops to guard POWs as part of the repatriation commission. Washington also insisted that the commission operate by unanimous decision. In addition, the United States stated that the armistice agreement must contain a definite provision for the release and transfer to civilian status of hard-core POWs.

Pearson was "very disturbed" by the rigid American counter-proposals, which injected several entirely new elements into the equation. He was "taken aback" by the idea that the repatriation commission should operate on the basis of unanimity, a position which "contrast[ed] sharply" with the Indian resolution.[53] When he learned that the American proposals – with an additional provision that all Korean POWs should be released rather than repatriated – had been delivered to Chinese and North Korean negotiators on 13 May, he was outraged. Alarmed that this might lead to a breakdown in the talks, he immediately instructed Wrong that "it should be made clear to the United States that we do not propose to follow them in the abandonment of the United Nations resolution which we accepted in good faith and would expect to carry out accordingly." [54] Later that day, with cabinet support, Pearson told Wrong to inform the State Department that there was "no disposition on the part of the government to defend the recent US Armistice initiative which introduced without consultation such important changes." [55]

Echoed by Washington's other principal allies in Korea, Canada's representations were not without impact in shaping the position adopted by the UNC when their 13 May counter-proposals were summarily rejected by the communists. In seeking Eisenhower's authority to moderate the American proposals, the acting secretary of state, Walter Bedell Smith, underlined the importance of allied support for the American effort in Korea, and warned that the "Korean negotiations are at a crisis point. Our position vis-à-vis the Allies is deteriorating daily." [56] On 19 May, Smith summoned the heads of the "old Commonwealth" missions, and presented them with a much more moderate set of proposals. Though these would be "the final UNC position," Smith assured them that they would be advanced in language that reflected communist terms, and in a secret session designed to "avoid ultimatum aspects." [57]

There were four main provisions in the amended UNC position: first, Korean POWs would be treated like their Chinese counterparts and would be turned over to the repatriation commission; second, the commission would resolve questions of substance by a majority of four and procedural issues by a simple majority; third, the UNC would maintain its opposition to using Polish and Czech troops to guard the POWs, and press for Indian troops; and finally, the UNC would insist on a provision that would release hard-core POWs from detention. This could be achieved by simply releasing those POWs 30 days after they were turned over to the political conference, or by transferring responsibility for them to the UN as envisioned in the Indian resolution. Ominously, Smith ending by emphasizing "that if it should come to a break-off in negotiations it cannot be expected that military operations can just sit where they are ... military operations will have to be intensified." [58]

These new UNC proposals were welcomed in Ottawa as a "distinct improvement." Pearson was "unhappy" only with the suggestion that the repatriation commission should resolve major questions by a majority of four as this contrasted directly with the terms of the Indian resolution. "[W]e should continue to stand by the resolution adopted by the Assembly on December 3," he explained. Fearful that the United States might seek to escalate the pressure on China should these proposals be rejected, Pearson was careful to set firm limits on Canadian cooperation. "In general, we consider that these new counter-proposals do provide a satisfactory basis for further negotiations, but we cannot, at this stage, accept being pinned down to agreement to them as a "final position" or to support any moves to break off negotiations if these proposals are not accepted." [59] But accepted they were, and on 27 July, 1953, military commanders at Panmunjom signed an armistice agreement bringing the war in Korea to an uncertain end.

To conclude, its worth reiterating that Canada's support for the American-led intervention in Korea was qualified almost from the start with real reservations about the direction of U.S. policy in Asia. These concerns reflected Canada's principal interests as a North Atlantic power and its view that effective Western policy in Asia must command the support of India and the other major Asian democracies. Acting effectively on these reservations was difficult for a smaller power like Canada, and during the important debates on crossing the 38th parallel and the UN's response to the Chinese intervention, its concerns were largely ignored and subordinated to the cause of allied unity. But not always, and in its efforts to advance the search for an armistice in Korea, Canada pursued a "pacific diplomacy" with results.

Endnotes

[1] Denis Stairs, *The Diplomacy of Constraint: Canada, the Korean War and the United States* (Toronto: University of Toronto Press, 1973), p. xi.

[2] Steven Hugh Lee, *Outposts of Empire: Korean, Vietnam, and the Origins of the Cold War in Asia, 1949-1954* (Kingston: McGill-Queen's University Press, 1995), pp. 26-27. ; See also, Robert Prince, "The Limits of Constraint: Canadian-American Relations and the Korean War, 1950-51," *Journal of Canadian Studies*, 27, 4 (Winter 1992-93). An earlier work of mine, also over-emphasized the similarities between Canadian and American policy in the first phase of the war. See Greg Donaghy, "The Road to Constraint": Canada and the Korean War, June to December 1950" in John Hilliker and Mary Halloran (eds.) *Diplomatic Documents and their Users* (Ottawa: Department of External Affairs, 1994), pp. 189-212.

[3] L.B. Pearson, *Mike: The Memoirs of the Rt. Hon. Lester B. Pearson*, Volume 2: 1948-1957 (Toronto: University of Toronto Press, 1973), p. 147.

[4] Record of Minister's Press Conference, 26 June 1950, Department of External Affairs (DEA) File 50,069-A-40, National Archives of Canada (NAC).

[5] Ian McGibbon, *New Zealand and the Korean War, Volume 1: Politics and Diplomacy* (New York: Oxford University Press, 1992), pp. 64-66.

[6] Unsigned memorandum from L.B. Pearson to the Prime Minister, 27 June and 4 July 1950, reprinted in Greg Donaghy (ed.) *Documents on Canadian External Relations (DCER), Volume 16: 1950* (Ottawa: Canada Communication Group, 1995), pp. 22-23.

[7] Cabinet Conclusions, 27 June 1950, RG 2, Vol 2645, NAC.

[8] Cabinet Conclusions, 28 June 1950, RG 2, Vol 2645, NAC.

[9] Washington to Ottawa, Tel No 1422, 28 June 1950, reprinted in Donaghy, *DCER, Volume 16: 1950*, p. 35.

[10] Unsigned memorandum from L.B. Pearson to the Prime Minister, 27 June and 4 July 1950, reprinted in Donaghy, *DCER, Volume 16: 1950*, pp. 48-50.

[11] New York to Ottawa, Telegram No 421, 30 June 1950, reprinted in Donaghy, *DCER, Volume 16: 1950*, pp. 39-40.

[12] Washington to Ottawa Telegram No WA-1444, 30 June 1950, reprinted in Donaghy, *DCER, Volume 16: 1950*, pp. 40-41.

[13] Washington to Ottawa, Telegram No WA-1447, 30 June 1950, reprinted in Donaghy, *DCER, Volume 16: 1950*, p. 42.

[14] Ottawa to Washington, Telegram Ex-1068, 5 July 1950, and Ottawa to Washington, Telegram Ex-1081, 6 July 1950 reprinted in Donaghy, *DCER, Volume 16: 1950*, pp. 52-57.

[15] Canadian Ambassador to Washington to SSEA, Tel No WA-1521, 12 July 1950, DEA File 50,069-A-40, NAC.

[16] Ottawa to Washington, Telegram Ex-1188, 13 July 1950, reprinted in Donaghy, *DCER, Volume 16: 1950*, pp. 61-62.

[17] A.D.P. Heeney, "Memorandum for the Minister", 18 July 1950, reprinted in Donaghy, *DCER, Volume 16: 1950*, pp. 67-68.

[18] David J. Bercuson, *True Patriot: The Life of Brooke Claxton, 1898-1960* (Toronto: University of Toronto Press, 1993), pp. 209-11.

[19] Cabinet Defence Committee Conclusions, 19 July 1950, reprinted in Donaghy, *DCER, Volume 16: 1950*, pp. 76-80.

[20] Cabinet Conclusions, 27 July 1950, reprinted in Donaghy, *DCER, Volume 16: 1950*, p. 93-94.

[21] Cabinet Conclusions, 2,3 and 7 August 1950, reprinted in Donaghy, *DCER, Volume 16: 1950*, pp. 98-104.

[22] L.B. Pearson to Dean Acheson, 15 August 1950, DEA File 50056-A-40, NAC.

[23] L.B. Pearson, "Memorandum to the Cabinet", 11 September 1950, reprinted in Donaghy, *DCER, Volume 16: 1950*, pp. 105-09.

[24] "Statement by Mr. L.B. Pearson, Secretary of State for External Affairs and Chairman of the Canadian Delegation to the United Nations General Assembly, made in the Plenary Session on September 27, 1950". S/S No 50/34.

[25] Ottawa to New York, Telegram 67, 4 October 1950, reprinted in Donaghy, *DCER, Volume 16: 1950*, pp. 170-73.

[26] Ibid.

[27] Washington to Ottawa, Telegram WA-2402, 5 October 1950, reprinted in Donaghy, *DCER, Volume 16: 1950*, p. 177.

[28] Delegation to the U.N. General Assembly to Secretary of State for External Affairs, Despatch 53, 9 October 1950, reprinted in Donaghy, *DCER, Volume 16: 1950*, pp. 182-83.

[29] New York to Ottawa, Telegram 351, 9 November 1950, DEA File 50,069-A-40, NAC.

[30] New York to Ottawa, Telegram 267, 11 November 1950, reprinted in Donaghy, *DCER, Volume 16: 1950*, pp. 228-29.

[31] R.A.D. Ford, "Soviet Motives in Korea," 21 November 1950, DEA File 50,069-A-40, NAC.

[32] "Memorandum by Deputy Under-Secretary of State for External Affairs," 9 December 1950, reprinted in Donaghy, *DCER, Volume 16: 1950*, pp. 273-74.

[33] Ottawa to London, Telegram 1867, 30 November 1950, reprinted in Donaghy, *DCER, Volume 16: 1950*, pp. 244-45.

[34] Ottawa to New York, Telegram 645, 22 December 1950, reprinted in Donaghy, *DCER, Volume 16: 1950*, pp. 321-22.

[35] Ottawa to Washington, Telegram EX-2708, 26 December 1950, reprinted in Donaghy, *DCER, Volume 16: 1950*, pp. 327-28.

[36] New York to Ottawa, Telegram 33, 7 January 1951, reprinted in Greg Donaghy (ed.), *Documents on Canadian External Relations, Volume 17: 1951* (Ottawa: Canada Communication Group, 1996), pp. 37-38.

[37] Washington to Ottawa, Telegram WA-216, 17 January 1951, reprinted in Donaghy, *DCER, Volume 17: 1951*, pp. 54-55.

[38] New York to Ottawa, Telegram 109, 23 January 1951, reprinted in Donaghy, *DCER, Volume 17: 1951*, p. 81.

[39] Rosemary Foot, *A Substitute for Victory: The Politics of Peacemaking at the Korean Armistice Talks* (Ithaca: Cornell University Press, 1990), pp. 152-53.

[40] Ottawa to Washington, Telegram EX-1759, 28 August 1952, reprinted in Donald Barry (ed.), *Documents on Canadian External Relations, Volume 18: 1952* (Ottawa: Canada Communication Group, 1990), pp. 152-53.

[41] New York to Ottawa, Telegram 143, 24 October 1952, reprinted in Barry, *DCER, Volume 18: 1952*, p. 173; and Pearson, *Mike*, p. 324.

[42] Secretary of State to Department of State, 12 November 1952 reprinted in *Foreign Relations of the United States, (FRUS) 1952-1954*, Volume XV, pp. 610-12.

[43] New York to Ottawa, Telegram 101, 28 October 1952 reprinted in Barry, *DCER, Volume 18: 1952*, pp. 176-178. See also Ottawa to New York, Telegram 100, 10 November 1952, reprinted in *ibid*, pp. 189-92.

[44] Dean Acheson, *Present at the Creation: My Years in the State Department* (New York: W.W. Norton, 1969), p. 700. A similar theme also permeates the memoirs of U. Alexis Johnson, *The Right Hand of Power: The memoirs of an American diplomat* (Englewoods Cliffs, New Jersey: Prentice Hall, 1984), p. 145.

[45] Secretary of State to Department of State, 12 November 1952, reprinted in *FRUS, 1952 1954, Volume XV*, p. 610.

[46] L.B. Pearson, *Mike*, p. 324.

[47] New York to Ottawa, Telegram 281, 14 November 1952, reprinted in Barry, *DCER, Volume 18: 1952*, pp. 197-200.

[48] Foot, *A Substitute for Victory*, pp. 155-56.

[49] Cited in Stairs, *The Diplomacy of Constraint*, p. 275.

[50] New York to Ottawa, Telegram 128, 1 April 1953, reprinted in Donald Barry (ed.), *Documents on Canadian External Relations, Volume 19: 1953* (Ottawa: Canada Communication Group, 1991), p. 63.

[51] Ottawa to New York, Telegram 51, 2 April 1953, reprinted in Barry, *DCER, Volume 19: 1953*, DCER 1953, p. 66.

[52] Ottawa to Washington, Telegram EX-827, 12 May 1953, reprinted in Barry, *DCER, Volume 19: 1953*, p. 77.

[53] Ottawa to Washington, Telegram EX-838, 12 May 1953, reprinted in Barry, *DCER, Volume 19: 1953*, p. 79.

[54] Cited in Steven Hugh Lee, "A Special Relationship?: Canada-U.S. Relations and the Korean Armistice Negotiations, January-July 1953," in Hilliker and Halloran (eds.) *Diplomatic Documents and their Users*, p. 222.

[55] Ottawa to Washington, Telegram EX-850, 14 May 1953, reprinted in Barry (ed), *DCER, Volume 19: 1953*, p. 82.

[56] "Memorandum by the A/Secretary of State to the President," May 18, 1953, reprinted in *FRUS, 1952-54, Volume XV*, pp. 1046-47; see also Foot, *A Substitute for Victory*, pp. 171-73.

[57] Washington to Ottawa, Telegram WA-1230, 19 May 1953, reprinted in *DCER, Volume 19: 1953*, pp. 87-88.

[58] "Memorandum of Conversation by the Deputy Assistant Secretary of State for Far Eastern Affairs (Johnson)," 19 May 1953, re-printed in *FRUS, 1952-54, Volume XV*, pp. 1052-56.

[59] Ottawa to Washington, Telegram EX-897, 21 May 1953, reprinted in Barry, *DCER, Volume 19: 1953*, pp. 89-90.

THE KOREAN WAR AND
THE SECURITY OF SOUTH KOREA

YONG-PYO HONG
JUNG ANG UNIVERSITY

The Korean peninsula was divided along the 38th parallel immediately after the unconditional surrender of Japan on August 15, 1945. The United States and the Soviet Union occupied the southern and northern parts respectively. Initially, it was a temporary division to facilitate the disarming of Japanese troops. However, the subsequent rivalry between the two superpowers, combined with the competition between the Communist forces and the right-wing conservative forces within the Korean political arena, brought about the establishment of two separate governments in 1948. The division of the Korean peninsula into North and South Korea eventually resulted in the outbreak of the Korean War in 1950.

After the North Korean Communist regime attacked South Korea on June 25, 1950, South Korea's primary aim was to enhance its security with the assistance of the United Nations which participated in the war. At the early stages of the Korean conflict, especially when South Korean and UN forces crossed the 38th parallel in October, 1950, South Korean President Syngman Rhee attempted to remove the main source of threat, namely the northern Communists. Rhee's desire to repel the Communists from the Korean peninsula was frustrated, however, after the intervention of Chinese troops in late October. Not only did UN forces have to retreat below the 38th parallel, but also shortly thereafter others within the UN Command, and most notably the US, began to seek a cease-fire based on the *status quo ante bellum.*

As a cease-fire became inevitable, while opposing any type of armistice short of removing the Communists, Rhee began to seek another way of ensuring South Korea's security—i.e., reducing the vulnerability of South Korea by concluding a bilateral security treaty with the US.[1] Thus, when the

---

[1] A state can seek to increase its security either by reducing its vulnerability or by removing or lessening threats. For this point, see Barry Buzan, *People, State & Fear: An Agenda for International Security Studies in the Post-Cold War Era* (London: Harvester Wheat sheaf, 1991), p. 112.

truce talks reached their final stages around April, 1953, difficult negotiations took place between South Korea and the US, which was unwilling to give such an explicit security commitment.

While examining the aspects of the Korean conflict from the perspective of South Korea—especially that of President Syngman Rhee who almost monopolized South Korea's war policy, this paper will focus on South Korea's effort to protect and enhance its security. In the first section, the security perception of South Korea before the war will be discussed. Secondly, this paper will study how South Koreans coped with the northern Communists' invasion, and why they strongly opposed an armistice while all other participants in the war advocated a cease-fire. The third section will analyze President Rhee's struggle with the US government at the last stage of the war to obtain stronger security commitments, especially a bilateral security pact between the two. Finally, this paper will examine the implication of the war on the security configuration of South Korea, and of the peninsula on the whole.

South Korea's Perception of Security Before The War

As the Republic of Korea (ROK) in the south and the Democratic People's Republic of Korea (DPRK) in the north had been created, both governments set forth unification as the utmost goal to achieve. Ostensibly, the leaders of both North and South Korea advocated to peaceful unification. It was highly unlikely, however, that they truly expected peaceful unification. A political solution of the Korean division had already proved impossible in the post-Liberation period. Above all, each claimed jurisdiction over the entire country as the only legitimate government in the Korean peninsula. Indeed, from early 1949, both Syngman Rhee in the South and Kim Il Sung in the North devoted themselves to preparing for unification by force.

On February 8, when the US Secretary of the Army visited Seoul, President Rhee straightforwardly expressed his intention to use force to unify the country. Rhee said that he would like to "increase the Army, provide equipment and arms for it, then in a short time move north into North Korea." He added that the UN's recognition of South Korea made it "legal to cover all Korea," and that he believed that "nothing could be gained by waiting." Of course, Rhee received a negative response from the US which was unwilling to be militarily embroiled in Korea.[2] Such an aggressive view of unification was attributable to a number of factors.

---

[2] *Foreign Relations of the United States, 1949, Vol. VII: The Far East and Australasia, Pt. 2*, pp. 956-58, February 8, 1949. (hereafter cited as *FRUS with year and volume number*).

First, Syngman Rhee had deep anti-Communist sentiments, identifying Communism with a disease which should be eradicated, and believed that the peace and security of Korea could be maintained only after the removal of the Communists.

Second, as implied in Rhee's conversation with the Secretary of the Army, President Rhee believed that, with recognition from the UN and the western powers, South Korea had the right to regain the land lost in the North.[3]

Third, fear of the Communist threat inside and outside the South seemed to force Rhee to contemplate a kind of pre-emptive war. Internally, in October, 1948, an ROK Constabulary regiment, instigated by Communist-indoctrinated junior officers, rebelled and occupied the southwestern cities of Yosu and Sunchon. The rising was soon suppressed, but disorder in the region continued as many Communists became guerrillas. These incidents demonstrated a considerable degree of Communist infiltration in the South, and caused fear and insecurity within the military and among the public. In addition, President Rhee's apprehension about the Communist threat further increased with the rapid "Communization" of China. Rhee believed that a Communist success in China was "bound to have unfavourable effects upon Korea," and that, before Korea became "another China," the Communists in Korea had to be removed.[4]

While eagerly seeking to unify Korea by military means if possible, the ROK President had to deal with the problem of the impending withdrawal of American forces from Korea, which had been due by the end of June, 1949. The South Korean government regarded the withdrawal of US troops as a great danger to its security. Thus, President Rhee wanted the retention of US forces until the defence forces of South Korea were capable of dealing with the Communist threat. And, if American forces should leave South Korea, Rhee suggested, the US should provide ROK forces with proper equipment in order to deter possible aggression from North Korea.[5] In addition, in May, 1949, Rhee requested one of the following commitments in return for the withdrawal: (1) the formation of a Pacific Pact similar to NATO; (2) an

---

[3] In December, 1948, the UN adopted a resolution which declared that "there has been established a lawful government [the ROK]....and that is the only such government in Korea." By February, 1949, such great powers as the US, Britain, and France had formally recognized the ROK

[4] Quoted in Robert T. Oliver, *Syngman Rhee and American Involvement in Korea, 1942-1960: A Personal Narrative* (Seoul: Panmun Book, 1978), p. 220.

[5] *FRUS, 1948, Vol. VI,* pp. 1331-32, November 19, 1948.

[5] *FRUS, 1948, Vol. VI,* pp. 1331-32, November 19, 1948.

agreement between the US and Korea for mutual defense against any aggressive nation, or (3) a public declaration by the US of a pledge to defend the ROK.[6] The South Korean effort to block US disengagement from Korea was not limited to such gentle proposals. As the final withdrawal of US troops became imminent, leaders of the ROK tried to increase the sense of crisis along the 38th parallel. They not only encouraged, but also probably initiated border fighting to insure the continued presence of the US.[7]

The border incidents, however, should not be understood only in terms of a South Korean attempt to delay the withdrawal of US forces. Throughout the spring and summer of 1949, both North and South Korea launched attacks and counter-attacks along the 38th parallel, and neither regarded the line as an international boundary. According to John Merrill's analysis, the size of the military units involved in the border engagements indicated that many of them were major battles, resulting in heavy casualties.[8]

Considering the seriousness of border clashes and guerrilla warfare within the South, it seemed hardly surprising that Rhee sought to launch a defensive war against the Communists before they struck first, believing that the best means of defence was offence. In addition, based on his perception that the source of Communist threat was the Soviet Union, the South Korean President believed that, when the Communists were removed from the North, as he put it, the "line of defense [against the Communists] must be strengthened along the Tumen and Yalu Rivers." For that purpose, Rhee needed more American military aid. Thus, in September 1949, President Rhee instructed his representatives in the US to lobby American statesmen and the public with the motto, "Give us the tools and we will do the job." In October, Rhee himself gave an address to American soldiers, saying that he would fight to the end against Soviet aggression, alone, if necessary, but "preferably with US and UN aid," describing Korea then as a "body cut in half." [9]

Needless to say, the proposal of war was not acceptable to the US which had been reluctant to be involved in military action in Korea. Far from providing additional arms, the Americans in Seoul were so fearful of the South undertaking a military offensive against the North that they distributed

---

[6] *FRUS, 1949, Vol. VII, Pt. 2*, pp. 1023-24, May 16, 1949.

[7] For this point, see Bruce Cumings, *The Origins of the Korean War, Vol. II* (Princeton University Press, 1990), p. 388.

[8] John Merrill, *Korea: The Peninsula Origins of the War* (Newark: University of Delaware Press, 1989), pp. 130-42.

[9] Oliver, *Syngman Rhee and American Involvement*, pp. 250-53; *FRUS, 1949, Vol. VII, Pt. 2*, 1093, October 31, 1949.

American ammunition only in quantities that could be used for a few days at a time. When ROK officials warned of an impending attack from the North, their US counterparts often suspected that they were exaggerating the Communist threat in order to request more aid from Washington, aid that would be used for a northern expedition. The US administration also repeated that, in the case of a South Korean attack against the North, all American military and economic aid would be terminated.[10]

Frustrated by American unwillingness to assist South Korean military action, Rhee wrote to Robert Oliver at the end of 1949:

> Koreans do want to fight the Communists and get the Russians out of the north. But unless they have the moral support of the United States, not to mention material support, nothing can be done ... [Communist] planes and everything else are all ready to come down to [S]outh Korea as soon as the harvest is under way. With what are we going to stop them? ... What we need is equipment to do the fighting ourselves.[11]

As indicated in the above letter, Rhee seemed to believe that a Communist military offensive was imminent, and that, therefore, it was necessary to first attack the Communists. All that held Rhee back was the knowledge that this would result in a break with the US, and that the ROK lacked sufficient offensive armament.

Indeed, Kim Il Sung in the north was preparing for a southern expedition to unify the country as Syngman Rhee perceived, fearing a surprise attack from the South. According to Russian documents regarding the Korean War,[12] Kim Il Sung also believed that peaceful unification was "impossible under the

---

[10] William Stueck, *The Road to Confrontation: American Policy toward China and Korea, 1947-1950* (Chapel Hill: The University of North Carolina Press, 1981), p. 164.

[11] Oliver, *Syngman Rhee and American Involvement,* pp. 259-60.

[12] On June 2, 1994, the Russian government handed over its documents on the Korean War, covering the period from January, 1949 to August, 1953, to the South Korean government. The materials were from the Archive of the President of the Russian Federation and the Archive of Foreign Policy of the Ministry of Foreign Affairs of the Russian Federation. The following examination of the North Korean attitude towards and preparation for a military offensive depends on the Russian archives, unless otherwise cited. For a useful analysis of the Russian archives in the light of the origins of the war, see Kathryn Weathersby, "New Findings on the Korean War," *Cold War International History Project Bulletin,* No. 3 (Fall 1993), p. 1 & pp. 14-18 and "The Soviet Role in the Early Phase of the Korean War: New Documentary Evidence," *Journal of American-East Asian Relations,* Vol. 3, No. 4 (Winter 1994), pp. 1-33; Hakjoon Kim, "Russian Archives on Origins of Korean War," *Korea Focus,* Vol. 2, No. 5 (September-October, 1994), pp. 22-31.

current situation," and concentrated on unifying the country by military means. In particular, as Rhee had worried, the Communization of China evidently encouraged Kim's ambition for a military unification of Korea. In January, 1950, he bluntly argued that: "Now that the unification of China has been achieved, it is time to liberate the South." Around this time, Terenti Shtykov, the Soviet Ambassador in Pyongyang, observed that Kim was "always" planning to attack the South.

Thus, the North Korean leader worried about a possible invasion, as did his southern counterpart. From early 1949, several intelligence reports suggested a southern military offensive was likely. In particular, around June, as the withdrawal of American forces from South Korea became imminent, Pyongyang feared Seoul's "freedom" in military operation. Thus, by September, 1949, Premier Kim believed that unless military action was taken at once, the unification of the country would be delayed, during which time the southern regime would build up strong armed forces, and overthrow the North. Accordingly, Kim tried to obtain approval of and military aid for military unification from the Soviet Union as eagerly as Rhee did from the US.

In a sense, Kim Il Sung and Syngman Rhee appeared to be involved in a zero-sum game where each feared a surprise attack by the other which would result in defeat, and thus became more eager to make a pre-emptive strike.

But the important difference between the two leaders in Korea lay in their patrons' responses. While the US, far from supporting South Korea in launching an invasion, continued to prevent one, the Soviet Union finally approved the North Korean plan to attack the South when Kim met Stalin in April, 1950, noting that the international environment had changed in their favour. North Korea then set up a three-stage invasion plan: to prepare and strengthen North Korean military capabilities; to propose peaceful unification to the South; and after the South's refusal, to launch a military offensive. Finally, after Seoul's refusal of Pyongyang's unification proposal of June 19, the North initiated an all-out war against the South on June 25, 1950.

The Outbreak of the War

When North Korea finally embarked upon military aggression to unify Korea on June 25, 1950, South Korea was so unprepared to cope with the superior Communist military forces that it was forced to withdraw from Seoul just three days after the outbreak of the war. Although the United States and the United Nations immediately decided to assist the South Koreans, the military situation was very disadvantageous at that stage: by August, UN forces had been forced into a narrow perimeter around Pusan, the very southern part of Korea.

However, largely encouraged by the participation of the US and 15 other nations under the UN flag, the ROK government saw an opportunity to ensure the security of South Korea by removing the main source of threat—i.e., the northern Communists. Thus, as soon as US forces arrived in Korea, President Rhee claimed that the North Korean attack had "obliterated the 38th parallel and no peace and order could be maintained in Korea as long as the division at the 38th parallel remained."[13] He also argued in his letter to the US President, Harry S. Truman, that "the time has come to cut out once and for all the cancer of imperialist aggression, the malignant growth artificially grown within the bosom of our country by world Communism.[14]

The South Korean hope for military unification expanded with the success of the Inchon landing on September 15, which shifted the balance of forces in favor of the UN Command. The subsequent UN counteroffensive forced the North Korean army to retreat north of the 38th parallel by the end of September. On September 27, the US government decided that it would shortly move its forces across the 38th parallel to destroy North Korean armed forces.[15] On October 1, ROK forces advanced into North Korean territory. A week later, American troops also crossed the 38th parallel with the UN resolution endorsing "all appropriate steps to ensure conditions of stability throughout Korea." When ROK units reached the Sino-Korean border of the Yalu River on October 29, as far as Rhee was concerned, the unification of Korea on his terms seemed close at hand.

The South Korean desire to destroy the Communist regime was frustrated, however, when Chinese forces intervened in late October.[16] UN forces were driven below the 38th parallel once again, and the military position finally stabilized close to that line.

As a military stalemate emerged near the 38th parallel in the late spring of 1951, the UN and the Communist sides began to seek to end hostilities by peaceful means. The UN/US position was that military unification became highly improbable, if not impossible, as a consequence of Chinese intervention. The Communists were also determined to start negotiations to end the fighting in Korea. The ROK, however, reacted to this move by vigorously demanding the removal of all Communist forces from Korea.

---

[13] *FRUS, 1950, Vol. VII*, p. 373, July 13, 1950.

[14] *Ibid.*, pp. 428-30, July 19, 1950.

[15] For a comprehensive analysis of the US policy to expand the war across the 38th parallel, see Rosemary Foot, *The Wrong War: American Policy and the Dimensions of the Korean Conflict, 1950-1953* (Ithaca, N.Y.: Cornell University Press, 1985), pp. 67-87.

[16] See Zhai Zhihai and Hao Yufan, "China's Decision to Enter the Korean War: History Revisited," *China Quarterly*, 121 (March, 1990).

President Syngman Rhee, as the popular symbol of Korea's struggle for independence as well as the recognized spokesman for the ROK, played a leading role in opposing all moves towards a cease-fire. He refused to consider any peaceful settlement short of the complete unification of Korea, repeatedly arguing that the 38th parallel became meaningless, and that the mission of the UN should remain the military unification of the Korean peninsula.[17]

The statement of June 23 by Jacob Malik, the Soviet Ambassador to the UN, that discussions should be started for an armistice, facilitated the launching of the truce talks. This development, however, was unacceptable to the Rhee government, and not surprisingly, soon after Malik's announcement, the South Korean President stated that the "so-called peace plan" which involved the division of Korea, and which left the aggressors in possession of parts of Korea was an "insult" to the country. He could not accept such a proposal as a "peace plan," he added, because the Communists were seeking to achieve what they had been unable to accomplish by force through diplomatic duplicity.[18]

Instead, the Rhee government suggested its own "peace plan" including the following points: Chinese forces must withdraw completely from Korea; North Korean troops must disarm; the UN must agree to prevent any third power from giving any assistance to the northern Communists, militarily, financially, or otherwise. Although the ROK government emphasized in announcing this proposal that South Korea did not oppose a cease-fire itself, it was tantamount to demanding surrender from the Communists.

President Rhee's opposition to an armistice was fully supported by many South Koreans. Despite disagreements among the political parties over Rhee's domestic policies, virtually all politicians supported Rhee's views on unification and his opposition to any settlement short of this objective. In June, the National Assembly passed unanimously a resolution condemning a cease-fire agreement as "appeasement." Not only pro-government but also anti-government newspapers carried editorials that were highly critical of a truce. The pro-opposition *Dong-A Ilbo*, for example, wrote in May that any cease-fire that allowed Communist forces to remain on Korean territory would become a "trap with which the Soviets would fool the US and other

---

[17] *Tamhwajip [Collection of Statements], Vol. I*, p. 50,
[18] *Ibid.*, pp. 285-86.

democratic nations." The US Embassy in Seoul confirmed these sentiments, observing that the "position of articulate [South] Koreans" must be regarded as "one of solid opposition" to an armistice without unification.[19]

The Korean armistice talks between the representatives of the UN Command, and the Chinese and North Korean Communists finally began on July 10, 1951. Through the first 10 months of these difficult negotiations, the two sides agreed on almost all issues designed to bring the war to an end. By May, 1952, there was only one unresolved issue—non-forcible versus automatic repatriation of prisoners of war—an issue that led to the cease-fire talks going into recess from October, 1952 to April, 1953.[20]

Regardless of developments in the armistice talks, however, the South Korean government maintained its intransigent attitude towards a peaceful settlement. Furthermore, President Rhee began to argue that, if necessary, South Korea would fight alone against the Communists to unify Korea. At the beginning of March, 1952, terming a cease-fire "a death sentence to the Korean people," Rhee argued that ROK forces would fight against the Communists single-handedly.[21]

Needless to say, Rhee's posture was unacceptable to the Truman administration which sought to bring the hostilities in Korea to a conclusion. Thus, on March 4, President Truman wrote to President Rhee, requesting assurances of continued ROK cooperation with the UN Command. In his reply, Rhee suggested that he would give the US such assurances on the conditions of the signing of a mutual security pact between the US and the ROK, and the speeding up of the expansion program for the ROK army.[22]

These conditions showed Rhee's concern for the future security of South Korea, which stemmed from his fear that South Korea would be vulnerable to North Korean threat if an armistice should be concluded. In other words, in the face of a growing awareness that a cease-fire was inevitable, Rhee began to shift his policy priority from removing the threat itself to diminishing the vulnerability of South Korea through US security commitment.

---

[19] *Dong-A Ilbo*, May 26 and June 6, 1951; Donald Stone Macdonald, *US-Korean Relations from Liberation to Self-reliance: The Twenty-Year Record* (Oxford: Westview Press, 1992), p. 48.

[20] For detailed analyses of the armistice negotiations, see Rosemary Foot, *A Substitute for Victory: The Politics of Peacemaking at the Korean Armistice Talks* (Ithaca and London: Cornell University Press, 1990); Sydney D. Bailey, *The Korean Armistice* (London: Macmillan, 1992).

[21] *Tamhwajip [Collection of Statements]*, Vol. I, pp. 72-74.

[22] *FRUS, 1952-1954. Vol. XV*, pp. 74-76, March 4, 1952; pp. 114-16, March 21, 1952.

The Truman administration felt it necessary to reassure the South Koreans that the US and the UN would not leave them exposed to any renewed Communist aggression. Thus, the US was willing to assist the ROK to increase its military defense capabilities, but with regard to Rhee's proposal for a security treaty, Washington believed that it would not be in the American national interest to negotiate such a treaty. Moreover, it also argued that so long as the US retained adequate military forces in Korea, there seemed to be no necessity for a formal defense agreement.[23]

Thus, when the truce talks reached their final stages around April, 1953, difficult negotiations took place between the ROK and US governments: the former was eager to obtain a bilateral security pact, but the latter was reluctant to give such an explicit security commitment.

The Armistice and South Korea's Search for a US Security Commitment

On 30 March, 1953, Chinese Premier Zhou Enlai made a statement which represented a Communist concession on the POW issue: he proposed to exchange those prisoners who wished to be exchanged, and to hand over the remainder to a neutral state, where their wishes concerning repatriation could be ascertained. The Chinese thus receded from insisting on automatic repatriation of all POWs. The UN side welcomed the proposal, and the armistice talks finally resumed at Panmunjom on April 26.[24] The repatriation of prisoners had been virtually the only barrier to the conclusion of these truce talks, and now with this Communist concession the last problem was almost resolved.

Being aware that an armistice agreement was imminent regardless of his position, Syngman Rhee began to consider enhancing the post-war security of South Korea by obtaining a mutual security pact through negotiations with the US. For this purpose, he insisted on a 'march north' more strongly, in order to threaten the US which wanted an end to the war in Korea as soon as possible, and thus to strengthen the South Korean bargaining position.

Immediately after the new Communist overture for a truce agreement, the South Korean government launched a public campaign against an armistice in order to demonstrate the strong and vocal support for its own view on the armistice issue. On April 2, the National Assembly passed a resolution opposing a settlement of the war without unification. Three days later,

---

[23] *Ibid.*, pp. 185-86, April 30, 1952; p. 189, May 2, 1952.
[24] See Foot, *A Substitute for Victory*, p. 168.

President Rhee made a speech in which he stated that, regardless of what happened at Panmunjom, the South Korean objective remained the same—to unify Korea. These public statements were reinforced by rallies and demonstrations and the shouting of slogans such as "Unification or Death," and "March to Yalu." Almost the whole of the South Korean press also supported the government's position on the armistice talks.[25]

While publicly rejecting the truce talks, the Rhee regime sought to negotiate with the US for a defence treaty. In early April, the Korean Ambassador in Washington, Yang You Chan, in a conversation with John Foster Dulles, the US Secretary of State, said that if there should be an armistice, a mutual security pact between the US and South Korea would "greatly relieve the fears and anxieties" of the South Korean people, who were "constantly afraid that the US and the UN would desert them." But Secretary Dulles responded that it would be better to consider such a pact "after the political conference had worked out a peaceful settlement for Korea."[26]

President Rhee thereupon sent a letter to President Eisenhower on April 9, a letter which was subsequently described by Eisenhower as "drastic in tone and extreme in its terms." In his letter, Rhee wrote that if a peace agreement allowing the Chinese to remain in Korea were to be arranged, he would have to ask all the nations, who did "not desire to drive the Communist forces up to the Yalu River," to withdraw from Korea. He added that, if the US wanted to take its forces out of Korea, it could do so. On April 24, Ambassador Yang delivered to the State Department an aide-memoir which indicated that President Rhee would withdraw the ROK military forces from the UN Command if a cease-fire agreement failed to expel the Chinese Communists from Korea.[27]

When Rhee said that he would fight alone, he might genuinely have meant it, considering his deep anti-Communism. Rhee was undoubtedly aware, however, that such a move would isolate him from the only real support South Korea had—i.e. the United States. Despite Rhee's declaration that the ROK was prepared to fight alone, he certainly knew that his forces could not successfully

[25] *Dong-A Ilbo*, April 2, 3, 6, 19, and 23, 1953; *Chosun Ilbo*, April 2, 1953; *Tamhwajip [Collection of Statements], Vol. I*, p. 178.

[26] *FRUS, 1952-1954, Vol. XV*, pp. 897-900, April 8, 1953. In the armistice talks, it was agreed that a political conference would be held within three months after the armistice for the peaceful settlement of the Korean question.

[27] Dwight D. Eisenhower, *The White House Years: Mandate for Change, 1953-1956* (London: Heinemann, 1963), pp. 181-82; *FRUS, 1952-1954, Vol. XV*, pp. 993-35, April 24, 1953.

attack North Korean and Chinese forces without the help of US troops.[28] Accordingly, his adamant attitude was interpreted by most American administrators as an attempt to "maximize his bargaining position" to obtain the fullest possible support from the US. Although Rhee repeatedly stated that he hoped the US would not consider his actions "a form of blackmail," US officials nevertheless perceived that the South Korean president was "bluffing." [29]

The US government could not completely ignore the possibility of Rhee's unilateral action, however. The South Korean President, immediately after the outbreak of the war, had granted the UN Command control over his troops only "during the present state of hostilities." Based on this fact, he was currently arguing, not unreasonably, that the signing of an armistice would "automatically mean withdrawal of ROK forces from the UN Command." Since Rhee's forces were holding two-thirds of the UN line by the spring of 1953, as General Clark feared, "a sudden decision by Rhee to remove them" from the UN Command would present "all sorts of nightmare possibilities." In addition, because Rhee's threat was based on his strong belief that the Communists must be removed from Korea, however exaggerated, American officials who met Rhee face to face often observed that he had a "burning sincerity and unshakable conviction" in expressing his view on unification.[30] As a result, his bluff or threat came to have greater credibility.

Although American policy makers felt that they had to take measures to prevent Rhee's possible unilateral action in light of Rhee's continued commitment to the 'marching north alone' theme, they were still not prepared to make a bilateral security relationship with the ROK. The US government rejected a security pact with South Korea for the following reasons: (1) a bilateral treaty would detract from the UN efforts in Korea; (2) a formal agreement would give legal effect to Communist control over North Korea; and (3) recent actions of the ROK in opposing the armistice would make it difficult to explain such a treaty to the American people and Congress. Above all, as Secretary Dulles confessed later, the US did not want a security pact with the ROK because it would involve America in "Asian mainland commitments."

In May, the Eisenhower administration, instead of the security treaty option, offered alternative measures for bolstering South Korean security, on the condition that Rhee provide sufficient assurances that he would not

---

[28] The weakness of South Korean forces was partly proved later when the Communists launched a major offensive against the ROK 2nd Corps in the east-central sector, and pushed them back 5 kilometres on a 12 kilometre front. Robert O'Neill, *Australia in the Korean War, 1950-1953, Vol. I: Strategy and Diplomacy* (Canberra: Australian Government Publishing Service, 1981), p. 358.

[29] *FRUS, 1952-1954, Vol. XV,* p. 942, April 26, and pp. 947-49, April 28, 1953

[30] *FRUS, 1952-1954, Vol.* XV, pp. 906-07, April 14 and pp. 1100-02, May 25, 1953; Mark W. Clark, *From the Danube to the Yalu* (New York: Harper & Brothers, 1954), p. 273.

violate the armistice terms. The measures were: (1) a "greater sanctions statement" by 16 members of the UN against possible future Communist aggression; [31] (2) discussions with South Korea for an agreement on military assistance; (3) a promise to attempt in the political conference to achieve a unified Korea and to secure rapid withdrawal of Chinese forces; and (4) military support for a 20 division ROK army. [32]

Rhee expressed great disappointment, however, at Washington's suggestions. He regarded a "greater sanctions statement" as far less valuable than a bilateral treaty. As for the US willingness to begin discussing a comprehensive agreement on military assistance, Rhee argued that if such an agreement were to be convincing to the Communists, it had to be concluded "now before [the] cessation of hostilities." [33]

In the face of Rhee's recalcitrant attitude towards the US position, the Eisenhower administration discussed at the end of May possible punishments and rewards for South Korea: (1) to support the previously devised "Plan Everready" to establish a military government under the UN Command in South Korea by taking President Rhee and his associates into custody; or (2) to agree on the withdrawal of the UN Command from Korea in the event President Rhee refused to cooperate in reaching or implementing an armistice agreement; or (3) to offer the ROK government a mutual defense treaty on the condition that the latter would agree to the provisions of the armistice agreement.[34]

---

[31] In November, 1951, in the midst of difficult armistice talks, the US prepared a "Great sanctions statement" to warn the Communists that a military retaliation would be imposed if they violated the armistice. After a series of negotiations between America and its allies, the text of the declaration was finalized in early 1952. The statement, which was issued later on July 27, 1953, made it clear that, if Communist aggression should reoccur, in all probability, it would not be possible to confine hostilities within the frontiers of Korea." See Foot, *A Substitute for Victory*, pp. 78-82; Gye-Dong Kim, *Foreign Intervention in Korea* (Aldershot: Dartmouth, 1993), pp. 331-42. For the full text of the declaration, see US Department of State, *The Record on Korean Unification, 1943-1960: Narrative Summary with Principle Documents* (Washington D.C.: US Government Printing Office, 1960), p. 132.

[32] *FRUS, 1952-1954, Vol. XV,* pp. 1086-90, May 22, 1953.

[33] *FRUS, 1952-1954, Vol. XV,* pp. 1097-98, May 25, pp. 1100-02, May 25, and pp. 1106-08, May 26, 1953.

[34] In April, 1953, General Clark had brought up to date "Plan Everready," which had been devised in May, 1952, as a preparation for the case of Rhee's unilateral action. Among US policy maker, General Collins, the Chief of Staff of the US Army, strongly favored the extreme measure to topple President Rhee. US officials seemed to expect to be helped by the Chief of Staff of the ROK Army, General Paek Sun Yup, if the plan were to be carried out. According to General Collins, General Paek "tacitly indicated that he would be prepared to back us [the US] if anything should happen which involves a split with Rhee." *Ibid.,* pp. 940-43, April 26, pp. 1112-14, 1114-19 and 1119-20, May 29, and pp. 1126-29, June 1, 1953; John Kotch, "The Origins of the American Security Commitment to Korea," in Bruce Cumings, ed., *Child of Conflict: The Korean-American Relationship, 1943-1953* (Seattle: University of Washington Press, 1983), pp. 244-47.

Washington policy makers opted to give President Rhee the carrot rather than the stick. The United States could neither give up South Korea after having fought three years to protect it, nor subvert the R.O.K government in the name of the UN—the very institution which had given the government its legality. Thus, Washington policy makers agreed to inform President Rhee that the US was prepared to discuss a mutual defense pact with the South Korean government "promptly after the conclusion and acceptance of an armistice" [35]

But Rhee was not satisfied with this proposal because he believed that his country's future security had to be assured prior to, not after, the signing of the armistice, a desire that reflected his fear that South Korea would be deserted after an armistice.[36]

In addition, Syngman Rhee, who was often described as a shrewd politician, must have realized that once the US achieved what it desired—i.e. a cease-fire—he would lose his bargaining power vis-à-vis the US.[37]

Rhee demonstrated his position more explicitly in a meeting on June 9 with General Maxwell Taylor, the Commander of the US 8th Army in Korea. Asked to specify US security assurances which would satisfy his requirements, he listed a mutual security pact with the US; and continued expansion of the ROK army to a 20 division ceiling, accompanied by the development of the navy and the air force. When Taylor said that a formal security pact would "take some time" to draft and to be ratified by the Senate, Rhee stated that all he wanted was a "simple statement in writing" that America would come to support South Korea if attacked. Taylor observed that Rhee seemed to "try to bring himself to an acceptance" of armistice provisions if the three points were satisfied, but "could not swallow the loss of face arising from a withdrawal from the uncompromising position" which he had taken publicly on the truce talks. The Commander concluded that Syngman Rhee could not find a "face saving means of escape," and that he needed help "to get over this hump." [38]

---

[35] *FRUS, 1952-1954, Vol. XV,* pp. 1122-23, and pp. 1123-24, May 30, 1953; pp. 1132-33, June 2, and pp. 1134-35, June 3, 1953.

[36] *Ibid.*, pp. 1149-51, June 7, 1953.

[37] In fact, when US officials were discussing the possibility of making a bilateral security pact with the R.O.K on May 29, a participant argued that: "it actually could be and really would have to be only a promise to negotiate a pact rather than the actual conclusion of a pact. We would have some time before a pact could possibly be concluded and could continue to use this as a pressure point with Rhee." *Ibid.*, p. 1119, May 29, 1953.

[38] *Ibid.,* pp. 1159-60, June 9, 1953.

The Eisenhower administration, while realizing that a speedy conclusion of an armistice might limit Rhee's possible unilateral action and that movement forward could also be helpful in convincing him of its inevitability, decided to provide Rhee with some "face-saving formula" through a high level meeting between America and South Korea. On June 16, Dulles informed Rhee that Walter Robertson, the Assistant Secretary of State for Far Eastern Affairs, would promptly go as an emissary to South Korea with the "full confidence" of Eisenhower and Dulles. Rhee's response to the suggested visit of Robertson was very positive.[39]

At Panmunjom, the Communists accepted the final proposal of the UN Command on the repatriation issue almost entirely at a meeting on June 4. This "far exceeded the most optimistic expectation" of the US. On June 8, a final text on the POWs was agreed between the UN and the Communists. General Clark expected that the armistice agreement would be signed, possibly on June 18. He also hoped that, with the reality of an armistice coming closer, "Rhee's bluffing would begin to dissipate." [40] But the General's expectation was completely undermined when the South Korean president released the anti-Communist North Korean prisoners on June 18— the very day when the armistice could have been concluded.

Between midnight and dawn on the morning of June 18, approximately 25,000 non-repatriate North Korean prisoners of war broke out of the United Nations Command camps at Pusan, Masan, Nonsan, and Sangmudae. Under the order of President Rhee, the ROK Provost Marshal, had prepared the release of the anti-Communists Korean POWs, with the tacit support of Paik Sun Yup, the Chief of Staff of the Army. The Korean security guards of the camps, who were supposed to prevent the prisoners' escape, aided and abetted the break-out by cutting the barbed wire and turning off the camps' lights. [41] The release of those non-repatriates was to undermine the basis of the final agreement between the two sides at Panmunjom on the POW issue, which had stipulated that a Neutral Nations Repatriation Commission would take charge of prisoners who did not wish to exercise their right to be repatriated.

Why did Syngman Rhee order the release of the Korean non-repatriates, and what were his aims in taking such an action? First, President Rhee considered those prisoners to be genuinely anti-Communist, and sincerely believed that they must be released from the POW camps without being

[39] *Ibid., Vol. XV,* p. 1164, June 10, pp. 1168-67, June 14, and p. 1188, June 16, 1953; Bailey, *The Korean Armistice,* p. 133.

[40] *FRUS, 1952-1954, Vol. XV,* pp. 1157-58, June 9, and pp. 1163-64, June 10, 1953.

[41] Sun Yup Paik, *From Pusan to Panmunjom* (New York: Brassey's, 1992), pp. 228-230.

turned over to the Repatriation Commission as stipulated in the proposed armistice agreement. In Rhee's view, if the prisoners were handed over to the Commission which included the "pro-Communist" India, these "innocent boys" would be urged not to remain in South Korea by the Communist "indoctrinators." [42]

Secondly, a number of US officials (especially some of the military) did sympathize with Rhee's position on the POWs. As early as February, 1952, according to the Australian Ambassador to the US, the UN Command contemplated permitting "a mass escape from the prison camps" by those prisoners who did not wish to be repatriated. In particular, General Clark, who was in charge of those prisoners, had "complete sympathy" for Rhee when the latter informed him that he might release the anti-Communist prisoners without involving the former. Such US sympathy for Rhee's stance undoubtedly encouraged Rhee to carry out his action.[43]

Thirdly, the R.O.K President's release of the Korean non-repatriates was stimulated by the agreement on June 8 between the UN Command and the Communists on the POW issue. Rhee was deeply concerned that, with this agreement, the armistice was indeed imminent. For Syngman Rhee, who had so vigorously opposed a cease-fire, it was not easy to accept without any protest what was happening at Panmunjom. Perhaps, he hoped that his aggressive action would cause the truce talks to be broken off indefinitely.

If not, he probably wanted to delay the Panmunjom agreement at least for some time during which he could negotiate with the US regarding the post-armistice security of South Korea. As noted earlier, the South Korean President was keen to obtain a mutual security pact before the signing of an armistice. Therefore, given the information that the Eisenhower administration was planning to send its emissary to South Korea, he was desperate to meet the American negotiator in advance of the conclusion of the truce talks. (In fact, the truce talks went into recess immediately after Rhee's release of non-repatriates, and did not reconvene until Rhee finished his negotiations with the US envoy.)

---

[42] *FRUS, 1952-1954, Vol. XV,* pp. 1197-99, June 18, 1953.

[43] O'Neill, *Australia in the Cold War,* p. 269; Clark, *From the Danube to the Yalu,* pp. 264-65; *FRUS, 1952-1954, Vol. XV,* pp. 1008-10, May 12, and pp. 1197-98, June 18, 1953. According to Bailey, there had been occasional unconfirmed reports that the US Central Intelligence Agency, and perhaps others, encouraged Rhee's unilateral action. See *Bailey, The Korean Armistice,* p. 134.

Finally, Rhee's release of the anti-Communist prisoners unequivocally showed the US that he had not been bluffing, and that he could take unilateral action to obstruct the truce talks. As a result, Rhee was able to reinforce, to some extent, his bargaining position vis-à-vis the US.

Faced with the embarrassing situation caused by the Korean President, the Eisenhower administration discussed several possible courses of action in Korea. As before, however, the United States had limited room for maneuver. The Americans did not wish to fight in Korea any more; but they could not abandon Korea itself, which would mean, in Eisenhower's words, "a surrender to the Chinese, handing them on a silver platter everything for which they had been fighting for three years." Whatever troubles the South Korean President caused, as the American President acknowledged, the US could not deny a simple fact that the Communists were "still the enemy," and that Rhee was a champion of anti-Communism.[44] At one time, Eisenhower wished the South Koreans would overthrow Rhee and replace him with a "more moderate and reasonable" leader. And US officials did discuss the possibility of establishing an "amenable" ROK government by utilizing the South Korean army. But they believed that there was little internal political and military disaffection with the South Korean President.[45]

The final choice was to persuade President Rhee to cooperate with the US. Consequently, on June 22, the US President's envoy, Robertson, left for Seoul to negotiate with President Rhee.

President Rhee was fully aware that the US envoy's visit was the last opportunity before the armistice in which he could obtain a bilateral military pact from the US. This was still deemed vital, not only to ensure the security of Korea, but also to help to save his face if he had to accept the armistice.

After arduous debate between the two sides, on July 4, Robertson proposed that Rhee "immediately begin negotiations to draft a mutual defense treaty" with South Korea although the ratification of such a treaty "would be subject to the advice and consent of the Senate." In addition, the US government promised to have a "high level conference" with President Rhee. In return, the US asked the Rhee government to support the armistice terms and to keep its armed forces under the control of the UN Command.[46]

---

[44] *FRUS, 1952-1954, Vol. XV,* pp. 1213-21, June 19, 1953; Eisenhower, *Mandate for Change,* pp. 185-186.

[45] Sherman Adams, *Firsthand Report; The Inside Story of the Eisenhower Administration* (New York: Harper & Brothers, 1961), p. 101; *FRUS, 1952-1954, Vol. XV,* pp. 1152-54, June 8, and pp. 1114-20, June 19, 1953.

[46] *Ibid., 1952-1954, Vol. XV,* pp. 1312-14, July 6, 1963.

President Rhee indicated that he was prepared to accept the US proposal, but asked "some evidence of congressional support" for a bilateral treaty so as to present it to his people as a fait accompli. The Rhee also wished to see a draft of the mutual security pact, which was given to him immediately. On July 8, the ROK president was informed that, at Eisenhower's personal discretion, Dulles had met with Senate leaders of both parties, and that the Senators declared themselves "willing to support ratification" of a security treaty.[47] At last, on July 9, President Rhee, in a letter to Robertson lukewarmly promised:

> Although we cannot sign [the] truce, we shall *not obstruct it*....We shall endeavor to cooperate fully and earnestly in [the] political and peaceful achievement of reunification of our nation....[emphasis added].

Two days later, Rhee confirmed in his letter to Eisenhower that he had decided not to obstruct, in any manner, the implementation of the armistice terms.[48]

The armistice agreement between the UN Command and the Communists was finally signed on July 27, 1953, putting an end to the long and difficult dispute between the two sides. Regardless of the conclusion of the truce talks, however, the controversies between the ROK and the US were yet to be finished.

A day after the formal end of the war, Secretary Dulles announced that he would visit South Korea to discuss with President Syngman Rhee the post-armistice problems between the US and South Korea. One of the main purposes of Dulles' trip to Seoul was to discuss in detail the US security commitment which had been promised to South Korea in return for Rhee's agreement not to disturb the armistice.

In the Rhee-Dulles meetings, which were held from 5 to 8 August, the issue of economic and military assistance raised few problems between the two sides. The US suggested a substantial economic aid programme including a $200 million grant. Militarily, the South Korean requested US approval for, and implementation of the 20-division army programme. This was also acceptable to the Eisenhower administration.[49] The Seoul and the Washington governments, however, found greater difficulty in resolving the issue of a mutual security pact.

In discussing a mutual defence treaty, President Rhee sought to make a treaty that could bind militarily the ROK and the US as tightly as possible. Accordingly, on reviewing a draft treaty prepared by Washington, he insisted that in the treaty there must be a pledge by the US government that in the case of an attack on South Korea, the US would act "automatically and immediately." Rhee also desired to insert a clause stating that the treaty would

---

[47] *Ibid.,* July 7, 1953; July 8, 1953.

[48] *Ibid.,* July 9, 1953.

[49] *Ibid., 1952-1954, Vol. XV,* pp. 1475-78, August 6, and pp. 1478-80, August 6, 1953.

endure "indefinitely." [50] The United States government, on the contrary, was not willing to enlarge its commitment on the Korean peninsula. When Rhee tried to add stronger language to the draft treaty, Dulles emphasized that the treaty had to be drafted in such a way as to guarantee the ratification of the US Senate. The Secretary asked President Rhee not to press the US government to add language which would not particularly add to the security of South Korea, but which would cause trouble with the Senate. Despite his repeated arguments and appeals, President Rhee failed to change the text of the draft treaty in the way he intended, and finally approved the draft presented by Dulles with minor changes.[51]

On August 8, Secretary Dulles and the ROK Foreign Minister, Yung Tai Pyun, initialed the draft Mutual Defence Treaty between the Republic of Korea and the United States. It was formally signed later on October 1 in Washington, D.C.[52]

Although the terms of the Treaty were less tight than he had hoped for, Syngman Rhee was delighted with the fact that the Mutual Defence Treaty was established at last. A day after its initialization, President Rhee made a statement that the benefits of the Mutual Defence Treaty would be "enjoyed by generations to come," and that neighbouring countries would neither look down on nor attack South Korea any more. He also tendered his thanks to America. The President added, nevertheless, that his soldiers had to prepare for the opportunity in which they could "march north."[53]

Implications Of The War For The Security Of South Korea

The Korean War is said to be the decisive turning point in modern Korean history. Its political, military, social, and economic impact on the Korean people are still difficult to ignore.[54] In terms of security, South Korea's basic security environment had been set up with the progress and results of

---

[50] *Ibid.*, August 6, 1953; Oliver, *Syngman Rhee and American Involvement in Korea*, pp. 426-28.

[51] *FRUS, 1952-1953, Vol. XV*, pp. 1466-73, August 5, and pp. 1481-88, August 7, 1953.

[52] For a full text of the Mutual Defense Treaty, see Se-Jin Kim, ed., *Documents on Korean-American Relations, 1943-1976* (Seoul: Research Center for Peace and Unification, 1976), pp. 185-86. According to the treaty initialed by both sides, it was stipulated in Article III that in the event of an armed attack on either Parties, each Party would act in accordance with its "Constitutional processes." As for the termination clause, which was provided in Article V, either Party could terminate the treaty one year after notice had been given to the other Party.

[53] *Tamhwajip [Collection of Statements], Vol. I*, pp. 314-15.

[54] For studies of the impact of the war in general, see B.C. Koh, "The War's Impact on the Korean Peninsula," *Korea and World Affairs*, Vol. 3, No. 3 (Fall, 1979), pp. 57-75; Sang-Seek Park, "Legacy of the Korean War," *Korea and World Affairs*, Vol. 15, No. 2 (June, 1991), pp. 302-16.

the war. The North Korean Communists' attack against the South, and the following bloody fighting between the two, critically deepened the antagonism between North and South Korea. The United States, the most important security partner of South Korea, was fully involved in Korea, making a bilateral defence treaty. Soviet and Chinese influence on North Korea had also been increased. Internally, public anti-Communist sentiment had been strengthened during the war perceived in the South as having been provoked by the Communists.

After the establishment of separate polities on the Korean peninsula in 1948, the unification of the country had been considered by the Korean people to be an overriding goal. The leaders of the two governments, Syngman Rhee and Kim Il Sung, had each tried to achieve unification by whatever means they deemed necessary, including military force. While perceiving that the other would launch a preemptive attack, the image of the other as the enemy had been increasing on each side. The Korean War turned that hostile image into reality. For Kim Il Sung, with his goal of military unification thwarted by the involvement of the US, his hostility against the US, together with his apprehension for its power, deepened further. President Rhee in the South, as his perception that the Communists would attack soon turned out to be true, strengthened his anti-Communist policy. His antagonism against China and the Soviet Union was also increased due to their assistance to the North. Accordingly, Rhee concentrated his efforts on finding ways to protect the South against Communists threats. As the war ended only with an armistice without creating a permanent peace, each side's perception of being threatened further increased and could not but continue.

In terms of US-Korea relations, the US, with its involvement in the Korean War, changed from a "minimum commitment" to a "maximum commitment" to the security of South Korea.[55] In early April, 1953, the US government excluded the option of a "complete withdrawal from Korea" from its possible courses of action. In NSC 170/1, which became the basis of US policy towards South Korea in the post-war period, the US set up its long-range objective regarding the Korean problem as to "bring about the unification of Korea ... under a free, independent and representative government, friendly toward the United States." As for the current objective, the NSC decided to maintain a position of strength in Korea by supporting the "commitment to oppose aggression," and by preventing the Korean peninsula "from coming under Communist domination either by subversion or by being overrun." [56]

---

[55] Joo-Hong Nam, *America's Commitment to South Korea* (Cambridge: Cambridge University Press, 1986), pp. 36-38.

[56] *FRUS, 1952-1954, Vol. XV: Korea,* pp. 839-40, April 2, 1953, and pp. 1620-24, November 20, 1953.

Above all, the US, despite its initial reluctance, concluded the bilateral defense treaty with South Korea, a treaty that has been the most important factor in South Korean security to this day.

Internally, after the Communist invasion of the South, anti-Communism became the main basis of the ideological legitimization of the ROK government. North Korea's provocation of the hostilities and the atrocities committed during the war deepened anti-Communist sentiment among the South Koreans. The following description may aid comprehension of the depth of anti-Communist feeling in South Korea caused by the war:

> The Korean War brought calamities to virtually everybody. Since Korea has an extended family system, almost everyone in Korea lost blood relatives. Others lost their property and still others were separated from their families. Many South Koreans held North Korea directly responsible for these calamities.[57]

Moreover, the war led to the liquidation of a large number of leftists who had threatened the stability of the South Korean government.

In a word, the experience of the war, and the continued existence of threats above the military demarcation line, whether they were military or political in nature, led both the rulers and the ruled in South Korea to place a high priority on security against Communists threats. And this legacy of the Korean War can be said to be the major reason why the Cold War confrontation between the two Koreas still remained on the Korean peninsula even after the collapse of the Cold War on the international scene.

---

[57] Park, "Legacy of the Korean War," p. 305.

Canada's Diplomatic Relations with North Korea, China, and Cuba

Eugene Lee

Sookmyung University

I. Introduction

North Korea (DPRK) is arguably one of the most isolated, unpredictable and xenophobic countries in the world. Canada established formal diplomatic relations with the DPRK only in February 2001, after fifty years of refusing to do so, in spite of the firm control of the DPRK over the northern part of the Korean peninsula.

The North Korean case seems unusual, given Canada's diplomatic tradition, similar to the British, of recognizing regimes in control of a given territory. It is also a notable exception to the Canadian policy of constructive engagement inspired by postwar liberal internationalism. It has been a widely accepted theme that, as a middle power heavily dependent on trade, Canada had a strong interest in preserving the peace and stability of the international system and emphasized in conducting its external affairs, based on values such as mutilateralism, compromise, accommodation and international obligation (Cooper 1997, 19-22). Constructive engagement with other countries regardless of their political differences has often been identified as one of the main features of postwar Canadian foreign policy. And it has been particularly conspicuous in Canada's relations with the People's Republic of China (PRC) and Cuba.

Whether or not to recognize the PRC was one of the most prominent diplomatic issues among Ottawa policymakers for the 20 years leading up to the recognition in 1970. Canada's relatively friendly and substantial ties with Cuba have been a highly controversial foreign policy issue ever since the Cuban revolution. They have raised a host of questions concerning some of the fundamental elements of Canadian foreign policy, including Canada's role in both East-West and North-South relations and its relations with the US. Despite numerous difficulties and controversies, however, Canada's engagement policy with the two countries was remarkably consistent. The same was not true in the case of North Korea.

There are a number of possible explanations for the North Korean exception, and it is the purpose of this article to look at some of them. Several examinations have been advanced.

As part of the UN forces, Canada fought against North Korea during the Korean War, and the two sides never signed a peace treaty. North Korea is a communist regime with an unusually belligerent attitude towards the outside world. The isolation of North Korea is largely self-imposed and it never showed any particular interest in establishing relations with Canada: a situation Canadians on their part did not feel compelled to rectify. Moral aversion to a notorious record of human rights' abuse and other negative images such as the dark terrorist state could explain the lack of Canada's interest in improving ties with the DPRK. And non-existent commercial opportunities in that country have contributed to Canadian indifference. Strong opposition from South Korea, which emerged in the 1970s as a major Canadian trading partner might have prevented Ottawa from approaching Pyongyang.

In the following, the validity of the above explanations will be examined in the context of the cases of China and Cuba. By doing so, it will also attempt to answer some broader questions. How does Canada decide to recognize and establish diplomatic relations with a foreign country? Why does it adopt engagement policy with certain regimes but not with others? Is there any consistently applied principle of Canadian foreign policy in engaging with regimes such as North Korea: communist, hostile, unpredictable and with poor human rights records?. Is there any factor in Canadian policy that can consistently explain its policy towards the regimes in question, or is it just a result of a series of historical accidents?

This paper suggests that the key, if not the only, factor that could consistently explain Canada's policy towards the PRC, Cuba and the DPRK was economic incentive. That is, Canada's policy of constructive engagement could be steadily maintained with China and Cuba to a large extent because there was substantial economic interest involved in their bilateral relations. On the other hand, North Korea offers no economic opportunity for Canada to deploy enough diplomatic resources and political energy to overcome all the difficulties in dealing with this exceptionally troublesome regime.

II. Recognizing China

1. To Recognize or Not to Recognize

When the People's Republic of China was proclaimed in October 1949, the question of recognition was immediately raised. Canadian embassy officials in China, led by Ambassador T.C. Davis and the second in command, Chester

Ronning, recommended that Canada recognize the PRC. They viewed the Kuomintang government (KMT) as corrupt and oppressive, and were sympathetic to Mao's revolution. Their views influenced the thinking within the Department of External Affairs. According to the DEA memoranda of 4 and 15 November 1949, the PRC fulfilled the usual requirements of international law for de jure recognition. Chester Ronning, who was in charge of the embassy in Nanjing, recommended that Ottawa recognize Mao's regime. In a statement in the House of Commons, Foreign Minister Pearson stated his position: "we reject completely the Marxist-Leninist principles... but we cannot reject the fact of China and its 450 million people." He stressed that recognition was not an approval but a simple acknowledgement of the state of affairs that existed, and stated that "if the fact of Communist control of China is demonstrated and [if] an independent... Chinese government, able to discharge its international obligations, is established there, which [is] accepted by the Chinese people..." then recognition should be accorded.[1] On 16 November 1949, the cabinet decided in principle to accord recognition to the PRC (Beecroft 1991, 43, 45-47; Holmes 1982, 136; Ronning 1974, 171).

Although Prime Minister St. Laurent favored recognition, he was hesitant to move immediately because of other considerations. Anti-communist sentiment was running high in North America at that time, and the opposition Conservative Party was against recognition. The attitude of the US was significant as well (Thompson 1971, 111). The US saw communism as a monolithic threat and made concerted efforts to isolate the PRC. US policymakers tended to consider the PRC as a Soviet puppet regime, and such perception became the root of diverging policies between the US and Canada.

Contrary to US policymakers, Canadians had different views about Asian Communism. The Canadian public, diplomats and press had little sympathy for the KMT. In Canada, it was generally believed that the Communist victory was a result not so much of doctrinal fervor among the Chinese people as apathy, disgust and lack of support for the KMT (Harrison 1957, 251). Canada had few close contacts with the KMT during the war, and did not get involved in the Western bloc's postwar efforts to bolster the regime. There was none of the feeling of having lost China, which deeply affected American thinking (Holmes 1965, 104). It was relatively easier for Ottawa to accept the reality and "attempt to find some constructive way of living with it" (Beecroft, 47).

From the outset, therefore, the basic Canadian policy was to recognize the PRC as the lawful government of China and to accept its UN membership. It was a matter of appropriate timing and method. The simple case for recognition was that the communist government was firmly established, and

---

[1] Statement by Lester Pearson in the House of Commons , 11 November 1949. In Mackay (1971, 337-78).

that refusing recognition would cause its continuing hostility towards Western nations, including Canada (Flaherty 1968, 183). There was no conscious decision to deny recognition.

For various reasons, however, Canadian recognition did not come until 1970. Canadians were not without reservations. The PRC's initial hostility towards the US made Ottawa uncomfortable. Moreover, recognition of Beijing seemed to carry the implication of accepting its territorial claim over Formosa, which was regarded important to the American defence perimeter in the Pacific, and to which millions of Chinese had fled from communist rule. There was a division among Canada's major allies, particularly between the US and the UK, concerning the PRC. This was another factor that complicated Ottawa's thinking. Canada did not want to undermine NATO unity and the US leadership, and sat uncomfortably in the middle (Beecroft 1991, 44).

Wanting to consult with other friendly countries, Ottawa deferred its decision until after the Commonwealth Conference held in December 1949. However, the conference showed a split of opinion among Commonwealth members. Some, such as India, Pakistan and the UK, did not wait for a common front and recognized the PRC between late 1949 to early 1950. By then, Canada's position became significant. Canada, unlike the UK, did not have any critical interest at stake, and was inclined to grant recognition; on the other hand, however, Canada was a country closely associated with the US. With Australia, New Zealand, Belgium, France and others still holding off, a Canadian decision for recognition might have had a catalytic effect (Holmes 1982, 136).

After the Commonwealth Conference, the general consensus in Ottawa was that recognition should be accorded in principle. However, the cabinet, mindful of the strong opposition from Washington, was reluctant to go ahead with recognition. A further delay was decided in March. The fact that the UK and others which recognized the PRC earlier were having difficulties did not encourage Ottawa (Ronning 1974, 177). Neither was there unanimous support for recognition in Canada. The then DEA under-secretary Drew said that recognition by the UK was no reason why the Canadian government should follow suit (Harrison 1957, 246). Although Canada had little reason to reject the PRC regime, it had no reason to rush. As more countries such as Norway, Sweden, and Denmark and the Netherlands later accorded recognition, Canada also prepared for negotiation with the PRC for simultaneous recognition and exchange of ambassadors. Not long after, however, the Korean War broke out, which profoundly affected China's external relations. The PRC becoming one of the belligerents on the side of North Korea complicated the situation.

Due to the Korean conflict, domestic political consensus became more difficult to achieve. The cabinet became divided and very cautious. The opinions in Parliament were split. It was ambivalent about recognizing the PRC and admitting it to the UN. The Conservative Party opposed any hasty action, and Canadian public opinion was also divided. Although Canada did not experience the consistently passionate anti-PRC sentiment that was found in the US, only a slim majority of Canadians supported the recognition of the PRC in the 1950s. Chinese policy was not influenced by any strong domestic constituency, and groups including academics, churches, and Chinese Canadians were not coherent. Canadian corporations did not have any large stake in the PRC, and did not forcefully lobby the government.

However, "the Korean War did not change Ottawa mandarins' consistent belief that the PRC should be recognized. If anything, it convinced them that recognition was essential to bring the PRC out of dangerous isolation and into the world community, thereby ensuring world peace" (Beecroft 1991, 54-55). However, "there never emerged a compelling popular mandate to act in any particular direction" (Evans 1991, 6). China was of limited interest to Canada, and Ottawa lacked any overwhelming incentive to take a large political or diplomatic risk by recognizing the PRC. Subsequently, a tendency set in to wait for the best timing both domestically and internationally, and the state of non-recognition lasted for twenty years.

As years went by, consensus was not formed in Canada. Canadian disquiet about China's menacing posture undoubtedly had an influence. Even into the 1960s, some politicians such as Prime Minister Diefenbaker strongly opposed recognition or UN Security Council membership of the PRC. The change in the Security Council representation was such a sensitive issue that Canada was hesitant to take any action without being sure of the consequences.

Other major events such as the off-shore shelling, Sino-India conflict, the Chinese intervention in the Vietnam War, and the Cultural Revolution affected Canadian policy. There were not so much compelling reasons to refuse recognition, but the problem was that they made the timing inappropriate to do something quite deliberately which had not been done before (Holmes 1982, 192).

Despite delays, the Canadian government considered recognition of the PRC sensible and inevitable, and kept the door open for eventual recognition. It also made efforts to dissociate itself from the US.

Until the Canadian recognition in 1970, arguments were frequently made that Canada was deterred by American pressure and that the case was a symbol of American dominance on Canadian foreign policy (Hanly 1968, 25-26; Tucker 1980, 29; Molot 1977, 230; Creighton 1970, 273). But attributing the delay mainly to the American factor is misleading. It is true that Canada had to be sensitive to the US position. The Korean War placed China firmly on the other side of the Cold War front, and the US became so deeply opposed to the PRC that recognition by any of the American allies was bound to appear as a slap on the American face than would have seemed the case before the war. However, Holmes maintained that Washington never threatened Ottawa in such a way as to prohibit Canada from recognizing the PRC. The US vigorously expressed concerns about Canadian action, but there was no diplomatic threat. With no vital interest at stake and given the importance of the US, Ottawa considered it undesirable to irritate Washington, particularly the Congress, simply for the sake of being different from the US. Holmes argues that it was in the interests of Canada to support its most important and trusted ally, to the extent that it was possible (Holmes 1982, 192; 1965, 118). Beecroft also observed that the importance of the US and the possible backlash from Washington far outweighed Canada's limited interest in China. It was considered unwise to undermine the position of the US, the most important ally of Canada (Beecroft 1991, 63-65). Whether it was a legitimate consideration for an important ally or a fear of retaliation and self-imposed restriction in policy options may depend on one's viewpoint. If there was a decision, or a non-decision, on the part of Canadians, it was their own choice. Canadians may well claim that their China policy was "made in Canada" (Evans 1991, 6).

As mentioned above, Canada's position was never a denial of recognition, but was always regarded as a temporary delay. There were successive reasons for postponement, each of which made sense when there were arguments for caution as well as for action. While recognition of the PRC was given serious consideration year after year, no further attempt was made to negotiate with Beijing until 1968.

2. Trudeau Recognizes Beijing

When Pierre Trudeau came to office in 1968, the China issue was again brought to the fore. As a politician, Trudeau perceived that Canada was too closely identified with the US, and that Canadian foreign policy was managed by politically non-responsive DEA officials. He wanted to depart from his predecessors' foreign policy. Trudeau described China's future as a world power and also a major potential threat largely because of its isolation. During the election campaign, he had declared his intention to recognize Beijing as soon as possible (*International Canada* May 1968, 58-59), and once elected, he launched a major foreign policy review, and redirected Canada's foreign policy away from the Atlantic and US-centered approach to pay more attention to the Asia-Pacific. Trudeau saw the China issue as an opportunity to assert his new foreign policy initiative, and made it one of his foreign policy priorities. In a May, 1968 statement, Prime Minister Trudeau stated, "we have an economic interest in trade with China... and a political interest in preventing tension between China and its neighbours... Our aim will be to recognize the People's Republic of China government as soon as possible and to enable that government to occupy the seat of China in the UN, taking into account that there is a separate government in Taiwan" (Frolic 1991, 190-92).

Trudeau's bold declaration raised a host of complex questions. The most difficult one was Beijing's determined effort to win Canadian acceptance of its claim to Taiwan as the main condition for mutual recognition. That the PRC wanted to establish diplomatic ties with Ottawa was one thing; whether it was possible to recognize the PRC 'one-China' policy without accepting its territorial claim over Taiwan was another. The Chinese could use Canada as a test case for major acceptance by the West of Beijing's territorial claim, by making it a prerequisite for recognition.

Canada could not accept it (Harbron 1974, 9). A Two-China policy would have been ideal for Canada; but it was unacceptable to Beijing. There was a consensus in Canada that establishing diplomatic relations with the PRC was necessary and desirable, but finding a mutually acceptable solution for the Taiwan issue was the crucial factor. DEA officials were charged with coming up with solutions for this difficult task. Various other considerations were factored in, such as the possible American response being one of them, and trade investments in China and Taiwan.[2]

At the end of 1968, the Canadian Embassy in Stockholm was instructed to approach the Chinese Embassy for negotiation. In February, 1969 the two sides agreed to start negotiations which dragged on for 20 months over the issue of Taiwan. The conditions that the Chinese put forward were: recognition of the PRC as the sole legal government of China, support for their claim to the Chinese seat in the UN, and acknowledgement of Taiwan as an integral part of Chinese territory. China wanted a clear Canadian position with respect to Taiwan, but Canadian terms were clear: recognize China without accepting all of Beijing's territorial claims. Canada was prepared to break diplomatic ties with Taiwan, but to go no further (*Canadian Annual Review for 1970,* 329).The prolonged negotiation came to a conclusion in October, 1970, thanks to the so-called Canadian Formula. According to the formula, the PRC reaffirmed that Taiwan was an inalienable part of its territory, while Canada 'took note of' this position. The formula allowed both parties to maintain the important principles they upheld (Harbron 1974, 14).

---

[2] For more information about the Canadian considerations before the start of the Ottawa-Beijing negotiation, see Frolic (1991, 195-97).

The terms of the Canadian recognition constituted an important precedent. In the months following the Ottawa-Beijing agreement, other countries followed suit, mostly adopting the Canadian formula (Thompson 1971, 115).

There were circumstances favorable to the successful conclusion of the negotiation. The Canadian position was always a temporary postponement of recognition, and Canada did not participate in the US-led embargo against the PRC. The Canadian government did not prevent individual contacts with the Chinese by academics, students, businessmen or journalists, and even government officials could visit the PRC on an unofficial basis. A direct relationship had been reestablished since 1959 as China purchased Canadian wheat. In Canada there was no articulate, anti-communist, American style China lobby. On the contrary, churches, academics, businesses were pressing the Canadian government to recognize the PRC. Trudeau's determination to push the issue forward was also important, and he provided the political energy to overcome many obstacles. It helped that the US position concerning China was somewhat softened as President Nixon considered a new foreign policy initiative of his own (Harbron 1974, 10; Molot 1977, 232). A change in Beijing's attitude was also a significant factor. The PRC, emerging from the Cultural Revolution, was interested in pursuing new diplomatic ties with the outside. Beijing's perception of the Soviet threat and its concern about the Soviet-American detente led it to see diplomatic contacts with the West and UN membership in a more positive light (Molot 1977, 234). In a way, therefore, it "[was] not the Canadian decision but the Chinese decision to let the exchange take place without demanding Canadian surrender on a matter of principle" (Holmes 1976, 169) that made it possible.

3. Economic Engagement and Human Rights

So far we have looked at the issue of recognition in the earlier years of the PRC. There is also an economic dimension and other political issues, which could shed light on the nature of Canada-China relations. Here, we briefly touch on the issue of human rights in China.

The Canadian awareness of being a Pacific nation was dramatically enhanced in the postwar years, although it took some time to manifest itself into concrete policy measures. Much of Canada's interest in the region lay in trade, and China's vast population appealed to many Canadians as a lucrative potential market. Canada participated in the Coordinating Committee for Multilateral Strategic Export Control (COCOM), which controlled the trade of strategic materials with communist countries, and the China Committee (CHICOM), which was set up in 1950 specifically for monitoring China trade (Nossal 1994, 20-21).

However, quite separate from the complicated legal, diplomatic, and political issues, the Canadian government in subsequent years actively sought to develop trade relations with China and a major breakthrough was made during the Diefenbaker era.

Being a conservative and anti-communist, John Diefenbaker, in opposition had vigorously opposed the recognition of the PRC. As a Prime Minister, his first statement on China was that he would support expanded trade with the PRC, although he maintained his opposition to diplomatic recognition of the regime (Beecroft 1991, 66). Subsequently, since the late 1950s, Canadian wheat sales led the way to gradual expansion of Canada-China trade. For instance, one of the most important trading developments for Canada during the early 1960s was the initiation of large-scale credit sales of wheat to China. In May 1961, the Wheat Board concluded with the PRC the largest grain deal in Canada's history, and the government set up a $50 million fund to underwrite the credit arrangements. Prior to this, transactions were on cash-basis. Throughout the 1960s, Canada was happy to sell surplus wheat to China, and it continued with generous credit arrangements. China became the second largest customer of Canadian wheat next to the UK, significantly contributing to the disposal of a huge surplus.

There were some objections in Canada to the grain deal with China on political or moral grounds. However, the prevailing arguments were that Ottawa's interest in engaging with the PRC was more than just opportunities for trade. According to this view, opening up the PRC had a far more significant implication: it was essential to sound and stable international relations. In the earlier years of Canada-PRC trade, Diefenbaker once stated, "There should be trade with Communist countries. There is no other way in which you can break down the walls of separation and suspicion."

The Canadian public strongly supported this position, and seventy percent of Canadians favored trade of non-strategic goods with China (Lyon 1968, 412). This policy of constructive engagement has largely been maintained by Ottawa, and may be considered as one of the policy principles in dealing with regimes of similar character. It also suited well with Canada's economic interests. There was an argument that the overriding consideration in wheat sales to China was the persistence of large surpluses of wheat in Canada. The sales were particularly popular in the Western provinces, which explained their stubborn loyalty to Diefenbaker's Progressive Conservative government. According to Lyon (1968, 420-23), the 1961 agreement was an outstanding commercial and political success. From then on, China proved to be a good market for Canada, especially for agricultural goods.

As we observed, there was an economic element in Canada's engagement policy towards China. Commercial engagement was maintained, regardless of diplomatic complications, political differences or questions of morality. Even during the Ottawa-Beijing negotiations on diplomatic recognition, the Wheat Board was conducting its independent negotiations with China to sell more wheat (Frolic 1991, 210). And, despite the nagging issue of human rights abuses in China in the ensuing decades, Canada had a tendency to downplay the issue. With an explosive increase in bilateral trade in the 1980s, both Liberal and Conservative governments regarded China as an opportunity, and showed reluctance to openly condemn Beijing's human rights abuses or act on its rhetoric. This policy was put to a serious test by the Tiananmen Square incident in 1989.

The Tiananmen incident somewhat changed the Canadian perception of China. Canada was forced to reconsider some of the major assumptions and beliefs upon which its China policy was based. In the end, however, the substance of Canadian policy did not change in any fundamental way. If anything, it gave Canada an opportunity to confirm its existing policy more clearly.

After the initial outrage, consensus emerged among Ottawa policymakers that isolating China was not the best policy. The arguments were similar to those made during the negotiations for diplomatic recognition. Condemning China was one thing; but it was too important politically and too vast in size to try to isolate.

The wisdom of constructive engagement again prevailed. Canada initially imposed limited sanctions against China, but they were soon watered down. The Conservative Party's Agricultural Minister Bill McKnight and Trade Minister Michael Wilson led separate trade missions to China in 1992. Subsequent visits by high level officials paid only lip service to human rights. China's explosive economic growth offered too tempting a market for Canada which was suffering a serious recession (Paltiel 1995, 16).

For the Liberal government, which returned to power in 1993, China became even more important in its foreign policy. When the Tiananmen incident occurred, the then opposition Liberal Party demanded that Prime Minister Mulroney impose sanctions against China. In early 1994, Chrètien stated in a public speech that Canada had never linked trade absolutely with human rights, signaling his government's intention to aggressively pursue increased trade with China. Other high-level officials made statements to that effect (Paltiel, 1995, 171, 173-74).

Concerning Chrètien's China policy, domestic opposition was minimal. Provincial governments were eager to jump on the Asia-Pacific bandwagon. Their interest were economic recovery and the opportunities in the growing Chinese market. In November 1994, the Liberal Prime Minister Jean Chrètien led to China the largest trade mission in Canada's history, including all provincial premiers and nearly 400 business representatives. Thereafter, it was back to business as usual.

The rationale behind Canadian policy toward China concerning trade and human rights is as follows. Human rights are important, but Canada has very little leverage to influence China on this matter. Condemning China will only undermine Canada's economic interest, while having little or no effect on the human rights situation there. Thus, it is only practical to continue with trade. Whatever the political complications, economic engagement seems to be a constant in Canadian policy towards China.

III. Engaging with Cuba
1. Revolution and the Aftermath

Canada's relationship with Cuba has deep historical roots, going back to the seventeenth century, and trade has been the underlying basis of Canada's interest in Cuba. Politics hardly affected this relationship, although their bilateral trade was not of vital importance to either side. From the late nineteenth century to early twentieth century, trade grew rapidly and Canadian investment thrived in Cuba. As early as 1910, a trade commissioner was posted in Cuba with the primary objective of developing trade. Canadian banks dominated Cuba's financial sector. The Royal Bank for instance had 65 branches in that country (Kirk and McKenna 1997, 3-9).

The trend did not change much in the postwar years. The External Affairs Department in 1949 defined Canada's ties with Cuba as "primarily commercial," and the main duties of the Canadian mission there included broadening Canadian trade opportunities.[3] Bilateral trade somewhat increased thanks to the postwar economic boom. By 1950, Cuba was Canada's second-best market in Latin America next to Brazil. In 1955, Canada and Cuba established full diplomatic relations. Through the 1950s, however, Canadian trade with Cuba slowly declined relative to the establishment of American dominance. For Canada, the Cuban market became of minor importance, although it had potential. The value of Canadian exports to Cuba represented only a fraction of its total. For Cuba, the relationship with the US became much more intense and important, politically and economically. In time, Canadian interests in Cuba were steadily edged out by those of the US (Kirk and MaKenna 1997, 8, 19-22).

---

[3] A letter to Ambassador E.H. Coleman from the Department of External Affairs, 11 March 1969. In Kirk and McKenna (1997, 8).

The Canada-Cuba relationship became more noteworthy after the Cuban revolution of 1959. Castro's hostile policy toward the US led it to break diplomatic ties in January 1961, and following the Bay of Pigs incident, the US imposed a full economic embargo against Havana in 1962. Cuba's support for insurgent movements throughout the region caused further tightening of the US embargo.

On the contrary, Canada was the only country in the Western Hemisphere to maintain full diplomatic relations with Cuba following the revolution. The then Prime Minister John Diefenbaker made it clear that Canada had no intention to impose an embargo on Cuba, and several reasons could explain this.

Canada had a radically different approach to the Castro regime. Canada was not a superpower with a face to save, did not have a powerful Cuban exile population that fled the revolution, and did not feel threatened by Castro. Castro was not hostile to Canada, and Canadian interests in Cuba, unlike those of the US, were not seized. Castro needed Canada in place of the US to keep access to international markets (Kirk 1995, 9-10). In addition, it is said that Canadians had different opinions concerning the nature of the Castro regime and the means to contain its aggressive tendencies, and Ottawa believed that an American embargo would drive Castro closer to the Soviet Union (Gotlieb 1994, 79; Preston 1965, 180).

Therefore, despite significant political difficulties, Diefenbaker's policy was consistent even during the Cuban Missile Crisis. In explaining this consistency, there was another factor that was of great importance to Canada. Diefenbaker's Cuba policy to a large extent reflected the desire to maintain independence from Washington and his enmity with Kennedy (Nossal 1994, 21). Kennedy's ignorance and insensitivity about Canada infuriated Diefenbaker. His Cuba policy survived domestic difficulties and heavy criticism from the US.

Prime Minister Pearson was on better terms with Kennedy and was more sympathetic to the US position, but did not alter the existing Canadian stance concerning Cuba. During his term of office, there were neither major diplomatic breakthroughs nor serious setbacks (Kirk and McKenna 1997, 72-73). He was not particularly friendly with Castro, but there remained fundamental disagreements concerning Cuba between Ottawa and Washington. His government maintained the view that the hard-line US policy was driving Cuba into the Soviet sphere, and that keeping normal diplomatic and commercial relations with Cuba might be a better approach than trying to isolate it. This policy also suited Ottawa's political and economic agenda. Canada's nationalistic sentiment prevented Pearson from moving too close to the US on such symbolic issues as Cuba. The appearance of an independent Canadian foreign policy was as important to Pearson as it was to his predecessor.

Economically, trade with Canada was important for Cuba. Although Canada was not particularly warm to the Castro regime, business went on as usual. Under the surface of diplomatic coolness, Canadian exports to Cuba dramatically increased.

2. Turning of the Tides

The Trudeau era was the most significant period in the development of Canada-Cuba relations. Trudeau sought to diversify Canada's external relations to Latin America and Asia, and the bilateral ties expanded in this context. Trade was at the top of his agenda, and he showed no ideological inhibition in promoting trade with Cuba. Trudeau declared: "Short of being at the state of war with another nation, we do not believe that curtailment of trade is in any sense conducive to a lessening of tensions between countries... We trade with Communist China. We trade with Cuba."[4]

Canada-Cuba trade expanded over tenfold during the 1970s. Toronto-Havana direct flights were inaugurated, and Cuba became the first foreign country permitted to fish in Canadian waters (Kirk 1995, 11). Canadian development aid was granted to Cuba for the first time, and there were many high level visits by both sides, which culminated in Trudeau's visit to Cuba in 1976. He became the first NATO leader to visit Havana. The visit was heavily criticized in Canada, and Washington also vehemently objected (Kirk and McKenna 1997, 111). Canada-Cuba relations were not without difficulties, however. Havana's human rights record was a source of tension, as Ottawa consistently expressed concern over the issue. There were disagreements between Ottawa and Havana on the latter's role in Angola. Eventually, bilateral relations suffered. In 1978, the Canadian International Development Agency's (CIDA) aid program was terminated due to intense opposition pressure. Going into the 1980s, trade started to decrease.

The tone of Canada's policy toward Cuba notably shifted when Brian Mulroney took office. Contrary to Trudeau, who tried to counterbalance Canada-US relations with its ties with other regions, Mulroney tried to integrate Canada into the US economic and political sphere as much as possible. Mulroney's top priority was the US, and he avoided anything that might offend Washington. The 'pro-American' prime minister supported the US position on Cuba, and was more critical than his predecessor about Havana's domestic and foreign policy. Canada's export credits, development aid, and humanitarian assistance for Cuba were all kept minimal. Cuban human rights records were cited as the main reason why Canada was cooling its diplomatic ties. From its peak in 1981, Canada's trade with Cuba declined and stagnated through the 1980s.

---

[4] Trudeau's remark quoted in the CIIA Monthly Report on Canadian External Relations. Vol. 8, no. 3, 84. Cited in Kirk and McKenna (1997, 98).

There was a symbolic event that characterized Ottawa's Cuba policy during the Mulroney years. When Cuba was hit by a devastating hurricane in 1993, Havana appealed to the international community for humanitarian aid, the first time since the revolution. While many countries in Latin America, Europe and Asia responded, the Canadian government initially gave no help to Cuba. It took intense pressure from NGOs and church groups for CIDA to eventually approve grants for medical supplies (Kirk 1995, 14; Kirk and McKenna 1997, 123, 144).

Subsequently, there were pressures for a policy change. Although the Canadian government did little to promote trade with Cuba, businesses recognized opportunities, particularly after the collapse of the Soviet bloc. By the end of Mulroney's tenure, Canada was Cuba's major trading partner and source of investment. Canadian firms established in Cuba the second-largest number of joint ventures after Spain, and Canada provided the largest number of tourists (Kirk and McKenna 1997, 136-138). Non-governmental sector groups, while aggressively involved in various aid programs, continued to lobby the government to change its Cuba policy. Canadian policy was ready for another shift.

The 1990s saw renewed interest in Cuba among Canadians. Many perceived tremendous business potential in sectors such as mining, agriculture and tourism in Cuba, and there was a steady increase in NGO and academic contacts between the two countries. The Cold War was long gone, and, since 1993, the Cuban economy showed signs of opening up to foreign investment. There came the realization that Canada should expand and consolidate its position in Cuba in case of the eventual lifting of the US embargo.

These factors provided the good foundation upon which the new Liberal government could build on. The Chrètien government made 'the promotion of prosperity and employment'[5] for Canadians one of the three key objectives of its foreign policy, and expanding trade was one of the most important means to achieve that objective. As his mentor Trudeau did, Chrètien considered Asia and Latin America as important counterweights to the US. The creation of two secretaries of state--for Asia-Pacific and for Latin America and Africa--reflected this policy of diversification. Canada-Cuba relations were revitalized in this context.

There have been some notable developments in bilateral relations since Chrètien's inauguration. For instance, the government announced in 1994 the resumption of ODA to Cuba. One of the reasons that Cuba has remained fairly high on the political agenda in the Chrètien government has been

---

[5] The Government of Canada. *Canada in the World: Government Statement.* 1995, p. 10.

NGOs' lobbying for ODA and their efforts to establish long-term projects in Cuba. CIDA resumed humanitarian aid to Cuba in 1993, for the first time since Cuba's involvement in Angola, as a result of persistent lobbying by non-governmental sector groups such as churches, universities, Canadian Foodgrains Bank, and the Canadian Labour Congress. In 1994, responding to the NGO lobby, the government removed Cuba from the list of countries ineligible for bilateral development assistance (Kirk and McKenna 1997, 155-56).

The most significant event in the official bilateral relations was Foreign Minister Lloyd Axworthy's visit to Havana in January 1997. The Axworthy visit, although it paid lip-service to human rights, was designed to shore up Canadian business connections and to consolidate political ties. A third of the Canadian premiers, mainly with business opportunities in mind, visited Cuba in the mid-1990s.

Diplomatically, the present government clearly maintains its traditional policy of constructive engagement with Cuba: sanctions are impractical and ineffective to achieve political objectives; the most effective way of promoting democracy and human rights is through trade and economic development, not through isolation. In reality, this means that trade takes precedence over human rights. Economic interest has been the driving force in the bilateral relationship in the current government (Kirk and McKenna 1997, 162, 173-74).

As was always the case in the past, the Chrètien government's Cuba policy is also influenced by its consideration of the US factor. Chrètien's pragmatic approach and active engagement with Cuba is to some extent a reflection of his desire to differentiate himself from Mulroney, who was perceived as extremely pro-American. His policy is also a reaction to unreasonable US policies manifested in the Torcelli Law or the Helms-Burton Act. Concerning Cuba, the appearance of independence vis-à-vis the US has become important for Chrètien as his predecessors. Thus, Chrètien's Cuba policy serves well the diplomatic, political and economic agenda of his government.

3. Canada's Trade with Cuba and the US Factor

Canada-Cuba relations since the revolution cannot be fully understood without considering the US factor, as they have been influenced directly by the hostility between Cuba and the US. This has been conspicuous in the area of trade. The US broke diplomatic ties with Cuba after the revolution and started imposing economic sanctions leading to a full embargo in 1962.

Canada's approach to Cuba was markedly different from that of the US. Rather than isolating Cuba, Ottawa considered engaging with the Castro regime more desirable, and Canada and Cuba kept their bilateral economic relations. Canada's trade with Cuba was somewhat restricted by the US embargo which prevented resale of American goods to Cuba through Canada, but other than that, as Mitchell Sharp stated in July 1963, the Canadian government placed no restrictions on trading non-military and non-strategic goods with Cuba (Girard 1980, 135).

Canada's trade with Cuba increased substantially after the revolution. Canadian exports to Cuba doubled from $15 million in 1959 to $30 million in 1961, and after a couple of years slump, the figure jumped to over $60 million in 1964. There was another sharp increase in Canadian exports to Cuba in the mid 1970s. Canadian imports from Cuba also dramatically increased in the 1970s, from around $10 million in 1970 to over $70 million in 1974. Bilateral trade increased over tenfold in the 1970s from $60 million to $600 million into the early the 1980s. Although Canadian trade with Cuba did not grow in the 1980s as was expected, Canada enjoyed a trade surplus vis-à-vis Cuba until the end of the 1980s. In 1991, Canada was Cuba's largest export market and fourth largest source of imports. In the same year, 130,000 Canadian tourists visited Cuba and spent $85 million. This steady flow of trade and investment between Canada and Cuba drew heavy criticism from the US.

The demise of the Soviet Union and the communist bloc in 1991 dealt a crippling blow to the Cuban economy. Hardship was inevitable given Cuba's extremely high economic dependence on Soviet aid and trade with the former Eastern bloc countries. Credits and subsidies from the Soviet Union to Cuba totaled some $38 billion between 1961 and 1984, and were up to $5 billion annually in the late 1980s. In 1989, over 81% of Cuban exports went to the Soviet bloc and over 85% of imports came from it. With the collapse of the Soviet Union, Cuba's trade with the Soviet bloc dropped to 7% of its previous level (Gotlieb 1994, 81). The Cuban economy shrank nearly in half within the following few years and became no longer sustainable.

In response to the economic crisis, the Castro government in 1993 took measures to fully liberalize possession of hard currency and to allow some free enterprise, and turned more actively to foreign direct investment to resuscitate the dying economy. It also made efforts to diversify its trade. Canadians saw the signs of opening, although limited, in the Cuban economy, and seemed to be fairly positive about the economic changes since 1993 (Kirk 1995). They saw opportunities to further expand their commercial ties with Cuba as in the following observation: "Cuba now beckons, with the Castro regime's desire for more open commercial relations with countries like Canada, a desire fueled by a desperate need for foreign currency, not democratic ideals" (Gotlieb 1994, 77). Although by 1994 Canadian exports to

Cuba decreased to one-third of the figures in the mid-1980s, Cuban exports to Canada substantially increased, thereby maintaining the previous level of two-way trade at around $300 million. This meant that Canada had recorded a trade deficit since 1991, the first time in over 30 years. Whatever havoc Cuba was experiencing, Canada was its third largest trading partner in 1994. Canadian companies wanted to keep their advantage as a major trade and investment partner for Cuba in case of the eventual lifting of the American embargo.

Americans seemed to be impressed more with Cuba's economic decline in the early 1990s. They tended to discount business opportunities in Cuba and saw its prospects bleak.[6] For them, the Castro regime was a revolution failed (Jorge and Cruz 1994, 17), and they did not show much willingness to alter the existing policy. If anything, Americans showed their determination to continue the policy of isolating Cuba, and the Cold War mentality seemed to remain strong among opinion leaders. Some argued that businesses should "realize their ethical and moral obligations and abstain from lending success to a regime that will be harshly judged by history..."(Suchlicki and Jorge 1994, ix). Some others likened Castro to Kim Il Sung, Hussein, Mao and Stalin and urged that the US should not reward the totalitarian regime by normalizing relations with Cuba (Horowitz 1994, 9-10).

Washington's policy seemed to reflect these sentiments. In October 1992, the US Congress passed "The Cuban Democracy Act," known as the Torricelli Law. It restricted US subsidiaries in a third country from having any business transactions with Cuba. In 1995, the US Congress legislated "The Cuban Liberty and Democratic Solidarity Act of 1995", sponsored by the Senate Foreign Relations Committee chair Jesse Helms. The so-called Helms-Burton Act again threatened punishment for Canadian subsidiaries of US firms doing business with Cuba. In this way, Canada's trade relations with Cuba came into the sphere of US extraterritorial sanctions. Ottawa responded to the Torricelli Law by passing in October 1992 an order under "The Foreign Extraterritorial Measures Act." It forbade any firm domiciled in Canada from complying with the US law (Gotlieb 1994, 85). Canadian response to Helms-Burton Act was similar. Clearly disagreeing with Washington, Ottawa strongly protested the extraterritoriality of the legislation.

Americans seem to perceive that Canada is profiteering with the Cuba trade while they are completely shut off from such opportunities. On the other hand, Canadians regard US policy as impractical, unworkable and hypocritical. For them, constructive engagement is the best possible option.

---

[6] See articles in Suchlicki and Jorge 1994.

This has been a source of strain between Ottawa and Washington. The US has often made attempts to impose on Canada its view of how to deal with the Castro regime, and Canadians feel its sovereignty challenged. Therefore, maintaining an independent Cuba policy vis-à-vis the US was a major consideration for Canada. Besides the lofty objective of promoting human rights and democracy in Cuba, the engagement policy has served well for successive Canadian governments, from Diefenbaker to Chrètien, both politically and economically.

IV. Implications for Canada-North Korea Relations
1. A History of Non-engagement

Canada's relationship with Korea started with missionary ties at the turn of the century. Canadian churches sent its first missionaries to Korea about a hundred years ago, primarily to the northern part. They contributed significantly to the welfare of Koreans who were suffering from the harsh Japanese colonial rule (Yoo 1987). After the division of Korea, isolation became the most prominent feature of North Korea's external relations. Since then, Canada had no access to North Korea and, for various reasons, refrained from actively making contacts with North Koreans, not to mention establishing diplomatic ties.

Canada's official involvement in Korea was concentrated in the postwar years through its role in the UN, while there were few bilateral relations between the two. Canada was represented in the Interim Committee and the UN Temporary Commission for Korea (UNTCK) in the late 1940s. When asked by the UNTCK, the committee made an important decision concerning the Korean peninsula. It decided in favor of the American proposal that UNTCK implement its program of popular election in such parts of Korea as were accessible to the Commission. Canada and Australia were the only two countries opposed to the idea, thinking that it would further complicate the situation in Korea. After the UN-sponsored election only in the southern part of Korea, Seoul was recognized by the West as the only legitimate government of Korea. Canada witnessed the formal inauguration of separate regimes in North and South Korea, which made permanent the partition of Korea. Canadians were prudent and cautious during the process, but could not influence the outcome on the Korean Peninsula.

The most intense Canadian involvement in Korean affairs happened during the Korean War, as Canadian troops joined the UN forces to fight against North Korea and China. Canada became part of the UN command, and later became involved in the Panmunjom and the Geneva Conferences to settle the

Korean issue. Canada withdrew two-thirds of its 6,000 troops by the end of 1954 and by mid-the 1950s, only a small number of Canadian troops remained in Korea. Canadian participation in Korea came to a virtual conclusion, and Korea was nearly forgotten by Canadians until the 1970s, when South Korea emerged in the international community as a rising economic star.

For half a century, 'no diplomatic relations' has perhaps been the only constant in Canadian policy towards Pyongyang, according to a Canadian foreign service official,[7] though there were some exceptions to this trend. For instance, the Canadian foreign policy community in the early 1990s made an attempt to involve Pyongyang in a track-two multilateral forum called the North Pacific Cooperative Security Dialogue (NPCSD) (Dewitt and Evans 1993). The North Korean delegation attended six of the seven meetings held under the auspices of NPCSD, and some high level North Korean officials were present at the initial meeting. They presented five papers and engaged in some of the discussions,[8] but the forum did not produce much in terms of changes in the state of Canada's relations with North Korea. The Council of Security Cooperation in the Asia Pacific (CSCAP) is another track-two regional multilateral security forum in which Canada and North Korea both participated. Canada and Japan co-chair CSCAP's North Pacific Working Group, where issues concerning the Korean Peninsula, among other things, are discussed. But CSCAP has made little impact on Ottawa-Pyongyang bilateral relations.

Commercially, Canada and the DPRK have had very little interaction. The Canadian government does not impose any formal trade embargo on North Korea, though there are some restrictions on military strategic items and dual-use products which are listed in Canada's Export Control List. Exporting these products requires a government permit. Canada is a signatory of the "Wassenaar Arrangement" which, established in 1996 in place of COCOM, controls 33 member states' export of military and dual-use products and technology to dangerous and unstable countries. The American "Trading with the Enemy Act" prohibits American companies from exporting to North Korea, and this puts restrictions on US-made products exported to North Korea through Canada.

---

[7] Interview with John Mundy, Director, Korea and Oceania Division, Department of Foreign Affairs and International Trade. 15 July 1998.

[8] Online interview with Paul Evans. 28 February 2000.

Canadian trade with North Korea has been negligible and there seems to be no long-term trend. Between 1967 (the year from which North Korean trade figures became available) and 1998, the total amount of bilateral trade fluctuated year to year from several hundred to around $60 million with the annual average approximately $7 million. Total Canadian exports to North Korea were zero in 1968 and 1970. Sale of cereals such as wheat occasionally pushed up the trade figures, but they were practically nothing in proportion to Canada's total trade. In 1998, Canadian exports to North Korea totaled around $1.9 million while the amount of imports was even smaller at around half a million dollars. Canadian exports to North Korea mainly consist of food and wood products. Canada exports some manufactures to North Korea, but the amount is negligible.

Table: Canadian Bulk Wheat (including durum) Exports to North Korea

Fiscal Year	Quantity (ton)
1987-88	28,000
1988-89	0
1989-90	0
1990-91	367,000
1991-92	296,000
1992-93	293,000
1993-94	0
1994-95	0
1995-96	0
1996-97	14,000
10-yr average	100,000

Source: The Canadian Wheat Board. The 1996-97 Annual Report.

As shown above, Canada and North Korea had virtually no political or commercial interaction in the postwar years. In quite a different setting, however, Canadian churches seem to have retained some sense of history and interest in North Korea. They renewed, albeit in a very limited way, contacts with North Korean church organizations in the early 1980s through venues such as the World Council of Churches.[9] This became an important connection that later helped Canadian church groups to quickly respond to North Korean appeals for food aid in recent famine years.

---

[9] Phone interview with Nan Hudson, The United Church of Canada. 13 August 1998.

2. Humanitarian Aid

Recently there has been some life in Canada-North Korea relations in areas involving humanitarian concerns. Failed socialist economic planning and massive floods in the summer of 1995 devastated the North Korean agricultural sector, and the ensuing food crisis prompted its government to make an unprecedented appeal for international assistance. In Canada, it was church groups that first heard this appeal partly because the appeal was first made by North Korea's Christian Federation at an international church group conference in January 1996.[10] At that time, the Winnipeg-based Canadian Foodgrains Bank (CFB) [11] was among the first to act. Encouraged by the farm and church communities, the CFB dispatched its program coordinator to North Korea for a fact-finding mission in May 1996, who subsequently reported pre-famine conditions there. By August 1996, six of the thirteen church partners of CFB raised $1.8 million to be used for a purchase of 4,350 tons of rice for North Korean flood victims.[12]

The CFB also requested CIDA to approve the use of CIDA matching funds[13] for aid to North Korea. However, the Canadian government refused as North Korea was on the list of countries ineligible for official aid. Ottawa felt it did not have enough information and was concerned about monitoring the distribution of food provided by aid agencies. Undeterred, another CFB delegation followed the shipment of the rice at the end of August to assess the situation in North Korea, and NGO groups kept lobbying the government with information obtained from the field.[14] For instance, returning in early September from his trip to North Korea, CFB program coordinator Al Kehler reported, "the current food shortage in North Korea is actually worse than the famine that hit Ethiopia in 1983/84." [15]

Eventually information obtained through UN agencies on flood damage estimates, human casualties and food requirements had some affect on the Canadian government's position. On 8 April, 1997, Don Boudria, Minister for

---

[10] Nan Hudson of the United Church of Canada was present at the conference. Interview with Nan Hudson.

[11] CFB is comprised of 13 church partners. It collects grain and cash donations from farmers, churches, the federal government and the public, and serves as a centralized grain banking and distribution system for international aid.

[12] CFB New Release. "Food Aid for North Korea Continues Despite Silence of Canadian Government." 21 August 1996.

[13] Under a contract with CIDA, food and cash donations raised by CFB are matched at a ratio of 4 to 1 by the Agency.

[14] Interview with Richard Fee, Director, Presbyterian World Services and Development. 11 August 1998.

[15] CFB News Release. "Politics Aside, Need for Food in North Korea Very Real." 10 September 1996.

International Cooperation, finally announced that CIDA would allow CFB to use up to $3.6 million of its allocations from CIDA for food aid to North Korea.[16] It was the first time that CIDA authorized the use of its funds for aid to North Korea, and this was followed by a CFB announcement the next day that it would commit $4.5 million, which included $2.5 million in CIDA funds, for aid to North Korea.[17] By the end of May 1997, the CFB shipped 13,500 tons of Canadian wheat worth $4.5 million to North Korea. It was the largest commitment of food aid by the CFB up to that time.[18]

In early June 1997, Boudria announced that Canada was sending additional shipments of food aid to North Korea. CIDA was to provide Canadian foodstuffs worth $2 million under the WFP, which was coordinating distribution of food to North Korean flood victims.[19] In August 1997, Diane Marleau, the new minister for International Cooperation announced that the Canadian government would provide $4.5 million in additional food aid to North Korea: $2.5 million through WFP and $2 million through CFB.[20] In October 1997, CIDA's Director of International Humanitarian Assistance Program visited North Korea as part of a World Food Program mission assessing the food crisis in that country.[21] Subsequently, Marleau in March 1998, announced that CIDA would provide additional food and humanitarian aid worth $4 million.[22] Responding to an appeal launched by the WFP, Marleau again announced in July 1998, that CIDA would provide $5 million worth of canned food to North Korea.[23]

By the end of 1998, CIDA contributed a total of $20 million for aid to North Korea, while the CFB provided over 44,000 tons of food aid worth $14.4 million.[24] Since the North Korean appeal for international assistance, aid to North Korea became the CFB's largest program, which is the largest

---

[16] CIDA News Release (97-46). "Canada to Provide Food Aid to North Koreans." 8 April 1997.

[17] CFB News Release. "Foodgrains Bank Comes Through with Commitments to North Korea." 9 April 1997.

[18] FB News Release. "Canadian Food Aids Sails for North Korea." 2 June 1997.

[19] CIDA News Release (97-65). "Canada Provides Food Aid to North Koreans." 5 June 1997.

[20] CIDA News Release (97-71). "Marleau Announces New Canadian Aid to North Korea." 10 August 1997.

[21] CIDA News Release (CIDA Update 23-3). "A CIDA official visits North Korea."

[22] CIDA News Release (98-17) "Diane Marleau Announces Additional Aid to Victims of North Korea's Food Crises." 23 March 1998.

[23] CIDA News Release. "Diane Marleau Announces Additional Aid to Victims of North Korea's Food Crises." 16 July 1998.

[24] CIDA News Release. "Diane Marleau Announces Additional Aid to Victims of North Korea's Food Crisis." 16 July 1998; CFB News Release. "Four Canadians to assess food need in North Korea." 9 October, 1998.

food aid donor in the world.[25] In the fiscal year 1998/99 alone, Canadian humanitarian aid to North Korea including grain, canned-food, and basic medical supplies totaled approximately $14.5 million, among which CIDA contributed $12.75 million (JETRO 1999). For the fiscal year 1999/2000, CIDA was to provide up to $15 million in humanitarian aid to North Korea.

As described above, enthusiastic responses by churches and NGOs to the North Korean appeal for assistance had some consequences for the state of Canada-North Korea relations. They were followed by provisions of government fund for aid and a CIDA official's visit to North Korea. Subsequently, there were some spill over effects on the bilateral relations into the political and deplomatic arena.

Some of the more noteworthy developments were the opening in mid-1998 of the Canadian interest desk in the Swedish Embassy in Pyongyang and the start of regular counsellor-level talks in Beijing since 1998. In the past, official contacts between Ottawa and Pyongyang were handled by the Canadian Embassy in Beijing. However, due to increased travel by Canadian aid personnel to North Korea, the Canadian government needed to provide consular services in the field. The counsellor-level talks were the first official bilateral diplomatic contact between the two countries since the end of the Korean War. However, Ottawa considered these contacts with North Koreans as "a modest development and its impact very limited." According to DFAIT's official position, these developments did not mean that Canada was upgrading its relations with Pyongyang. The agenda of the talks was mainly concerned with consular interests, and if anything, Ottawa saw it as a venue to reconfirm the traditional position: Pyongyang should improve its relations with Seoul before things move on any further.[26]

The Canadian government's recent policy on North Korea so far described was largely reactive, responding to pressures from the WFP, the Red Cross, the CFB, church groups and other NGOs, and preferring the status quo, rather than taking any initiative. North Korea mainly represented a humanitarian agenda for Ottawa. All in all, the basics of Canada's traditional policy seemed unaffected: "Canadian interest in North Korea is part of Canadian interest in South Korea and the region." [27] And the result of DFAIT's departmental review of North Korea policy in 1998 seemed to have stayed within the framework of that traditional policy.

---

[25] Interview with Richard Fee.

[26] Interview with Margaret Huber, Director General, North Asia and Pacific Bureau, DFAIT. 15 July 1998.

[27] Interview with John Mundy.

3. Canada's Non-engagement with North Korea: Possible Explanations

Canada's policy toward Mao's China and Castro's Cuba could be characterized as that of constructive engagement. The justification for establishing and maintaining relations with such aggressive, oppressive or morally suspect regimes was that we could hope to promote values such as democracy, human rights and stability in those regimes not by isolating them but only through engagement. Why, then, has Canada's policy towards the DPRK been that of consistent non-engagement? As was suggested in the introductory section, there could be a number of possible explanations. We now examine them based on our review of the Chinese and Cuban cases.

The Korean War may have been the deciding factor that determined the tone of Canada's policy in the ensuing decades. Canada and the DPRK had fought against each other during the Korean War and never signed a peace treaty at the end of the war. Is the fact that Canadian soldiers died fighting North Korean invaders in a war enough reason for total lack of diplomatic contact between the two countries? The answer would be in the negative, if we look at the Chinese case.

China was also involved in the Korean War on the side of North Korea, which was identified by the UN as aggressor. Canada, as a part of UN forces, fought against the Chinese army. The war was a setback for the Ottawa policymakers who championed the cause of recognizing the PRC, but did not change Ottawa's long-term policy of recognizing the PRC. In fact it is quite normal that two belligerent states reestablish diplomatic relations once the hostilities are over. So the North Korean exception cannot be explained by the Korean War factor.

North Korea is perhaps one of the most isolated and xenophobic communist regimes in history with intense hostility and suspicion towards the West. Its ideological fanaticism and oppression of its own population was unusual even among the former Eastern bloc countries. Its erratic behaviour was well demonstrated in numerous incidents involving violence and terrorism. North Korea was active in helping communist revolutions in many African countries, by providing them with military advisors and other resources. It is considered one of the worst human rights abusers in the world. However, both China and Cuba displayed similar characteristics in the earlier period of their revolutions.

China showed its aggressive external posture in the offshore shelling incident, in 1958, and border conflicts with Russia and India. It was involved in the Vietnam War. The Cultural Revolution, the culmination of Mao's revolutionary fervor, drove much of the Chinese population into mass hysteria and brutal suppression. Cuba in a similar way, tried to export revolution to other Latin American countries, and its involvement in the

Angolan civil war was a major political sore in its relations with Western countries. Both China and Cuba have very poor human rights records. But these phenomena did not prevent Ottawa from recognizing them and Ottawa did not change its consistent nature of engagement towards the two regimes.

It may be that Ottawa's non-recognition and non-engagement with North Korea has been the result of Seoul's efforts. Ever since the division of Korea, the two Koreas waged an intense diplomatic warfare with each other over the title of the sole legitimate government on the Korean Peninsula, and Seoul was extremely sensitive about other countries recognizing or establishing relations with Pyongyang. Seoul's diplomacy concerning North Korea was to gain the upper hand over Pyongyang in the international arena by isolating the latter as much as possible. South Korea devoted much of its resources and energy to dissuade others from pursuing relations with Pyongyang.

Canada was also a target of this intense diplomatic effort, and Seoul seems to have been quite successful over the years. An informed Canadian academic observes that foreign service officials in Ottawa tend to see North Korea through Seoul's prism, and that this is particularly true with the staff in the Korea division and those who have served in Seoul. According to this view, Canadian officials' perception of North Korea is shaped to a large extent by their significant exposure to Seoul's viewpoint and their personal relations with their South Korean counterparts.

When we consider Canada' policy towards the PRC and Cuba, however, opposition from Seoul does not seem to fully explain Canada's North Korea policy. Since even Washington could not prevent Canadians from engaging with Cuba and the PRC, could Seoul have kept Ottawa from engaging with North Korea? Canada's heavy dependence on the US has often been believed to be the main determinant of its foreign policy. It has been suggested by some that the twenty-year delay in Canadian recognition of the PRC was the result of US opposition. It is not clear whether, or to what extent, the US actually put pressure on Canada about China. But as we have observed, although Canada was sensitive to the US position, Ottawa held a remarkably consistent view of China and was unswerving in its policy of diplomatic recognition. The delay was mainly due to a series of events that made the timing of recognition awkward.

Canada's consistent engagement policy in defiance of US pressure becomes more apparent in the Cuban case. After the Castro revolution, Washington made attempts to impose its position on Canada concerning Cuba. It was strongly critical and directly expressed its displeasure to Ottawa when Canada did not follow the US policy so much so that Canadian policy towards Cuba has been to a large extent a reflection of its determination to maintain an independent foreign policy. This has been one of the most important foreign policy issues for Canadians throughout the postwar years. Even strongly anti-communist Diefenbaker maintained close ties with the Castro regime, defying the US embargo in 1960 and subsequent pressures from the Kennedy Administration. On many occasions, the Canadian government made clear its disagreement with the US on Cuba.

All in all, the American position did not have a critical impact on Canada's relations with China and Cuba. If the US factor had any impact at all on Canadian policy, it did not work in a way which compelled Ottawa to conform to the US policy line. It worked to the contrary. Keeping some distance from US policy was politically important for Canadian leaders who did not want to appear subservient to Washington, and to appeal to Canadian nationalism. Therefore, it is hard to believe that Seoul imposed its policy of isolating North Korea on Ottawa against its will.

South Korea is not a "bullying superpower" and dealing with Seoul did not provoke a strong sense of nationalism among Canadians. In any event, if Canada had had an important policy agenda of its own in the Korean Peninsula, it is doubtful that South Korean pressure would have been so effective. Ottawa went along with Seoul's diplomatic offensive because it suited the Canadian interest.

Despite the above-mentioned obstacles and numerous other snags, Ottawa exerted persistent efforts to overcome them, and established and expanded relations with China and Cuba. On the contrary, Ottawa and Pyongyang never made any attempt to normalize their relations. One of the factors that made a difference in Canadian policy towards China and Cuba was the personality of the prime ministers. Trudeau was a driving force behind Ottawa's recognition of the PRC. Concerning Cuba, there have been discernable policy swings depending on the policy agendas of the prime ministers. North Korea policy was hardly affected by personalities.

What, then, is the factor that could explain Canada's consistent engagement policy with China and Cuba on the one hand, and its consistent non-engagement with North Korea? Why the North Korean exception? What is lacking, or present, in the case of North Korea? Is there any principle or motive that can consistently explain Canada's policy towards the three regimes in question? Economic incentive is the probable answer.

Canada had a clear economic interest in China and Cuba. China, with its vast size and population, represented an enormous potential market, and from the early postwar years, Canada had a significant interest in the Chinese market. Their bilateral relations started, before anything else, with trade. Canada's exports to China took off from the late 1950s with the sale of Canadian wheat, and from then on, bilateral trade shot up, and the Cultural Revolution did not seriously affect them. Even the Tienanmen incident did not fundamentally alter the relationship.

We have observed that Canada's relationship with Cuba has been anchored primarily on trade and investment. Although trade with Cuba has not been vital to Canada, Canadians have nonetheless been quite interested in commercial opportunities in certain sectors, and successive Canadian governments identified Cuba as an important market. For Cuba, Canada was always important economically in the postwar years. The Cuban Missile Crisis did not affect the rapidly growing Canada-Cuba trade and, since the imposition of the US trade embargo, Canada became one of the most important trade and investment partners for Cuba.

The main difference between the above two regimes and North Korea is that the latter offers virtually no commercial opportunity for Canada, or any other country for that matter. Canada's lack of economic interest in North Korea seems to have been the factor that had made Seoul's attempt to keep it from approaching North Korea so effective. As Canada's economic ties with South Korea flourished, Canada's commitment to South Korea grew stronger, and Pyongyang was effectively written off from Ottawa's policy agenda. Ottawa had no incentive to jeopardize its ties with Seoul for the sake of the principle of constructive engagement.

The main tenor of Canada's constructive engagement policy is that, as the former minister of foreign affairs, Andre Ouellet once stated, the most effective way of promoting democracy and human rights is through trade and progress in the economy of the concerned country. Based on that assumption, Canada vigorously pursues commercial initiatives in a number of countries irrespective of their human rights records. Trade is a crucial element of engagement policy, and this position goes back to the early postwar period. Therefore, when there is little opportunity for trade and little hope for economic progress, constructive engagement as a policy principle does not seem to be in effect. North Korea is the case in point.

V. Conclusion

This paper examined Canada's diplomatic relations with the PRC and Cuba from the early postwar years to the present, in order to draw some implications for explaining its policy of non-recognition and non-engagement towards North Korea. There has been a striking contrast in Ottawa's policy toward China and Cuba, on one hand, and towards North Korea, on the other. Canada has consistently sought to be engaged with the former. On the contrary, Canada has never made serious attempt to improve relations with Pyongyang. With Cuba and China, Ottawa has been proactive; Canadian policy towards North Korea has been reactive.

There have been numerous obstacles that made it difficult for Ottawa to have normal diplomatic relations with these regimes. It took twenty years for Canada to recognize the PRC. Canada-Cuba relations suffered in varying degrees over the following decades after Castro's revolution. Despite those difficulties, however, Canada constantly maintained an engagement policy with them. North Korea is a conspicuous exception. The Canadian tradition of recognizing a regime in control has not been applied to North Korea. Engagement policy--to build trust and to promote peace, stability and democracy--has not, applied to North Korea as well. This paper has suggested that Canada's lack of economic interest in North Korea is a key factor in explaining a near complete absence of its diplomatic initiative. It is not to argue that economic factor solely determined the outcome of Canada's policy towards the three regimes in question. Canadian policy would be the result of a combination of different factors. Foreign policy is to a large extent path dependent and historically embedded, where government's action or inaction may often be a matter of expediency in the given circumstances. The establishment of South Korea as America's client regime and its subsequent recognition by Western countries set the course of Canada-DPRK relations. Pyongyang's ideological fanaticism, xenophobia and intransigence has certainly been exceptional; so has Seoul's effort to isolate its rival fierce. When these factors combined, there was little room for constructive engagement.

Engagement policy is applied on the assumption that it is the best way to reduce tension and promote values such as democracy and human rights. In practice, such policy necessarily entails promotion of economic interaction. Engagement opens up commercial opportunities, although it may not be the primary objective. Engagement often continues without knowing when or to what extent it will take effect. China or Cuba changed not by virtue of engagement policy but because of some other internal or external dynamics. But as long as one's own security is not directly threatened by the regime, engagement is perhaps more pragmatic than economic sanctions of which the effect is equally suspect. Conversely, when there is no economic incentive at all, enthusiasm for engagement may diminish. In this sense, economic incentive, not any moral or legal principles, seem to consistently explain Canadian policy toward China, Cuba and North Korea. And economic interest being the undercurrent, Ottawa would have little incentive to take any initiative ahead of others to improve relations with Pyongyang.

There have been some developments in Canada-DPRK relations since the end of 1999. In December, three DFAIT officials, along with Canadian academics, visited North Korea. In return, in early March, 2000, four North Korean foreign service officials, led by the director responsible for Canada and Latin America, visited Canada. They were the first official exchange of visits by the two countries. These events did not happen in isolation, but in a broader context. In recent months, Pyongyang has been showing some sign of opening up and willingness to engage with the outside world. As a result, a number of countries have recently come into active contact with North Korea. Talks between Washington and Pyongyang have been going on with a view to lifting the US economic embargo and establishing diplomatic relations, on condition that Pyongyang abandons its nuclear weapon and missile development program. The so-called 'Perry Report' presented in October 1999 outlines this process. Pyongyang opened a consulate general in Hong Kong in February 16. A French government delegation visited Pyongyang in early February. North Koreans and the Filipinos are discussing their diplomatic normalization. As perhaps the most noteworthy development in this flurry of diplomatic activities, Italy, became the first among the G7 members to establish full diplomatic relations with North Korea on 4 January 2000. Then on 8 May, Pyongyang announced that it would resume diplomatic relations with Australia, which were suspended since 1975.

Ottawa's response to Italian recognition of the DPRK seemed rather cool. DFAIT considered it a positive sign but an insignificant event." DFAIT has no particular assessment of the Italian recognition. There are many things about which we have no 'official' opinion," [28] According to a DFAIT official, he doubted that Italy's recognition would have any impact at all on Canada's North Korea policy. DFAIT also downplayed the newsworthiness of the official visits, as they were too junior a level. Another DFAIT official's statement revealed Ottawa's position: "We have begun a process of broadening dialogue with the DPRK, along the lines of [Korean] president's 'engagement policy.' As we have had so little contact with the DPRK until

---

[28] Online interview with Eber Rice, Counsellor, Canadian Embassy in Seoul. 23 February, 2000.

now, the initial stage is simply a getting-to-know-you process, and our main goal was to expose the DPRK visitors to Canada..." [29] Certainly, the historic inter-Korean summit on 13 June 2000 could be a big push for Canada.

The reasons for Ottawa's recognition of Pyongyang in 2001 await analysis, but our discussion permits some observations. We suggest that Canada is essentially reactive to external conditions concerning the DPRK, and for a longtime found no compelling rationale to take strong diplomatic initiatives or to rush into establishing diplomatic ties. In the case of China and Cuba, there was a strong sense among Canadians that they could do something special.

Canadian recognition of the PRC was considered as a significant diplomatic achievement. According to one assessment, Ottawa pursued a difficult policy without alienating Washington; showed off a newly independent foreign policy, diplomatic skills, and the potential to be more than just a middle power (Frolic 1991, 210). Canada's Cuba policy offered a similar sense of self-assurance that it can have an independent foreign policy and defy its superpower neighbor over an important principle. With North Korea, there was little room for Canada's meaningful role, and any decision by Ottawa was likely to end up as the diplomacy of "catching-up".

---

[29] Online interview with Glenn Sheppy, Director, Korea and Oceania Division, DFAIT. 22 March, 2000.

References

Beecroft, Stephen. 1991. "Canadian Policy towards China, 1949-1957: The Recognition Problem." Paul Evans and B. Michael Frolic, eds. *Reluctant Adversaries*. Toronto: University of Toronto Press.

Cooper, Andrew. 1997. *Canadian Foreign Policy: Old Habits and New Directions*. Toronto: Prentice Hall.

Dewitt, David and Evans, Paul, eds. 1993. *The Agenda for Cooperative Security in the North Pacific*. Toronto: Centre for International and strategic Studies.

Evans, Paul. 1991. "Introduction: Solving Our Cold War China Problem." Paul Evans and B. Michael Frolic, eds. *Reluctant Adversaries*. Toronto: University of Toronto Press.

Evans, Paul. 2000. "It's Time to Open the Door" *The Globe and Mail*. February 25.

Evans, Paul and Frolic, B. Michael. eds. 1991. *Reluctant Adversaries*. Toronto: University of Toronto Press.

Eayrs, James. 1959. *Canada in World Affairs 1955-57*. Toronto: Oxford University Press.

Flaherty, Frank. 1957. "Canadian Interests in the China Trade." *International Journal* 12 (Summer).

Frolic, B. Michael. 1991 "The Trudeau Initiative." Paul Evans and B. Michael Frolic, eds. *Reluctant Adversaries*. Toronto: University of Toronto Press.

Gotlieb, Alan. 1994. "Canada-Cuba Trade Relations: Problems and Prospects." Jamie Suchlicki and Antonio Jorge, eds. *Investing in Cuba: Problems and Prospects*. London: Transaction Publishers.

Hanly, Charles. 1968. "The Ethics of Independence." Stephen Clarkson, ed. *Independent Foreign Policy for Canada?* Toronto: McClelland and Stewart Ltd.

Harbron, John D. 1974. "Canada Recognizes China." *Behind the Headlines*. 33 (October).

Harrison, W. E. C. 1957. *Canada in World Affairs 1949 to 1950*. Toronto: Oxford University Press.

Holmes, John. 1965. "Canada and China: the Dilemmas of a Middle Power." A. M. Halpern, ed. *Politics toward China: Views from Six Continents*. Toronto: McGraw-Hill.

Holmes, John. 1982. *The Shaping of Peace, Vol. ?*. Toronto: University of Toronto Press.

Horwitz, Irving. 1994. "Ethical and Political Consequences of the American Embargo of Cuba." Jamie Suchlicki and Antonio Jorge, eds. *Investing in Cuba: Problems and Prospects*. London: Transaction Publishers.

JETRO. 1999. "The Canada-North Korea Relations report." May.

Jorge, Antonio and Cruz, Robert David. 1994. "Foreign Investment Opportunities in Cuba: Evaluating the Risks." Jamie Suchlicki and Antonio Jorge, eds. *Investing in Cuba: Problems and Prospects*. London: Transaction Publishers.

Kirk, John and McKenna, Peter. 1997. *Canada-Cuba Relations: The Other Good Neighbor Policy*. Miami: University Press of Florida.

Kirk, John. 1995. *Back in Business: Canada-Cuba relations after 50 years*. Toronto: the Canadian Foundation for the Americas.

Lyon, Peyton. 1968. *Canada in World Affairs 1961-63*. Toronto: Oxford University Press.

Mackay, R. A., ed. 1971. *Canadian Foreign Policy 1945-54*. Toronto: McClelland and Stewart Ltd.

Masters, Donald. 1959. *Canada in World Affairs 1953-55*. Toronto: Oxford University Press.

Molot, Maureen Apple. 1977. "Canada's Relations with China since 1968." Norman Hillmer, ed. *Foremost Nation*. Toronto: McClelland and Stewart.

Nossal, Kim R. 1982. "Business as Usual: Relations with China in the 1940s." Kim R. Nossal, ed. *Acceptance of Paradox*. Toronto: Canadian Institute of International Affairs.

Nossal, Kim R. 1994. *Sanctions in Canadian and Australian Foreign Policy*. Toronto: University of Toronto Press.

Paltiel, Jeremy. 1995. "Negotiating Human Rights with China.' Maxwell Cameron and Maureen Appel Molot, eds. *Canada Among Nations 1995: Democracy and Foreign Policy*. Ottawa: Carleton University Press.

Preston, Richard A. 1965. *Canada in World Affairs 1959-61*. Toronto: Oxford University Press.

Ronning, Chester. 1974. *A Memoir of China in Revolution*. New York: Pantheon.

Suchlicki, Jamie and Jorge, Antonio, eds. 1994. *Investing in Cuba: Problems and Prospects*. London: Transaction Publishers.

Thompson, Dale and Swanson, Roger. 1971. *Canadian Foreign Policy: Options and Perspectives*. Toronto: McGraw-Hill Ryerson Ltd.

Yoo, Young Sik. 1987. *Earlier Canadian Missionaries in Korea: A Study in History 1888-1895*. Toronto: The Society for Korean and Related Studies.

KOREA'S POLITICAL REGIONAL DIVISION IN THE POST DEMOCRATIZATION ERA: PARTISAN CAUSES AND THE PROCESS OF CHANGE

MYUNGSOON SHIN
YONSEI UNIVERSITY

I. Introduction

Korean society is often regarded as the most homogenous of societies. Due to its small size and homogenous composition, it has never suffered serious problems arising from racial, linguistic or cultural differences. Despite such external homogeneity, Korea is beset by severe problems of regionalism. The reason why this so-called regionalism is of such importance in Korea is due to the detrimental effects it ultimately has on the political, economic and social sectors by undermining national unity and social integration. Therefore, few oppose the argument that for the future development and consolidation of democracy in Korea, regionalism must be eradicated. However, the existing debates have concentrated on the regional conflict between the Young Nam (North and South Kyungsang Provinces) and Ho Nam (North and South Cholla Provinces) regions. With the static and the regions' emotional approach constituting the mainstream of scholarly discussions, it is difficult to avoid the criticism that the existing analyses have succeeded in presenting only normative rather than more realistic solutions.

This study, suggesting that the regionalism we see today emerged in the post-democratization period since 1987, and that regionalism in this era is markedly different in its causes and nature from that witnessed during the period prior to the democratization process, limits the period under analysis to that following the 13th general elections in 1987. It maintains that despite the variety of factors contributing to regionalism, it is mainly the pursuit of power by party leaders centered around the "3 Kims", (Kim Dae Jung, Kim Young Sam and Kim Jong Pil) and the continual appearance of regional parties as a tool toward fulfilling the party leader's ambitions. These have prevented the emergence of national or policy-oriented parties and perpetuated the reproduction of regionalism. In addition, the study aims to reveal that regionalism has not been fixed statically on the Young Nam vs Ho

Nam regions but that it has undergone a series of dynamic transformations centered around the party and its leader.

This study focuses on four aspects of the research question. First, it looks into the cause of regionalism in the period prior to democratization in 1987 using historical, social psychological, economic, and political approaches and intends to critically examine their relevance and limits in explaining the regionalism that has emerged after democratization. Second, it deals with the question of what characterizes regionalism in post-democratization Korea and how it is distinguishable from that prevailing prior to the democratization process. Third, it analyzes the cause of regionalism in the post-democratization era from a political perspective, and the process of change it has undergone using the election results and party types. Fourth, keeping in mind the dynamics of cause and change in regionalism, it offers prospects for the future and searches for a realistic solution to eradicate regionalism focusing on party politics.

II. Reviews and Critique of Existing Research on Regionalism Prior to Democratization

Korea's regionalism, which has deep historical roots, has gained prominence in academic circles only after the 13th General Elections in 1987. Although the general elections was a long sought achievement of the Korean democratization movement, the election results revealed a deep seated regional cleavage between Young Nam and Ho Nam regions, resulting in the subsequent failure of democratic forces to bring about a regime change.

Research on regionalism has been dealt with primarily by historians, psychologists, and some social scientists, who focused on its historical origins, biases held by regional inhabitants, realities of regional emotions, and its role as a cause of social conflict as manifested in imbalance of regional economic development and discrimination in government official recruitment. However, these studies are limited in the sense that they do not provide a fundamental answer to the question of why regionalism has become so prominently manifest in the post-democratization era. Although regionalism in the post democratization era is a direct manifestation of latent regional conflict extending back into history, a new approach is needed in order to explain the strengthening of the political nature of regionalism that is different from the past.

1. Historical Approach

In the studies of Korean regionalism, many scholars have used the historical approach which examines the origins and development of regionalism.[1] Although common ground is to be found among scholars using the historical approach in that they look at regional emotions and regional discrimination for the causes of regionalism, there seems to be no consensus on the date of its emergence. Generally, they tend to regard the period in which Wang Gun, the founding father of the Koryo dynasty, officialized government official recruitment discrimination against the Ho Nam region through the document called "Hoon Yo Shib Cho" as a critical historical point in which regionalism emerged. In the process of establishing the Koryo dynasty, Wang Gun fought critical battles with Kyun Won of the post-Paekche Kingdom, today's Ho Nam regions, for power, After his victory, Wang Gun made explicit in his official recruitment policy that he would discriminate against those from the south - the Ho Nam region - because of their sly and treacherous nature and their tendency to revolt.[2] During the Chosun dynasty, prevailing negative images on Ho Nam region residents coupled with incidents such as the Chong Yeo Ryp's revolt imposed severe disadvantages in the political advancement of those with a Ho Nam background.

In the Japanese colonial period, Ho Nam region residents were the most widely exploited and suffered the most. These historical facts are often mentioned by those advocating the historical perspective to be the causes of regionalism.[3]

The strength of the historical approach lies in its understanding of the problem based on a rigorous verification of historical materials. Its weakness is that, in the light of the fact that traditional regionalism developed through a structure of discrimination by the central government against Ho Nam region rather than that between Young Nam and Ho Nam regions, it does not explain why present regionalism does not reflect the tradition of central government and specific regions. It also does not provide an answer as to why traditional regionalism did not become manifest prior to the democratization process. Such limitations signify that although regionalism has historical roots, other more fundamental and practical reasons are behind the recent overt manifestation of regionalism as a political issue.

---

[1] More detailed debate on the historical approach is to be found in Ko Heong Hwa, *Research Data on Regional Emotions of Koreans* (Seoul: Sung Hwa Sa, 1989), pp. 49-65; Song Bok, "Historical Explanation of Regional Conflict: Through the Chosun Dynasty," Korean Sociology Association (ed.), *Korean Regionalism and Regional Conflict* (Seoul: Sung Hwa Sa, 1992), pp.13-26; Moon Suk Nam, "Historical Background of Regional Gap: From Liberation to 1960s," Korean Sociology Association (ed.), *Ibid.*, pp. 33-43; Lee Byung Hyu, "The History of Regional Conflict," in Kim Chong Chul and Choi Jang Gip et al., *Study on Regional Emotions* (Seoul: Hak Min Sa, 1991), pp. 83-121; Kim Kwang Joo, "Regionalism in Korea: Historical Analysis," *Kum Ho Mun Hwa* no.29 (1989), pp. 166-181; Shin Bok Ryoung, "Historical Background of Korean Regional Emotions: The Ho Nam Phobia," Korean Sociology Association (ed.), *Reexamination of Modern Korean Politics: Pre-Modernism, Modernism, Post-Modernism* (Seoul: Han Eul, 1996), pp.110-137.

[2] Ko Heong Hwa, *Ibid.*, p. 52; Song Bok, *Ibid.*, pp. 19-21.

[3] Ko Heong Hwa, *Ibid*, pp. 53-65.

2. Social Psychological Approach

The social psychological approach to regionalism has mostly been undertaken by research in the disciplines of psychology. This approach generalized regionalism as biases or collective hostility against people from particular regions and analyzed regionalism through research aimed at understanding the emotional feelings or discriminative attitudes brought forth when considering people from certain regions as business partners, friends, close neighbors, or spouses of family members.[4]

The social psychological approach measures the psychological regional conflict as formed through the social discrimination and socialization process. An important concept utilized in the analysis is the so-called "social distance".

Table 2-1. Social Distance between Regional Inhabitants (%)

1 \\ 2	SE	KK	KW	CB1	CN1	CB2	CN2	KB	KN	CJ	North	Average
SE	4.6	4.6	5.2	6.5	7.2	38.6	39.2	14.4	12.4	7.8	12.4	13.9
KK	7.7	3.4	3.9	5.2	5.2	39.9	40.8	9.4	9.9	8.6	15.9	13.6
KW	21.7	13.2	4.7	6.6	6.6	47.2	49.1	14.2	16.0	19.8	32.1	21.0
CB1	12.0	7.2	10.4	4.0	5.6	48.8	50.4	13.6	15.2	19.2	40.0	20.0
CN1	7.2	3.2	4.5	2.7	2.7	32.4	35.1	6.8	7.2	5.4	10.4	10.7
CB2	14.7	9.6	11.9	7.3	7.3	2.8	9.0	31.6	31.1	14.7	32.8	15.7
CN2	9.7	6.9	9.3	8.0	7.3	6.6	3.1	25.6	25.6	8.3	18.0	11.7
KB	13.8	10.1	9.8	9.8	9.8	53.2	55.4	3.4	5.8	16.8	31.2	19.9
KN	23.0	15.2	11.1	9.8	9.8	51.4	55.7	9.8	3.4	15.2	27.0	21.0
CJ	15.6	13.3	13.3	13.3	11.1	48.9	60.2	15.6	15.6	0.0	33.3	21.8
North	10.3	10.3	3.4	6.9	6.9	37.9	37.9	17.2	13.8	10.3	3.4	14.4
Total	13.4	9.0	8.4	8.1	7.8	45.2	47.7	16.9	17.0	12.4	23.8	

Source: Na Kan Che, "Social Distance between Regional Inhabitants," Korean Sociological Association, (ed.), *Korean Regionalism and Regional Conflict* (Seoul: Sung Hwa Sa, 1992), pp. 85-86.
1: Target Province, 2: Native Province
SE: Seoul, KK: Kyung Ki, KW: Kang Won, CB1: North Chung Chong, CN1: South Chung Chong, CB2: North Cholla, CN2: South Cholla, KB: North Kyung Sang, KN: South Kyung Sang, CJ: Che Ju, North: North Korea (DPRK).

---

[4] Hong Dong Shik, "Regional Emotions," Korean Sociological Association, (ed.), *op. cit.*, p. 68. Prominent works in this field are Na Kan Che, "Social Distance between Regional Inhabitants," Korean Sociological Association, (ed.), *op. cit.*, pp. 79-100; Min Kyung Hwan, "Regionalism from a Social Science Perspective," Kim Chong Chul, Choi Jang Gip et al., *op. cit.*, pp. 171-182.

The social psychological approach measures the psychological regional conflict as formed through the social discrimination and socialization process. An important concept utilized in the analysis is the so-called "social distance". Table 2-1 is the result of a 1988 study investigating social distance among regional inhabitants from various perspectives.[5]

From the table, we can see that social distance is felt to a minor degree for the surveyed people's own region whereas social distance is felt more strongly by people from other regions against those from Ho Nam region. Specifically, social distance existing between the Young Nam and Ho Nam region residents are especially strong. This signifies that the core of regionalism in Korea lies at the conflict between the Young Nam and Ho Nam regions, and from a broader perspective, at the conflict between Ho Nam and non-Ho Nam regions.

The social psychological approach is significant in that the approach keyed into the social distance felt between regional inhabitants through focusing on social relationships and conflicting psychological issues, and thereby presented some important standards and concepts in explaining the phenomenon of regionalism. Also to its credit is the need for a socialization process it proposes, to overcome the hostility experienced by residents of differing regions. However, the social psychology approach also fails to answer the question of why regionalism has manifested itself so suddenly in the aftermath of the democratization process while held latent during authoritarian regimes. It also comes under criticism for overlooking regionalism in other regions by concentrating simply on Young Nam vs Ho Nam, and Ho Nam vs non-Ho Nam regions.

3. Economic Approach

An oft cited source of regionalism is the difference in the level of economic development between regions. In the Korean case, the starting point of the economic approach differs from scholar to scholar, some tracing it back to the Japanese colonial era, some maintaining that it originates from the failure of the land reform conducted during President Syngman Rhee's era, while others point to the delivery process of economic aid. Generally, however, most scholars advocating the economic approach tend to view Hirshman's 'unbalanced growth strategy', adopted by the Park Chung Hee regime in the

---

[5] There is also research on the mutual reciprocity between regional inhabitants from a psychological perspective. Ko Heong Hwa, Kim Hyun Sub, "Korean's Regional Prejudice," in Ko Heong Hwa, *op. cit.,* pp. 289-300; Kim Hye Suk, "Stereotypes and Biases between Regions: Does Generational Transition Exist?" Korean Psychology Society, (ed.), *Regional Emotions from Psychological Perspectives: Regional Stereotypes and its Resolution* (Seoul: Sung Hwa Sa, 1988), pp. 123-164; Kim Kuk Jin, "Regional Emotions and its Resolutions," Korean Psychology Society, (ed.), *Ibid.,* pp. 221-249.

1960s as the beginning of the widening gap.[6] In their view, President Park's economic development strategy was an effort to compensate for the lack of legitimacy of his regime through economic achievement, and perpetuated the economic gap between the regions, resulting in the marginalization of certain regions.

Scholars who have attempted the economic approach have delved into the issue of regional economic gap by setting and measuring varying standards. For example, they explained the regional economic gap through presenting and analyzing various standards across the regions such as gross regional production, percentage of primary industry, level of industrialization, proportion of manufacturing industries, ratio of poor people, level of budgetary independence of the local governments, level of urbanization, per capita resident income, deposit and credit extension of banks, etc.[7]

The fact that regional economic differences account for an important source of regionalism is indisputable. Explaining the regional hostilities between the Young Nam and Ho Nam regions through the gap in economic development levels is also very persuasive. Despite such strengths, when one considers the fact that Seoul and Kyung Ki province were the regions that have developed the most, with Young Nam not far behind, while Chung Chong and Kang Won provinces were as much marginalized as the Ho Nam region, this approach fails to explain why regionalism of the past did not develop between Kyung Ki and the Seoul region vs. the other regions, but in fact, developed around Ho Nam and Young Nam. This is a crucial weakness of the economic approach.[8]

---

[6] Cho Min, *Research on Resolution of Regionalism: Plans to lay the Foundations for Reunification* (Seoul: National Reunification Institute, 1995), pp. 29-37; Kim Kwang Soo, "Cholla Province in Korean Politics," *Korean Political Science Review* vol. 20, no. 1 (1986), pp. 85-107; Kim Moon Cho, "Formation and Characteristics of Korean Regionalism," Korean Sociological Association, (ed.), *op. cit.*, p. 157. However, there are scholars who raise the question of the effectiveness of government policy in this respect. Lee Kap Yoon for one argues that Pusan and Tae Gu avoided the damages of the Korean War and thus most of the capital, labor and market were concentrated on this region, thereby aiming at the assertion that particular regions were selected simply based on its connections with the government leader merits reexamination. Lee Kap Yoon, *Election and Regionalism in Korea* (Seoul: Oruem, 1999), pp. 48-49.

[7] Kim Man Heum, "The 6th Republic and Deepening of Regional Emotions," Kim Chong Chul, Choi Jang Gip et al, *op. cit.*, pp. 155-167; Kim Man Heum, *Reexamination of Korean Politics: Democracy, Regionalism, Localism* (Seoul: Pul Vit, 1997), pp. 201-224; Ma In Sup, "Social Support Base of Political Party", Yoon Jung Suk, Shin Myungsoon and Sim Ji Youn (eds.), *Korean Party Politics* (Seoul: Bummoonsa, 1998), pp. 303-304.

[8] Lee Kap Yoon, *Ibid.*, p. 47; Son Ho Chol, *Modern Korean Politics: Theory and History* (Seoul: Sa Hwe Pyoung Ron, 1997), p. 465.

In addition, the approach is not able to explain why in the face of static or even decreasing economic differences in the 1980s (compared to the 1960s and 1970s which witnessed an ever widening gap between the regions),[9] regionalism should so rapidly erupt after democratization. Considering the strong support given to the ruling party in major elections during the authoritarian regimes of the past by Ho Nam region, Kang Won and Chung Chong provinces, despite their relative economic weakness, substantial difficulties are encountered in attempting to explain regionalism using an economic approach. Also, the cycle of support and withdrawal of support toward the ruling party shown by the Chung Chong, Taeku and Pusan regions in the elections of the post-democratization era is also difficult to explain by economic approach. The weaknesses of this approach reveals that regionalism in post democratization Korea cannot be explained simply by the economic differences existing between the regions.

4. Political Approach

Analysis of regionalism using the political approach emerged mainly in the post-democratization period. The reason why regionalism began to gain such prominent attention by political scientists who prior to democratization did not show much interest, was mainly because regionalism as revealed in the 13th National Assembly Elections was, unlike that of the past, being very much political in nature. In addition, political scientists have come to seriously address the issue of how election results in which regionalism seemed latent would affect Korean politics as a whole.

In the case of political analysis, it is possible to classify it into two approaches. One is a tendency to approach the issue of regionalism from a macroeconomic and structural point of view, and research dealing with the legitimacy of authoritarian regimes, regional discrimination in the distribution of political power, effects of government institutions and electoral rules, all fall into this category.

The other approach deals with the subject matter based on microeconomic and functional premises, and research focusing on the power struggle between political leaders, region-centered election strategies, voting behavior across regions, and the nature of regional issues from a rational choice perspective are within this category. Such classifications are only for purposes of understanding the trends and perspectives of research and, in reality, most research can be said to hold a structural functional position.

The relevance and limits of the political approach to regionalism prior to democratization will be examined, focusing mostly on research citing the legitimacy issue of authoritarian governments and regional conflict arising from distribution of political power as the main source of regionalism.

An abundance of theories has been put forth mostly by political scientists, claiming that authoritarian regimes of the past have politically manipulated

---

[9] Refer to tables in Lee Kap Yoon, *Ibid.*, pp. 45-46.

regional emotions in order to lay the ground for successive reigns and solidify their power bases in the face of weak legitimacy.[10] Such theories were able to gain credibility through specifically revealing the practice of exclusive government recruitment policy and regional discrimination in the advancement of high level government officials during authoritarian regimes.[11] More specifically, Table 2-2 shows that in the hometown distributions of the ministers and high level officials of past administrations, Young Nam has the highest percentage with 31.6% and 31.4% while Ho Nam has a meager 13.6% and 12.6%. Such figures give evidence to the fact that a personnel recruitment policy markedly in favor of the Young Nam region while discriminating against the Ho Nam region was indeed in existence. Also, under the Syngman Rhee and Jang Myoun regimes during the 1950s

Table 2-2. Birth Places of Ministers and High Ranking Officials in Successive Governments (%)

1	Ministers						High Ranking Officials					
2	SE KK	CC	YN	HN	KW CJ	North	SE KK	CC	YN	HN	KW CJ	North
RHEE	42.5	12.6	19.0	4.0	7.1	14.8	33.2	16.0	18.8	6.2	6.5	19.3
CHANG	22.0	16.0	21.0	21.0	--	20.0	16.3	16.3	25.5	16.3	1.0	24.6
PARK	15.2	16.3	29.8	15.3	7.0	16.4	14.1	13.9	30.1	13.2	7.7	21.0
CHUN	24.6	13.2	33.0	14.1	4.7	10.4	19.4	12.3	41.2	12.6	5.4	9.1
ROH	17.3	12.4	45.8	12.0	4.5	7.9						
KIM	17.6	18.0	40.9	15.1	1.5	6.8	20.8	14.7	41.2	14.7	2.0	6.6
Total	23.2	14.8	31.6	13.6	4.1	12.7	20.8	14.6	31.4	12.6	4.5	16.1

Source: Choi Young Jin, *Korean Regionalism and Politics of Identity* (Seoul: Oruem, 1999), pp. 105-106; Lee Kap Yoon, *Election and Regionalism in Korea* (Seoul: Oruem, 1999), p. 56; Kim Man Heum, *Reexamination of Korean Politics: Democracy, Regionalism, and Localism* (Seoul: Pul Vit, 1997), p. 178.
RHEE: Rhee Syng Man, CHANG Chang Myoun, PARK: Park Chung Hee, CHUN: Chun Doo Hwan, ROH: Roh Tae Woo, KIM: Kim Young Sam
SE: Seoul, KK: Kyung Ki, CC: Chung Chong, YN: Young Nam, HN: Ho Nam, KW: Kang Won, CJ: Che Ju, North: North Korean region

---

[10] Kang Myung Koo, " Elections and Regional Conflict: Process of Structralization and Regional Civil Society," *Korean Political Science Review* vol. 27, no. 2, (1993), pp. 76-96; Choi Jang Gip, "Regional Emotions as an Ideology," *Criterion and Prospects of Democracy* (Seoul: Na Nam, 1996), pp. 387-389; Ro Byung Man, "Formation and Causes of the Political Structure of Regionalism: Beyond Regional Emotions and Conflict," *Korean Political Science Review* vol. 32, no. 1, (1998), pp. 71-76.

[11] Prominent works in this field include Kim Man Heum, "Study on the Political Division of Korea: Structural Approach of the Political Process of Political Division," Seoul National University Ph.D. Dissertation, 1991; Kim Yong Hak, "Regional Gap of Elite Recruitment and Replacement: Micro Causes and Macro Results," Kim Jong Chul, Choi Jang Gip et al, *Ibid.*, pp. 258-284.

and 1960s, there was a high ratio of officials with a Seoul or Kyung Ki province background rather than those hailing from the Young Nam region. On the other hand, the Park Chung Hee and Chun Doo Hwan regimes, the percentage of high ranking officials from Young Nam shot up suddenly, supporting the claim that a discriminative personnel recruitment policy favoring the Young Nam region was adopted in order to maintain the authoritarian regime.

However, as with the economic approach, research citing regional discrimination in the distribution of political power during the authoritarian regimes as the source of regionalism cannot explain why regionalism suddenly manifested itself in the aftermath of democratization. Also as the above table reveals, the current political approach fails to explain why under the Roh Tae Woo and Kim Young Sam governments in which legitimacy was not at issue, officials from the Young Nam region were able to achieve greater political advancement than their Ho Nam counterparts. Although it is true that the exclusive government recruitment policy did operate as a factor in stimulating regionalism, it can not be deemed as the direct cause of regionalism. The fact that discriminative recruitment policy was more in use even under a democratized regime should be seen more as a consequence rather than the cause of regionalism. Therefore, in order to search for the direct cause of regionalism in the post-democratization era, factors other than the legitimacy issue of authoritarian governments and discriminative recruitment policy should be looked into.

III. The Causes and Characteristics of Regionalism during the Democratization Process

Compared to the past, the regionalism that became manifest during the democratization process was distinctly political in nature.[12] Although it is undeniable that regionalism during this period emerged from a background of historical, social, and economic regional discrimination and marginalization, such a distinct political characteristic signifies that this is a phenomenon markedly different in its nature from that of the past. If this is so, the question of how to characterize regionalism in the post-democratization era can be raised, coupled with the necessity to clarify the political circumstances and the factors that set off regionalism. This section characterizes regionalism in the post-democratization period to be "political regional division" and finds as its causes the mutual interaction and dynamics between political actors centered around party leader, party, and voters, and the political results focusing on election circumstances and results.

---

[12] This point is well illustrated in Ko Heong Hwa , previous work, pp 314-334. When the research materials available are examined, while there were few researches on regionalism prior to the 1987 Democratization, they increased dramatically in the years after. Especially of note is that while research papers or books on regionalism from a political perspective were almost nonexistent before 1987, numerous works appeared after this point. This means that the Korean political scientists defined regionalism as a political issue after the 13th Presidential Elections and began to focus on it.

1. The Concept of Political Regional Division

Scholars who have studied existing regionalism in Korea have established its nature and analyzed its characteristics through various different concepts and terminology. While the term regionalism was generally accepted, from the psychological perspective, "regional emotions"; from the social science perspective, "regional conflict"; from the economic perspective, "regional gap"; and from the political science perspective, "regional hegemony"; were widely used.[13] However, even today, there is no concrete consensus on the definition of regionalism, a mixture or a variety of terms being used to denote a concept.[14]

This study defines the regionalism that emerged in the post democratization period as "political regional division." This is because the nature of the regionalism that appeared during this period is fundamentally political, and because election results clearly revealed a pattern delineated across regional lines. On the other hand, regionalism prior to democratization was latent with regional hostilities arising from historical, social psychological, and economic causes, which found no political expression. In the regionalism after democratization however, in a situation where the "democracy vs anti-democracy" issue was no longer the dominating one, the fact that a regional division structure was created through a firm solidarity between the party leaders, party, and regional voters, led regionalism in this period to be characterized as political regional division.

The characteristics of the political regional division can be more clearly understood when the election results before and after democratization are compared. Table 3-1 gives the results of the presidential election held during

---

[13] Nam Young Shin was the first scholar to use the term "Regional Hegemony." This term appears in his works *Regional Hegemony and Korea: Advice for Social Integration and Development* (Seoul: Se Mul Sa, 1991), and *Study on Regional Hegemony* (Seoul: Hak Min Sa, 1992). In these works, Nam Young Shin defines regional hegemony as "a political ideology where people from a particular region existing as a part of a state, take the lead in national governance thereby obtaining, maintaining and strengthening the political power". In addition to Nam, another scholar who has recently defined the term in relation to elections is Lee Nam Young. In "1998 Local Elections and Regionalism: Compared to the 15th Presidential Elections," Cho Chong Bin, (ed.), *Korean Elections III* (Seoul: Pu Lun Kil, 1999), he refines the concept by defining regional hegemony as "a phenomenon in which parties whose power bases are in Young Nam and Ho Nam vie for power through stimulating regional emotions", and defines political regional hegemony as "the phenomenon in which political ideology and policies disappear and regional issues become dominant."

[14] Choi Han Soo, "Assessment of 6.27 Local Elections: Examination of Party Support and Regionalism," *Korean Political Science Review* vol. 29, no. 3, (1995), p. 146.

Table 3-1. Presidential Election Results by Region during the Third Republic (%)

Election / Region	5th Presidential Elections (1963) Park Chung Hee	5th Presidential Elections (1963) Yoon Bo Sun	6th Presidential Elections (1967) Park Chung Hee	6th Presidential Elections (1967) Yoon Bo Sun	7th Presidential Elections (1971) Park Chung Hee	7th Presidential Elections (1971) Kim Dae Jung
Seoul	32	68	47	53	40	60
Kyung Ki	37	63	44	56	50	50
Kang Won	45	55	55	45	61	39
N Chung Chong	45	55	52	48	58	42
S Chung Chong	45	55	49	51	55	45
Pusan	50.4	49.5	67	33	56	44
N Kyung Sang	61	39	71	29	76	24
S Kyung Sang	67	33	75	25	74	26
N Cholla	54	46	46	54	37	63
S Cholla	62	38	49	51	35	65
Che Ju	66	34	64	36	58	42
Total	51	49	55	45	54	46

Source: *Shin Dong A*, (June 1971); Choi Young Jin, *op. cit.*, p. 139.

the Third Republic (the Park Jung Hee regime). The table shows that in the 5th Presidential Elections, candidate Park Jung Hee of the ruling party recorded the highest percentage of votes in the regions south of the Chung Chong provinces. Candidate Yoon Bo Sun of the opposition party won the most votes in the regions north of the Chung Chong provinces, demonstrating a "North-South division" across the nation. In the 6th Presidential Elections, votes won by the ruling and opposition party showed no major regional divisions, while in the 7th Presidential Elections, an "East-West division" appeared across the country, with candidate Park Jung Hee and Kim Dae Jung showing dominant followings in the Young Nam and Ho Nam regions respectively.

However, regional influences on election results during this period are markedly different from the political regional division which appeared after the democratization process.

First of all, the North-South division of the 5th Presidential Elections is not the result of regional conflicts but rather, results in the traditional "Yeo Chon Ya Do" (Urban areas favor the ruling party while the countryside favors the opposition party) phenomenon.[15] Also the election was issue-centered as a result of the ideological controversy and Park's agriculture-oriented policy.[16] Second, as can be seen from the fact that regionalism was not a major factor in the 6th Presidential Elections, regionalism at the time was a temporary phenomenon by nature. Third, although it is true that the ruling and opposition parties exploited regional emotions during the 7th Presidential Elections as an election strategy, regionalism did not play a decisive role in the four National Assembly elections prior to the 13th National Assembly Elections. Also, in the Ho Nam region, the degree of voting based on regionalism was relatively weaker.[17] This clearly indicates that regionalism during this period and the political regional division in the post-democratization years differs substantially.

In short, we can infer that regionalism in the pre-democratization years, although latent, did not manifest itself as a source of sharp regional conflict in the political arena, and therefore is differentiated from the political regional division that has appeared in the post-democratization period.

In order to understand more specifically the characteristics of political regional division, it is necessary to examine the election results of the main party candidates across the major cities and provinces in the 13th Presidential Election in 1987, which was a result of the hard won constitutional amendment by the democratization movement.

---

[15] The phenomenon of "Yeo Chon Ya Do" is a hypothesis presented along with the "Chon Ko Do Jo" phenomenon by Professor Yoon Chon Joo based on the theory of modernization. In effect, it is a hypothesis maintaining that in the rural areas, support for the ruling party is high where in the urban areas support for the opposing party is high. Such a phenomenon is attributed to the voting behavior of the residents of the rural areas, who are strongly influenced by the pressures and mobilization of government organizations or social organizations. For more information, refer to Yoon Chon Joo, *Korean Political System: Political Situation and Participation* (Seoul: Seoul National University Press, 1987); Yoon Chon Joo, *Korea's Elections* (Seoul: Seoul National University Press, 1981).

[16] Cho Ki Sook, "Rational Voter Model and Analysis of Korean Elections: Yeo Chon Ya Do, Regionalism, and Party Voting," Lee Nam Young , (ed.), *Korean Elections I* (Seoul: Na Nam, 1993), p. 415; Choi Moon Sung, "Examination of the 15th Presidential Elections Outcomes: Influence of the Ideology Controversy," Ku Bum Mo, *New Horizon of Korean Political Science* (Seoul: Na Nam, 1994), pp. 512-543.

[17] Kisuk Cho, "Regionalism in Korean Elections and Democratization: An Empirical Analysis," *Asian Perspective* vol. 22, no. 1, (Spring 1998), p. 138; Lee Kap Yoon, *op. cit.*, pp. 37-38.

Table 3-2. Election Results of the 13th Presidential Elections by Region (%)

Candidates Region	Roh Tae Woo (DJP)	Kim Young Sam (RDP)	Kim Dae Jung (DPP)	Kim Jong Pil (NDRP)
Seoul	30.0	29.1	32.6	8.2
Pusan	32.1	56.0	9.1	2.6
Taeku	70.7	24.3	2.6	2.1
Inchon	39.4	30.0	21.3	9.2
Kwangju	4.8	0.5	94.4	0.2
Kyung Ki	41.4	27.5	22.3	8.5
Kang Won	59.3	26.1	8.8	5.4
N Chung Chong	46.9	28.2	11.0	13.5
S Chung Chong	26.2	16.1	12.4	45.0
N Cholla	14.2	1.5	83.5	0.8
S Cholla	8.2	1.2	90.3	0.3
N Kyung Sang	66.4	28.2	2.4	2.6
S Kyung Sang	41.2	51.3	4.5	2.7
Che Ju	49.8	26.8	18.6	4.5
Total	36.6	28.0	27.1	8.1

Source: Made by author based on the Central Election Management Commission's Homepage (http://www.nec.go.kr) data.
DJP: Democratic Justice Party, RDP: Reunification Democratic Party, PPD: Party for Peace and Democracy, NDRP: New Democratic Republican Party.

Table 3-2 clearly demonstrates that in the election results of the 13th Presidential Elections, particular parties are given dominant support in certain regions. Ro Tae Woo of the Democratic Justice Party (DJP) in North Kyung Sang Province and Taeku; Kim Young Sam of the Reunification Democratic Party (RDP) in South Kyung Sang province and Pusan; Kim Dae Jung of the Party for Peace and Democracy (PPD) in North and South Cholla Provinces and Kwangju, and Kim Jong Pil of the New Democratic Republican Party (NDRP) in South Chung Chong province, all received from 23.3% to 67.3% more votes than their national average. This signifies that unlike the past, political regional division is manifest, showing clear voting differences across regions centered around particular candidates and parties. Under the authoritarian regimes of the past, the division between democracy vs. anti-democracy was dominant, and regionalism was suppressed in the prevalent competition between the Taeku and North Kyung Sang province, the power base of the ruling party and other regions.[18] After democratization however, a more diversified four political regional division of North Kyung Sang including Taeku vs South Kyung Sang including Pusan vs. Ho Nam (North and South Cholla provinces including Kwang Ju) vs. South Chung Chong was formed centered around party leader and party.[19] Such differences between regionalism prior to democratization and political regional division after democratization an analysis from a different perspective.

Of some note here is that the Ho Nam region's support for Kim Dae Jung was absolute. Such absolute support, going over 90% in South Cholla and Kwang Ju, comes from both marginalization and regional discrimination of Ho Nam and protest against the forceful suppression of the Kwang Ju uprising by the Chun Doo Hwan regime in 1980.[20] However, such voting behavior by the Ho Nam residents resulted in strengthening other regions' hostility against Ho Nam and opened up the possibility of a new political regional division, i.e. Ho Nam vs. non-Ho Nam.[21]

2. Causes of Political Regional Division

The next question to be asked is what factors contributed toward the development of the political regional division. Several persuasive arguments have been presented, mainly by political scientists concerned with the causes behind the phenomenon.

First, the most oft-cited cause, related to the political situation, is the weakening of national issues and the rise of the regional issues. This argument maintains, that due to democratization, the confrontational structure of "democracy vs anti-democracy" has been weakened, and the parties and party leaders, having lost their most important instrument of partisan competition, came to search for a new issue or a political cleavage which they could utilize.

---

[18] Son Ho Chul (1997), *op. cit.*, p. 466.

[19] According to an opinion poll conducted at the time, about 79.1% of voters voted based on the candidates' home provinces. Kim Hyung Kook, "A Geopolitical Study on the Voting Behavior of the13th Presidential Elections," Kim Kwang Oong, (ed.), *Korea's Election Politics* (Seoul: Na Nam, 1990), pp. 207-232. This reflects the fact that the regional variable was a major influence in the elections.

[20]For more information on the Kwang Ju Democratization Uprising and Regionalism refer to Chung Gun Sik, "Kwang Joo Democratization Uprising and Regionalism," Kim Jong Chul, Choi Jang Gip, et al., *op. cit.*, pp. 133-153.

[21] Shin Bok Ryong stresses that regionalism is not simply a problem between the Young Nam and Ho Nam provinces, but one between Ho Nam and non-Ho Nam regions based on Ho Nam phobia. Shin Bok Ryong, *op. cit.*, pp. 113-114.

In such a situation, they keyed into the regionalism issue that was latent up to then. For example, in the case of the Chun Doo Hwan regime, its inherent legitimacy weakness, resulting from having come to power through a coup d'etat, coupled with the regime's authoritarian rule to strengthen its power was enough to rouse the resistance and antagonism of the entire nation. In this situation, opposition parties could become unified through a nationwide issue of anti-regime and democratization. However, as democratization progressed rapidly, such regime-related issues were weakened, and with no other suitable national issue to take its place, regionalism emerged as the dominant issue.

Second, the 3-Kims' political capabilities, and differences in home provinces, are presented as arguments related to the political actor argument. For example, Kim Young Sam and Kim Dae Jung won considerable popular support in the process of leading the anti-authoritarian regime movement and especially the powerful support of their home provinces. In this situation, the failure of the opposition parties' 2-Kims to present a unified front (single candidate) had a major influence in the emergence and deepening of political regional divisions.[22] In other words, regionalism latent during the period prior to democratization was able to emerge due to the existence of powerful political leaders like the 3-Kims who were sharply different only in terms of their home provinces.

Third, a cause related to election strategies is the argument of divide and rule of opposition party strategy, and the instigation of regionalism.[23] The ruling party that experienced powerful popular resistance during democratization realized that within the existing democracy vs. anti-democracy structure it had no chance of winning the presidential election. In addition, candidate Roh Tae Woo, compared to the opposition parties' Kim Young Sam or Kim Dae Jung, enjoyed low popularity, which added to his unfavorable election prospects. The ruling party, in response, came to believe that dispersing the democratic forces by pursuing both strategies of the division of opposing parties and the instigation of regionalism simult-aneously, was the only way to stay in power. Thus, political regional division came into being.[24]

---

[22] The failure of the opposition parties to produce a unitary candidate is a natural result seen from the perspectives of a politician bent on their pursuit of power. In the case of Kim Dae Joog, he recognized that the "4 candidates competition", simultaneous running with Kim Young Sam as opposition candidates, was more advantageous than a unitary candidate. Lee Gap Yoon, *op. cit.*, p. 116; Son Ho Chul (1997), *op. cit.*, p. 473.

[23] For more information on election strategies and regionalism, refer to Chong Young Kook, "Regionalism and Election Strategies: the 14th Presidential Elections," *Korea and International Politics* vol. 9, no. 2, (1993), pp. 33-46.

[24] The pardon and reinstatement granted to Kim Dae Jung at the time was part of the ruling party's strategy to divide the opposing sectors. Ji Byoung Moon, et al., *Development and Dynamics of Modern Korean Politics* (Seoul: Park Young Sa, 1997), p. 411.

Finally, an important cause that should be pointed out related to the party is the personalization of parties or regionalization of parties. The fact that the parties took the form of 'regional' parties centered around party leaders in the post democratization years, thereby failing to create a national party or policy-oriented parties. This is an important factor in explaining the regional voting behavior of voters to this day. Even though the democracy vs. anti-democracy issue between the ruling and opposition parties was weakening, no policy differences between the parties has emerged. Especially because the Reunification Democratic Party, Party for Peace and Democracy, and New Democratic Republican Party were all personal parties of the 3-Kims, there was little possibility of parties themselves becoming the standard voters went by.[25] In other words, whereas the ruling Democratic Justice Party was more of a ruling bloc party formed around the North Kyung Sang province and Taeku during the Park Jung Hee and Chon Doo Hwan regimes, the rest of the opposition parties were personal parties centered around the 3-Kims. As a result, in the 13th Presidential Elections, as can be seen from the election results in Table 3-2, regional voting based on individual candidate rather than party identification was a major factor, giving evidence to a structure of severe regional division.

Therefore, we can conclude that the political regional division demonstrated in the 13th Presidential Elections held after the democratization process was a phenomenon produced by a complex interaction among factors such as the composition of political leaders, their voter mobilization strategy, personal parties, and regional parties in a situation where regional conflict arising from regional biases and economic gaps of the past was latent. Above all however, the problematic relationship between the political leaders and their parties, in which the party system failed to outgrow the personal and regional parties, was the overriding cause of the vicious cycle of political regional division.

IV. The Transformation Process of the Structure and Nature of Political Regional Division

The factors contributing to the emergence of political regional division in the years after democratization are diverse. However, it is clear that personal parties or regional parties closely related to political leaders lay at the core of the political regional division problem. This means that there is a good possibility of the change of structure and nature of Korea's political regional

---

[25] From such a perspective, Cho Ki Sook criticized the modernization theory based on a rational choice theory maintaining that the regional voting behavior was a result of rational choice in a situation where no policy differences existed between the parties. Cho Ki Sook, *Rational Choice: Korean Elections and Voters* (Seoul: Han Ul Academy, 1996), pp. 132-143.

division depending on the change of political situations or choice of the political leaders. At the same time it also implies that political regional division is a dynamic phenomenon definable from varying perspectives rather than a static one fixed around the Young Nam and Ho Nam regions. In this section, I will analyze how the structure and nature of political regional division, established in the 13th Presidential Elections has since evolved in relation to the issue of political parties.

1. The Roh Tae Woo Administration Era

Although it cannot be denied that the ruling DJP in 1988 was a successor of the preceding authoritarian regime, it can not be categorized as a personal party centered around Roh Tae Woo. For these reasons, the DJP had a good chance of success in penetrating the conservative voters with their aim of stability. In contrast, because the opposition parties showed characteristics of personal parties centered around their respective leaders, they were able to win support from particular regions. However, as a reaction against this, their logic of checks and balances had little room to mobilize national support, and revealed the limitations of a personal party, thereby failing to bring about a regime change.[26] As a result, in the 13th Presidential Elections, in which one ruling party competed against three personal opposition parties, the political regional divisions of North Kyung Sang province and Taeku (DJP) vs. South Kyung Sang province and Pusan (RDP) vs. North and South Cholla provinces, Kwang Ju, and Ho Nam (PPD) vs. South Chung Chong province (NDRP) were created.

This structure of political regional division continued into the 13th National Assembly Elections held in April of 1988.[27] As can be seen in Table 4-1, the DJP and NDRP received a greater percentage of votes compared to the 13th Presidential Elections, while those received by the RDP and PPD decreased. When the earned votes rate of each party is compared across the major provinces and cities it is to be noted that with the exception of the NDRP, the DJP, PPD, and RDP all witnessed decreased total votes from their supporting regions. Therefore, it can be said that compared to the 13th Presidential Elections, the degree of political regional division decreased in the 13th National Assembly Elections.

---

[26] Ji Byung Moon, et al., *op. cit.*, p. 417.

[27] Following the 13th Presidential elections, there were some discussions on integration of the opposing parties. However due to leadership system problems and the status of Kim Young Sam and Kim Dae Jung, the idea was scrapped. Ji Byung Moon, et al., *Ibid.*, p. 420. This reveals the strongman party characteristics of both parties.

This can be explained first, by the fact that unlike the presidential election, in the general elections, the candidates were mostly from the same region. Second, this was a result of a substantial portion of voters favoring the opposition parties choosing not to exercise their voting rights. This is because they lost their sense of political effectiveness resulting from the failure to achieve a regime change in the 13th Presidential Elections.

Table 4-1.   Result of the 13th National Assembly Elections: Percentage of Votes and Number of Seats

Party Region	Democratic Justice Party	Reunification Democratic Party	Party for Peace And Democracy	New Democratic Republican Party
Seoul	26.2 / 10	23.4 / 10	27.0 / 17	16.1 / 3
Pusan	32.1 / 1	54.3 / 14 (-1.7)	1.9 / 0	6.8 / 0
Taeku	48.2 / 8 (-22.5)	28.4 / 0	0.7 / 0	13.2 / 0
Inchon	37.5 / 6	28.3 / 1	14.1 / 0	15.5 / 0
Kwang Ju	9.7 / 0	0.4 / 0	88.6 / 5 (-5.8)	0.6 / 0
Kyung Ki	36.1 / 16	22.9 / 4	15.9 / 1	18.2 / 6
Kang Won	43.6 / 8	21.6 / 3	4.0 / 0	20.2 / 1
N Chung Chong	43.6 / 7	16.0 / 0	0.4 / 0	33.3 / 2 (+19.8)
S Chung Chong	30.2 / 2	15.0 / 2	3.8 / 0	46.5 / 13 (+1.5)
N Cholla	28.8 / 0	1.3 / 0	61.5 / 14 (-22.0)	2.5 / 0
S Cholla	22.9 / 0	0.8 / 0	67.9 / 17 (-22.4)	1.3 / 0
N Kyung Sang	51.0 / 17 (-15.4)	24.5 / 2	0.9 / 0	16.0 / 2
S Kyung Sang	40.2 / 12	36.9 / 9 (-14.4)	1.0 / 0	10.3 / 0
Che Ju	36.0 / 0	27.1 / 1	6.0 / 0	3.4 / 0
Total	34.0 / 87	23.8 / 46	19.3 / 54	15.6 / 27

Numbers in the parentheses are differences from the 13th Presidential Elections.

In effect, the 13th National Assembly Elections were held after the 13th Presidential Elections in a situation where there were no major political issues. And in its election results, a political regional division was formed identical to that of the 13th Presidential Elections, with each party receiving absolute support from its own support region while the DJP and RDP were not even able to win a single seat in the Ho Nam region. The PPD faced the same fate in the Young Nam region. This clearly reflects that at the core of political regional division lies the conflict between the Young Nam and Ho Nam regions.

The structure and nature of the political regional division beginning since democratization and continuing into the 13th National Assembly Elections started to undergo changes during the Roh Tae Woo regime. The Roh administration, which had been heavily constrained by the divided government (opposition parties had the majority in the National Assembly), combined the DJP, RDP and NDRP to establish a giant ruling party, the

Liberal Democratic Party (LDP) in February 1990. A new player entered the game in the 14th National Assembly Elections held in March 1992, namely the National Party (NP) created by Chung Joo Young. Thus, the scene was set for some changes.

First of all, the unexpected, and sudden merging of the three parties, regardless of differing policies and political orientations, was achieved through the decision of the political leader, thus clearly reflecting the personality party characteristics of the RDP and NDRP.[28] Kim Young Sam of the RDP made the decision with the intent of running in the Presidential Elections as the ruling party's candidate, having recognized the difficulty of taking power in a four-party structure. Kim Jong Pil of the NDRP joined the merger in order to raise his status as a core leader of the ruling party. Such were the calculations behind the grand alliance of the conservative forces.[29]

Although the NP, which suddenly appeared on the scene with leader Chung Joo Young and Hyundai corporation as its backer, differentiated itself in terms of policy as an economy-oriented party, is a classic example of the establishment of a political party by a single person.

Table 4-2. Results of the 14th National Assembly and 14th Presidential Elections: Earned Votes Rate and Number of Seats

Party / Candidate Region	14th National Assembly Elections			14th Presidential Elections		
	LDP	DP	NP	Kim Young Sam	Kim Dae Jung	Chung Joo Young
Seoul	34.8 / 16	37.2 / 25	19.1 / 2	34.6	37.8	18.0
Pusan	51.8 / 15	19.4 / 0	10.2 / 0	73.3	12.5	6.3
Taeku	46.9 / 8	12.1 / 0	28.6 / 2	59.6	7.8	19.4
Inchon	34.3 / 5	30.8 / 1	20.4 / 0	37.3	31.7	21.4
Kwang Ju	9.1 / 0	76.4 / 6	3.9 / 0	2.1	95.9	1.2
Taejoun	27.6 / 1	25.5 / 2	21.3 / 0	35.2	28.7	23.3
Kyung Ki	37.1 / 18	31.9 / 8	19.6 / 5	36.3	32.0	23.1
Kang Won	38.8 / 8	11.7 / 0	31.9 / 4	41.5	15.5	34.1
N Chung Chong	44.6 / 6	23.8 / 1	21.5 / 2	38.3	26.0	23.9
S Chung Chong	43.4 / 7	20.2 / 1	16.0 / 4	36.9	28.6	25.3
N Cholla	31.8 / 2	55.0 / 12	4.8 / 0	5.7	89.1	3.2
S Cholla	25.2 / 0	61.6 / 19	5.0 / 0	4.2	92.1	2.1
N Kyung Sang	49.0 / 14	6.8 / 0	17.7 / 2	64.7	9.6	15.7
S Kyung Sang	45.6 / 16	8.7 / 0	20.4 / 3	72.3	9.2	11.5
Che Ju	34.1 / 0	19.9 / 0	0.0 / 0	40.0	32.9	16.2
Total	38.5 / 116	29.2 / 75	17.4 / 24	42.0	33.8	16.3

LDP: Liberal Democratic Party, DP: Democratic Party, NP: National Party.

---

[28] Lee Jung Hee, "Factionalization of Korean Party Politics" Korean Political Science Society, (ed.). *op. cit.*, p. 179.

[29] Kim Young Myoung, *Revised Modern Korean Political History* (Seoul: Ul Yoo Moon Hwa Sa, 1999), p. 289; Oh Myung Ho, *Understanding Modern Korean Political Science* (Seoul: Oruem, 1999), pp. 447-448.

In the case of the merger of the three parties, although there was a strong element of grand alliance of conservatives to block the emergence of radical forces, more pertinent was the political intent to exclude and marginalize the Ho Nam region. In the case of the NP, although Chung Joo Young could claim Kang Won province connections, the party was politically insignificant in terms of importance and influence. Therefore, in the 14th National Assembly Elections, the overall political regional division structure was projected to be Ho Nam vs non Ho Nam regions within which Young Nam vs. Ho-Nam was especially prominent. This is due to the fact the the Chung Chong provinces, the support base of Kim Jong Pil, supported the ruling party. More specifically, with the Chung Chong provinces, in effect, breaking away from the political regional division, the regional division structure came to be constructed around the Young Nam vs Ho Nam confrontation. Such a structure continued into the 14th Presidential Elections. Compared to the political regional division displayed in the 13th Presidential and National Assembly Elections, its structure narrowed down to a divisional structure between Young Nam and Ho Nam.

The reason why the regional divisional structure between Young Nam and Ho Nam deepened and took roots in the 14th National Assembly and Presidential Elections was due to the failure of the party system to outgrow its personal party characteristics centered around Kim Dae Jung and Kim Young Sam. In the 14th National Assembly and Presidential Elections, the LDP, originally a regional alliance party, came to assume the characteristics of a personal party centered around Kim Young Sam. In the case of the Democratic Party (DP), which was formed by merging the PPD and those who left the former RDP in the process of the merge between the three parties, was still a personal party centered around Kim Dae Jung. Such developments led to the perpetuation of the Young Nam vs Ho Nam political regional division. In the case of the NP, the party leader Chung Joo Young hailed from Kang Won province, so that the influence of such connections was minimal.

2. The Kim Young Sam Administration Era.

Kim Young Sam, having come to office through the 14th Presidential Elections, initiated political reform under the flag of a civilian government in order to eradicate the ills of previous authoritarian regimes. In the process, the North Kyung Sang province and Taeku forces who were at the center of the merger of the 3 parties suffered some suppression, and Kim Jong Pil's Chung Chong forces were marginalized. However, in the early days of the Kim Young Sam administration, popular support of the government was so high that these factions were not able to openly to express their discontent.

There is some controversy in evaluating the political reforms by the Kim

Young Sam administration, and the view that there were definite limitations to the reforms which were conducted more by the personal decisions of Kim Young Sam rather than through the relevant rules and procedures is dominant.[30] Especially from the standpoint of the party, it is at this juncture that the regional alliance nature of the LDP came to change into that of a personal party.

In contrast, with the defeat of the 14th Presidential Elections and consequent political retirement of Kim Dae Jung, the DP changed from a personal party to a regional party based on Ho Nam.

Table 3-5. Results of the 1995 Local Elections by Region (%)
ULD: United Liberal Democrats

Election Party Region	Governors/Majors			Small city majors		
	LDP	DP	ULD	LDP	DP	ULD
Seoul	20.7	42.4		35.0	47.9	3.8
Pusan	51.4	37.6		59.3	4.0	1.6
Taeku	16.9		22.1	26.3		5.6
Inchon	40.8	31.7	27.5	34.8	36.4	14.4
Kwang Ju	10.3	89.7		11.9	83.0	
Taejun	20.9	10.8	63.8	17.3	18.1	57.0
Kyung Ki	40.6	29.6	10.2	31.0	32.8	5.8
Kang Won	34.2		65.8	29.7	15.8	8.7
N Chung Chong	23.3	24.5	36.4	30.7	13.9	22.6
S Chung Chong	19.2	12.9	67.9	24.8	7.0	53.6
N Cholla	32.8	67.2		23.6	54.7	0.9
S Cholla	26.4	73.6		13.9	50.5	0.3
N Kyung Sang	37.9		27.7	27.9	7.7	3.4
S Kyung Sang	63.8		36.2	33.7	8.0	
Che Ju	32.5	24.3		40.9	10.2	
Total	33.3	30.1	17.3	31.8	28.8	8.0

In the case of the ruling party, internal resistance was inevitable with political power shifting from North Kyung Sang province and Taeku to South Kyung Sang province and Pusan and transformation from a regional alliance

---

[30] Choi Jang Gip, "Democratization of Korea: Implementation and Reform," Choi Jang Gip, Lim Hyun Jin, (eds.), *Challenge of the Civil Society: Korean Democratization and State, Capital and Labor* (Seoul: Na Nam, 1993), pp. 27-51; Kil Seong Heum, "Basic Direction of New Korea Political Reform," Han Lim Science Institute, (ed.), *New Korea Policy Task* (Seoul: Na Nam, 1993), p. 20-39; Son Ho Chul, "Civilian Government and Political Reform: Characteristics and Limitations," Son Ho Chul, *50 Years of Korean Politics since Liberation* (Seoul: Se Kil, 1995), pp. 263-283.

party to a personal party. In this situation, Kim Jong Pil left the LDP and established the United Liberal Democrats (ULD) several months before the local elections in 1995 with the joining of the North Kyung Sang faction who were alienated from the LDP. Therefore, the 1995 local elections were held in a structure where two personal parties, the LDP and ULD, and one regional party, DP, competed against each other. Table 3-5 shows the election results providing evidence of a political regional division, where the LDP came out strong in South Kyung Sang province, the DP in the Ho Nam region and ULD in the Chung Chong region.

These results reveal how the existing political regional division of Ho Nam vs. non-Hon Nam or Young Nam vs Ho Nam changed through the local elections into a triangular structure of South Kyung Sang province and Pusan (LDP), vs Ho Nam (DP) vs Chung Chong (ULD).

In addition, the unexpectedly good showing of the ULD in the traditional ruling party support base of North Kyung Sang province, and the election of the ULD candidate as mayor of Taeku, demonstrates the power shift from North Kyung Sang province and Taeku to South Kyung Sang province and Pusan and the resistance against the personal party of the LDP centered by Kim Young Sam. The overwhelming support given to the ULD by North Chung Chong province, where previously Kim Jong Pil by himself had not been able to obtain dominant support, added to the developments shaping the new political regional division. In other words, the political regional division at the time is characterized by the division within the Young Nam region and the emergence of the Chung Chong region, becoming diversified from the existing confrontation structure of Young Nam vs Ho Nam.

These political regional divisions underwent new changes in the months preceding the 15th National Assembly Elections as Kim Dae Jung, encouraged by the local election results, reentered politics, creating the National Congress for New Politics (NCNP) in July 1995, which resulted in the disintegration of the existing DP into the NCNP and DP. The LDP also changed its name to the New Korea Party (NKP).

Kim Dae Jung's political comeback retriggered the rise of regionalism at a time when overall political regional division was weakening.[31] The emergence of a personal party in the form of the NCNP at a time when the DP, no longer showing the characteristics of a personal party, fared well overall in the local elections due to the alliance of politicians who opposed the three-party merger.[32] Traditional factional politics led to the eventual demise of the minority DP and provided the opportunity for strengthening political regional divisions. At the same time, it exposed Korea's bent toward personal parties.

---

[31] Son Ho Chul (1997), *op. cit.*, p. 469.

[32] Kim Young Myoung, *op. cit.*, p. 306.

Therefore, in the 15th National Assembly Elections, with the exception of the DP, all parties which participated in the elections were personal parties centered around the 3- Kims again.

The political regional division as evidenced in the 15th National Assembly Elections were very similar to that of the 13th National Assembly Elections with the exception of Taeku. All 3 Kims received full support from their home provinces, sweeping most of the seats. The NKP in Young Nam and Pusan, the NCNP in Ho Nam, and the ULD in Chung Chong provinces, emerged dominant, creating a political regional division of Young Nam and Pusan (NKP) vs Ho Nam (NCNP) vs Chung Chong and Taeku (ULD).

In short, as can be seen from Table 3-6 , the resistance expressed by North Kyung Sang province and Taeku against the Kim Young Sam government in the 1995 local elections, turned around to support for the NKP in North Kyung Sang province in the 15th National Assembly Elections, while Taeku's antagonism toward the ruling party was strengthened. In North Kyung Sang province, while the NKP took 11 (57. 9%) out of the 19 seats, they managed to take only 2 (15.4%) out of the 13 seats in Taeku. The fact that from the remaining 11 seats, the ULD took 8 and Independents took 3, gives evidence to this claim.

This development points toward some changes in the political regional division, with the Taeku region which harbored feelings against both the Kim Young Sam government and Ho Nam province, allied with the ULD, which represents the Chung Chong region. However, the meager 9 seats won by the DP despite a relatively high polling rate of 11.2%, through its appeal to the eradication of regionalism and "3-Kim" politics, demonstrates the difficulty of national and policy-oriented parties surviving under an electoral system of First-Past-The-Post and the personal party system.

The structure and nature of the political regional division created in the 15th National Assembly Elections again underwent change in the 15th Presidential Elections in 1997 as the NCNP and ULD came together to present Kim Dae Jung as a unitary candidate from the opposition parties. Under the recognition that control of power would be difficult in the political regional divisional structure, Kim Dae Jung induced an alliance with Kim Jong Pil to the so-called "DJP (Dae Jung and Jong Pil Kim) Alliance." The alliance was possible basically because of the strong "personalparty" characteristics of both parties. This enabled them to overcome or ignore the vast differences existing between the political lines held by the parties and the past relationship of the party leaders. In contrast, the ruling party began to undergo changes in its partisan characteristics, with the selection of Lee Hae Chang, a non-Young Nam politician, through a presidential candidate selection competition, and a party name change to the Grand National Party (GNP).

Table 3-6.   Results of the 15th National Assembly Elections and Number of Seats by Region

Party Region	NKP	NCNP	LDU	DP
Seoul	36.5 / 27	35.2 / 18	11.3 / 0	13.5 / 1
Pusan	55.8 / 21	6.4 / 0	5.5 / 0	17.1 / 0
Taeku	24.5 / 2	1.4 / 0	35.8 / 8	4.0 / 0
Inchon	38.2 / 9	29.5 / 2	14.5 / 0	11.0 / 0
Kwang Ju	7.5 / 0	86.2 / 6	0.8 / 0	2.0 / 0
Taejun	21.5 / 0	11.4 / 0	49.8 / 7	11.6 / 0
Kyung Ki	33.2 / 18	27.4 / 10	18.6 / 5	13.9 / 3
Kang Won	37.3 / 9	6.7 / 0	23.6 / 2	14.5 / 2
N Chung Chong	31.7 / 2	8.9 / 0	39.4 / 5	8.9 / 0
S Chung Chong	28.9 / 1	6.1 / 0	51.2 / 12	7.9 / 0
N Cholla	23.4 / 1	63.7 / 13	0.5 / 0	5.8 / 0
S Cholla	17.7 / 0	71.0 / 17	1.3 / 0	0.8 / 0
N Kyung Sang	34.9 / 11	1.6 / 0	0.6 / 2	6.9 / 1
S Kyung Sang	46.5 / 17	4.2 / 0	4.7 / 0	14.7 / 2
Che Ju	37.2 / 3	29.4 / 0	1.2 / 0	2.0 / 0
Total	35.4 / 121	25.3 / 66	16.2 / 41	11.2 / 9

While the NKP was a personal party centered around Kim Young Sam, the GNP with Lee Hae Chang at its head showed strong characteristics of a regional party. This means that while in the case of the NKP, Kim Young Sam maintained close ties with the regional voters, in the case of the GNP, ties began to be formed between the regional voters and the GNP as a regional party, rather than with any individual in the name of Lee Hae Chang. Therefore, the 15th Presidential Elections can be seen as a direct competition between one regional party (GNP) and one personal party coalition (NCNP and ULD).

Table 3-7. Results of the 15th Presidential Elections by Region (%)

Candidate/party Region	Lee Hae Chang (GNP)	Kim Dae Jung (NCNP+ULD Coalition)	Lee In Jae (NPP)
Seoul	40.9	44.9	12.8
Pusan	53.3	15.3	29.8
Taeku	72.7	12.5	13.1
Inchon	36.4	38.5	23.0
Kwang Ju	1.7	97.3	0.7
Ulsan	51.3	15.4	26.7
Kyung Ki	35.5	39.3	23.6
Kwang Won	43.2	23.8	30.9
N Chung Chong	30.8	37.4	29.4
S Chung Chong	23.5	48.3	26.1
N Cholla	4.5	92.3	2.1
S Cholla	3.2	94.7	1.4
N Kyung Sang	61.9	13.7	21.8
S Kyung Sang	55.1	11.0	31.3
Che Ju	36.6	40.6	20.5
Total	38.7	40.3	19.2

In the elections, with the ruling party beset by difficulties caused by the economic crisis, and the military service exemption controversy of candidate Lee Hae Chang's son, as well as Lee In Je's decision to run for the presidency independently from the GNP, meant that Kim Dae Jung of the bi-partisan coalition won the election by the slimmest margins; only 1.6% of the popular vote. There is some controversy about whether or not to interpret this outcome as a Ho Nam vs non-Ho Nam election or a Young Nam vs Ho Nam and Chung Chong one.

Externally however, there is no doubt that despite their hostility against the Ho Nam region, Chung Chong voters supported Kim Dae Jung, thereby creating a Young Nam vs Ho Nam and Chung Chong regional division structure. This, with respect to the 15th Presidential Election outcome, it is significant that the GNP was able to win back the anti-ruling party support of Taeku by changing from a personal party centered around Kim Young Sam to a regional party embracing the whole Young Nam region. Also worth mentioning is that in the bi-partisan coalition between Kim Dae Jung and Kim Jong Pil, Chung Chong province voters were able to support Kim Dae Jung despite their hostility to Ho Nam province because of Kim Jong Pil. This signifies that in Korea's political regional division, party leader (person) and regional party (region) are at the center and that by the change of the leader such a structure is susceptible to change.

V. Regional Divisions in the Future

Due to the first ever regime change between the ruling and opposition party in the 15th Presidential Elections, changes in the structure and nature of political regional divisions were predicted. This was because many expected the chronic regional conflict between Young Nam and Ho Nam to be alleviated by the change of regime. Such claims were based on the prediction that the only means of abating the resistance and regional emotions harbored by Ho Nam residents is through the control of power by Ho Nam province, and once this is achieved, ways to reduce the regional gaps would be sought.

These prospects for weakening political regional divisions were strengthened by the results of the opinion polls conducted in the early days of Kim Dae Jung's administration. In them, Young Nam province gave high marks to both Kim Dae Jung personally and his style of governance, and also showed great support for the NCNP.

For example, in the early days of Kim Dae Jung's administration, while nationally, 78.9% showed satisfaction with his administration, Pusan and South Kyung Sang province showed an 81.7% satisfaction level, higher than the national average.[33] Also, in terms of party support, while the GNP obtained 27.9% in Pusan and South Kyung Sang province, and 30.1% in Taeku and North Kyung Sang province, the NCNP was not far behind with 26.6% and 21.3% respectively.[34]

Table 5-1. Results of 1998 Local Elections by Region

Election /party Region	Governors/Mayors(%)			Small city majors(Number)			Local Assembly Members(Number)		
	NKP	NCNP	ULD	NKP	NCNP	ULD	NKP	NCNP	ULD
Pusan	45.1	11.4		11			43		1
Ulsan	42.7		7.9	3			9		
N Kyung Sang	72.0		28.0	14	1	2	44		5
S Kyung Sang	74.6	12.8		14			41		
Kwang Ju		67.2			5			14	
N Cholla		100.0			9			32	
S Cholla		100.0			15			42	1
Taejun			73.7		1	4			14
N Chung Chong	25.9		74.1		2	6		3	17
S Chung Chong	15.4		84.6			11		1	30
Total	40.6	34.5	15.3	74	84	29	224	271	82

Despite such predictions however, when the results of the 1998 Local Elections, the first election held after the regime change, were examined, one finds that the political regional division has not been alleviated and is as strong as ever. As can be seen in Table 5-1, in the case of provincial governors and metropolitan mayorality elections, the GNP swept the seats in Young

---

[33] *Han Kyeu Re* Newspaper, 11 February, (1998), p. 2.

[34] *Kyung Hyang* Newspaper, 7 October, (1998), p. 4.

Nam, the NCNP in Ho Nam, and the ULD in Chung Chong. Moreover, the fact that with the exception of North Chung Chong province and South Chung Chong province governors, the GNP was not able to run a candidate in any of the regions supporting the ruling party. Moreover, the poor showing of 10% received by candidates representing the NCNP and ULD in the Young Nam provinces reveals that political regional division has become in effect more pronounced after the regime change.

The same phenomenon was also to be witnessed in the small city mayoralty and Provincial Assembly elections, where NCNP and ULD under cooperation managed to together obtain a seat or two in Young Nam, while the GNP failed to win even a single seat in the Ho Nam and Chung Chong regions.[35] Considering these election results, many pundits suggest that even if a change of regime is achieved and the 3 Kims retire from the political scene in the near future, political regional divisions will continue for some time.

Korea is thus faced with the question of how to approach the problem of political regional division. Previous arguments have pointed to the inability of existing parties to overcome the limitations of the personal party and regional party as the cause of the current manifestation of political regional divisions.

In short, Korea's political regional division emerged in the process of creating the personal parties of the 3 Kims during the democratization period, and in the subsequent years a vicious cycle continued, where no workable solution was found amid the absence of a new and national political issue and the lack of effort by the parties to transform themselves into policy-oriented or national parties. Therefore, the search for solutions to political regional divisions might well focus on the party system.

Table 3-7. Typology of Korean Parties in the Post Democratization Years

Region Party Leader	Strong	Weak
Strong	Type C: Quasi-personal Party, Quasi-Regional Party, Quasi-Policy Party(Person»Party, Person»Region, Party^1 Region)	Type A Personal party (Person=Party=Region)
Weak	Type D: National Party, Policy-oriented Party (Person^1 Region^1 Party)	Type B: Regional Party (Person^1 Region, Person^1 Party, Region=Party)

[35] Lee Nam Young, who has made a comparative analysis on the regionalism as was manifested in the 2nd Local Elections with the 15th Presidential Elections, pointed out that in a situation where hostility is felt by other regions toward Ho Nam province, regional variables played a critical role in determining the election results. Lee Nam Young, *op. cit.*, pp. 15-41.

Based on our discussions to this point, the most critical elements in classifying Korean Parties in the post-democratization years are individual person (party leader) and region. With these two standards, classification of parties into 4 types is possible.

First in type A, parties that have formed close ties between the party leader, party, and region. Examples like the parties of the 3 Kims, fall into this category. Type B consists of parties where its leaders are not solid representatives of certain regions, and ones which do not show signs of personalization of party, but demonstrate instead close ties between the party and the region. The Democratic Justice Party of the past and the present GNP fall into this category. Parties of type C are ones in which the political leaders show some connection to the region and party, but are not based on regional support. Finally, those included in type D are parties which do not have connections between the party leader, party and region, and which compete nationally through policy agendas. Parties coming closest to this ideal are the existing minor parties such as the People's Victory Party in the 15th Presidential Elections.

Our own conclusion is that the reason Korea even now witnesses the continuation of regional political divisions is due to the fact that the parties were unable to develop into national or policy-oriented parties, succeeding only in transforming from a personal party to a regional party and vice versa. Therefore, critical in projecting the future of political regional divisions and searching for its solutions, the task is to focus on ways to increase the possibility of national and policy-oriented parties emerging amidst the shifting of personal parties to regional parties caused by the disappearance of political leaders having regions as their bases of power.

Based on the analysis of the present study, it is difficult to foresee an easy, short term change in the structure and nature of regionalism even when continuous transfer of power between political parties is effected, when the 3 Kims leave the political scene, and regional emotions improve.

Thus, there is still some hope that from a long-term perspective, political regional divisions will be alleviated and eventually eradicated. As the influence of the Kims, which acted as the nucleus of political regional division increasingly weakens and finally disappears with the passing of time, the existing personal parties will change to regional parties. It seems likely that in the new climate, it will become more and more difficult for regional parties to monopolize the seats in local or National Assembly elections. In other words, although political regional divisions will continue for some time in the Presidential elections, with the decreasing influence of the regional parties in local and National Assembly elections, there is more room for national or policy-oriented parties to emerge. It is highly likely that a new national issue such as class consciousness will surface by experiencing both economic development and crisis. More important, if the political sector is unable to achieve change and reform, it will be confronted with the resistance of a future civil society. This means that ultimately, with the importance of regional issues decreasing, the existing parties have no choice but to become national and policy parties.

There are numerous questions to be dealt with in regard to the emergence of national and policy-oriented parties. In such issues as promoting democratic practices within parties related to candidate nomination, establishment and management of party organizations, the appropriate role of party headquarter and local branches, the failure of existing parties to assume proper roles and functions within the limitations posed by personal parties and regional parties, should be criticized and corrected.[36] However, the most important point to emphasize in dealing with partisan issues related to political regional divisions, is to create an institutional mechanism which might prevent the emergence of personal and regional parties brought about by political leaders such as the 3 Kims.

Some solutions seem possible. First of all, in order to solve the problem of personal parties, two kinds of institutional mechanisms are needed. One is a legal mechanism which militates against the change of party membership of National Assembly members. The reason that parties could be quickly created and maintained by the 3 Kims in the past was due to the behavior of National Assembly members who could be mobilized to participate in the creation of a new party. National Assembly members frequently changed party membership from opposition to ruling party to receive favorable support from the government, contributing to the perpetuation of personal parties.

Therefore, if a legal mechanism prohibiting or limiting the change of party membership of National Assembly members could be instituted, it would play a major role in preventing the emergence of personal parties and maintain the continuance of parties. If a total ban on party membership change is difficult, then legal mechanisms should be instituted that allow it only when the member has explicitly declared his/her intention to the voters during the election campaign period, or force members who have left their parties to remain as independents.[37] The other mechanism is one which

---

[36] For a more detailed discussion of party system reform, refer to Chong Young Dae, "15th Presidential Elections and Task of Korean Party Politics," Korean Political Science Society, (ed.), *op. cit.*, pp. 212-227; Chang Hoon, "From an elite centered closed political organization to an citizen centered open organization," *Idea* (Summer 1999), pp. 70-88.

[37] For example, in the case the 14th National Assembly, among the 237 members elected from their constituency, 130, over half, have changed their parties. Lee Young Hee, *op. cit.*, p. 177. And the reason for this is due to the emergence of personal parties centered around the 3 Kims. For example, this occurred when Kim Young Sam changed the Democratic Liberal Party into a personal party based on South Kuyng Song province of Pusan, and when Kim Dae Jung and Kim Jong Pil created the NCNP and ULD respectively.

enables the decrease of the power of party leaders. Most criticisms against Korean parties are directed at the excessive power concentrated in the party leader. Therefore, ways to limit the influence of the party leader in matters of candidate nomination, political funds, and management of party organization, in addition to means of encouraging the participation of backbenchers must be approached from various angles. For example, with respect to candidate nomination, the party leader can be divested from his right to declare his preferences or make the ultimate decision, being limited to simply confirm candidates selected through primary elections. Laws to prohibit any party leader from receiving or raising funds could also be considered.

IV. Conclusions

This paper has defined regionalism in the post-democratization period as "political regional division" in that it is inherently political, and shows clear regional divisions in terms of candidates and parties supported, unlike the regionalism of the era preceding democratization. With this definition, based on the outcomes of elections held since the 13th Presidential Elections, the study has examined the causes and changes of political regional divisions focusing on the relationship between the party and the political leader. Research findings have revealed that although Korea's regionalism is a phenomenon with deep historical roots, brought about by the complex interaction of various factors, the ultimate cause lies with the Korean political parties which are unable to outgrow the limitations of personal and regional parties centered around the 3 Kims. In addition it has been shown that the structure of political regional divisions underwent dynamic changes according to the choices and decisions made by the party leaders.

This study predicts that in the short term, even when the 3 Kims retire from the political scene and some transfer of government between political parties is effected, political regional divisions will not disappear in the absence of new circumstances that enable the emergence of national and policy-oriented parties. In the longer term, however, there exist the possibility of the decline of political regional divisions. Specifically, measures to penalize the change of party membership among National Assembly members, decrease the power of the party leader, and impose sanctions against the instigation of regionalism might occasion change for the better.

Research on Korea's regionalism up to the present has been conducted from various angles, but were mostly focused on the regional conflict between the Young Nam and Ho Nam region, stressing the emotional aspects and failing to capture its changes from the static approaches they have adopted. Also by concentrating only on analyzing the phenomenon of regionalism itself, they have failed to suggest practical solutions. In the present study, the problematic nature of the Korean party system, characterized by personal parties and regional parties has been emphasized as the key cause of political regional divisions.

Korea, like Canada, experiences the politics of regionalism.

KOREAN-CANADIAN TRADE:
BEFORE AND AFTER THE ASIAN FINANCIAL CRISIS

JAE-DONG HAN
UNIVERSITY OF WESTERN ONTARIO

I. Introduction

Korea and Canada rank within the top ten among each other's trading partners. Both are highly open economies, and foreign trade accounts for the lion's share of aggregate expenditures. In terms of resource endowment, Korea and Canada are very complementary.

Even a cursory look at the absolute volume of Canada-Korea trade leads both Koreans and Canadians to appreciate the rapid growth of bilateral trade (See Figure 1). However, detailed statistical analysis shows Korean and Canadian trade authorities are far apart in many aspects of their assessment of the current situation regarding the bilateral trade. In this paper, I attempt to have a closer look at the conditions surrounding the Korean-Canadian bilateral trade. I will examine the Korean as well as the Canadian statistical data, which in fact prove to be quite different. Other related issues will be briefly discussed although in the present paper, our focus is kept on the overall macroeconomic view.

I will also set up a quantitative model for Korean-Canadian trade respectively, and estimate the two models with quarterly data from 1980-99 collected by Statistics Canada, which are more comprehensive than the Korean data. I will attempt to interpret the regression results, and in the process of interpretation, I will test the validity of some conventional wisdom about Korean-Canadian trade. I will also try to infer some practical policy implications.

II. Korean-Canadian Bilateral Trade: Two Different Perspectives

Korean authorities have expressed two major concerns about Korean-Canadian bilateral trade: first, as shown in Figure 1, based upon the Korean trade data, the absolute amount of Korean exports has shown a trend toward stagnation or decrease since the late 1980s. As a result, according to the Korean trade data, the share of Korean exports to Canada as a percentage of total Korean exports has been sharply declining from over 3% in the mid 1980s to about 1.5% in the mid 1990s. On the other hand, they note that Korean imports from Canada have shown quite a different trend. The absolute amount has been in line with the growth of the overall Korean imports from the world. Thus the share of Canada in Korean imports has been more or less stable at around 2% throughout the 1980s and the 1990s. Figure 2 shows the Canadian share of total Korean exports and imports. One can easily draw a sharp downward sloping trend-line for Korean exports to Canada while a slightly upward sloping trend-line can be drawn for Korean imports from Canada.

The gap between the stagnating exports and the growing imports has put Korea in the position of a balance-of-trade deficit with respect to Canada. Furthermore, as shown in Figure 1, which is based on Korean trade statistics, Korean trade deficits have been growing rapidly. This is the second concern voiced by Korean authorities.

Why do trade deficits worry the policy makers? It would take a simple-minded, outmoded Mercantilist to abhor trade deficits as a robber of national wealth, but even in the modern Keynesian framework of macroeconomics, trade deficits are regarded as "leakage" or "withdrawal" from the circular flow of income and expenditures on domestic products. An increase in imports and the resultant trade deficits are regarded as depriving the nation of jobs. If an X amount of imported goods are produced in domestic firms using domestic factors of production, there would be a higher level of employment or utilization of human and physical capital.

Persistent and growing trade deficits for one side may lead to disputes between the trading partners which often strains the goodwill between them. Disgruntled policy makers might well ask their foreign counterparts to make efforts, non-market oriented, to rectify the current situation and stem the trend in the future.

However, Canadian trade authorities have a quite different view: Canada has been experiencing deficits in Canadian-Korean bilateral trade, and the trade deficits have been growing since the early 1980s. Figure 3, which is based on trade statistics collected by the Canadian customs authorities, makes this point.

According to the Canadian data, despite its declining trend, the share of Canadian imports from Korea in Canada's total imports is higher than the share of Canadian exports to Korea in Canada's total exports. In a word, Canada is extending more than its fair share of courtesy and goodwill toward

Korea among its many trading partners. Figure 5 shows that a growing share of U.S. products dominated the Canadian import market in the 1990s, and Figure 6 shows that in the face of rapid advancement by Chinese exporters, the decreased Korean share of total Canadian imports is no worse than that of Japan or Hong Kong.

In fact, our simple juxtaposition of the two data sets shows that the differences in viewpoint between Korean and Canadian authorities stem from the differences in the statistical data on which their analyses are respectively based. The largest gap between Canadian and Korean data lies in the Korean exports to Canada, or the Canadian imports from Korea. In addition, the gap is growing as shown in Figure 4, which is based on both Korean and Canadian statistical data.

One obvious reason for the difference is that, in collecting the data, the Korean trade authorities use the CIF basis method while the Canadian trade authorities adopt the FOB method. In a word, only the merchandise explicitly heading for Canada is captured as Korean exports to Canada in the Korean statistics, while all the merchandise 'originating' from Korea without regard to their immediate shipping location are captured as the imports from Korea in the Canadian statistics. The difference between the two is the amount of goods that go through a third country or countries before they get to Canada.

For two reasons, this kind of circuitous movement of Korean export products has been increasing. First, increasingly globalized Korean multinational enterprises have been setting up subsidiaries overseas since the 1980s. The base merchandise may therefore originate from Korea, but pick up value-added features through stages of processing in a third country or countries. Some of these products are classified by the Canadian customs authorities as Korean for their "country of origin". Second, in the early 1990s, the North American Trade Agreement (NAFTA hereafter) led Canadian customs to reinforce the above practice of assessment of the country of origin. Today, Canadian customs authorities have a reputation for their thorough and elaborate scheme for the assessment of the country of origin of imported goods.[1]

At a different level, the NAFTA treaty among Canada, U.S. and Mexico might compound international trade with non-member countries, such as Korea. It is reported that some Korean firms supply their merchandise for

---

[1] Refer to *Integration and Trade in the America*, Inter-American Development Bank, October 1999.

Canada via the U.S.[2] In principle, Korean goods carry differential tariffs between U.S. and Canada when they come to Canada over the border. Despite some anecdotal cases where differential tariffs are being charged, there is no evidence that the Korean firms can cut down on the combined total tariffs by sending their merchandises via the circuitous route.

Then, what is the incentive for this circuitous kind of export? The answer is probably found in U.S.-Canadian differences in transactions or marketing costs, which stems from economies of scale in marketing, so that a U.S. marketing company with Canadian branches may have cost advantages over a potential Canadian direct importer of Korean products. As an increasing number of U.S. marketing giants are taking over the Canadian market, the intra-firm shipment of Korean merchandise over the border may lead to an increase in the gap between the CIF and the FOB statistics. It would be an interesting future research project to further investigate what opportunities for profitable arbitrage NAFTA provides for international trade in its member countries.

There is also some agreement of views on bilateral trade between Canada and Korea: the trade has exhibited considerable fluctuation, and the degree of fluctuation has been increasing in recent years.

III. A Statistical Analysis of Korean-Canadian Trade

Naturally our next questions are, "What has caused the fluctuations and changes in trade between Canada and Korea?" and "Can they be fully explained by economic variables?" These are interesting for two reasons: First, they shed light on our understanding of the causes of changes in the Canadian-Korean bilateral trade. By employing the right analytical tools of statistical studies, we can test whether and to what extent a particular factor affects the trade. Second, analysis should dispel any lingering doubts about the fairness of each party in the bilateral trade.

As there are many factors that affect exports and imports, this question can be best dealt with using the technique of multivariate regression analysis which basically separates the impact of each determinant while controlling - holding constant- all others. Economics and statistics theories behind the quantitative analysis in this paper are given in 'Appendix 1: Technical Notes'. Specific information on data and their sources is given in 'Appendix 2: Data'. Here I will present the summary of the regression results and their implications.

---

[2] Computer chips are a good example in where the circuitous exports to Canada, via U.S., are larger than the direct exports to Canada. Refer to a recent report by Mr. J. G. Lee, Toronto KOTRA.

1. Canadian Imports of Korean Merchandise

First, we must construct a functional relationship between imports or exports and their determinants. The functions are based on the general demand model of international trade. In terms of time horizon, a change in any determinant may induce a response over multiple periods of time; it would take time for the change to ripple through and finally die down. These long-term cumulative effects will be fully captured by the so-called 'Partial Adjustment Model of Trade', which is fully explained in Appendix 1.

The variables that we adopt to explain the changes in the exports or imports are basically the national income of the importing countries, the price level of both countries, the price index of international competitors for the exporting nation, and the foreign exchange rates or the currency exchange rates between the two countries. We may also come up with non-economic variables which pick up the impact of policy or structural changes.

The higher the national income level of Canada, the larger its import demand for Korean products. On the other hand, the price level or the aggregate average prices of the Korean export products is measured by the producer price index of the manufacturing industry, which is the mainstay of Korean exports.

The higher the Korean producer price index, the lower the Canadian demand for Korean manufactured commodities. The price level of Canadian major export products is measured by the Commodity Price Index. The prices of competitors' products faced by the Korean exporter in the Canadian market are measured by the Canadian Implicit Index of Merchandise Imports. Of course, the Korean export products are included in the computation of the Implicit Index. However, given the relatively small weights of the Korean products in the Canadian imports, we can safely assume the overall import price index is, by and large, independent of the Korean producers price index. Thus the Canadian Implicit Index of Merchandise Import variable allows us to measure the so-called 'Cross-Price Elasticity': To what numerical degrees are the Korean exports to Canada affected by a percentage change in the prices of the substitutes from international competitors?

Second, we run the multivariate regression technique to estimate the coefficient of the export and import functions. To measure the elasticity of each variable, we have taken the logarithmic values of data. In this case, the estimated value of the coefficient of an explanatory variable gives a direct measure of what percentage changes in the exports or imports will be brought out by a percentage change in that explanatory variable.

The regression results for the estimation of the Canadian imports from Korea can be summarized as follows:

A 1% Increase in Explanatory Variables	leads to a change in Canadian Imports from Korea by	Short-run Elasticity	Long-run Elasticity
Canadian GDP		1.23 % (+)	2.93% (+)
Korean Producer's Prices		0.74% (-)*	1.76% (-)*
International Competitors' Prices		2.15 % (+)	5.11 % (+)
Value of Canadian Dollars against Korean Won		0.22% (+)*	0.52% (+)*

Note: * Its t-value is less than 1.99, and thus is statistically insignificant. We cannot reject the null hypothesis that they have no impact on the imports.

As shown in the detailed technical report of the regression in Appendix 3.2, the (partial) adjustment coefficient is 0.57, meaning that it takes about a year for the trade to fully adjust to a changing factor.

All of the estimators are found to have the right signs. The most important determinants for Canadian imports from Korea turn out to be the Canadian GDP, and the International Competitors' Price Index. On the other hand, the prices of Korean exports themselves and currency exchange rates have virtually no significant impact. In other words, the base price elasticity is low, and the cross elasticities are very high.

These results bring a set of interesting interpretations for the underlying causes of the somewhat wildly fluctuating Korean exports to Canada. First, we note that the magnitude of the estimated income elasticity is larger than one: The Canadian demand for Korean outputs is highly income elastic. This suggests that as long as the Canadian economy is growing, its demand for Korean products will grow and the growth rates will exceed that of the Canadian GDP. In the long-run, this is good news as the Canadian economy is expected to grow in a solid manner. However, it also suggests that Canadian imports of Korean products are highly cyclical: At a downturn of the Canadian business cycle, the demand for Korean products will take a deeper cut than the overall business. In the medium term, this feature means a wide swing in the performances of Korean exports to Canada, amplified by the Canadian business cycle. This is the major explanation for the apparent instability of post-1980 Korean exports.

A relatively small magnitude of the estimated price elasticity seems to contradict the conventional wisdom that the rising costs of Korean export industry are the major cause for the apparently sliding Korean exports in

Canada. It may seem puzzling that Korean exports were, all in all, unaffected by the rising price level of the export industry.

My interpretation for this apparent paradox is that the rising price index or weighted-average prices of a mixture of disparate outputs may reflect, to a certain extent, the improving quality of Korean outputs, or the changing composition of low versus high value-added products within the manufacturing industry which covers various types of merchandise. Canadian consumers are willing to pay higher prices for some Korean products as long as they are of an improved quality or are new products. The increase in export revenues more than offsets the shrinking exports of the conventional Korean outputs of a relatively low quality.

This may be evidence that the Korean export industry as a whole has been scoring a success in moving upward along the ladder of quality and unit prices in the Canadian market, though caution should be exercised in applying the above result to Korean products of a fixed quality over time. The base price elasticity might be higher than our results indicate if we estimate the export function with a break-down of the industry classification or on an individual product level.

On the other hand, the relatively large magnitude of the estimated cross (price) elasticity implies that Korean exports are faced with fierce competition from other countries. A 1% increase in the price index of international competitors to Korea leads to a 2.5% increase in Canadian imports from Korea within 3 months and over 5% on a cumulative basis over a year or so. A higher price level of competitors induces Canadians to switch the demand from competitors to Korean producers. This formally confirms the argument that developing countries such as China and Vietnam have been eroding the traditional Korean base in the Canadian market.

The combination of the two results as regards to the price elasticities seems to suggest that, for the Korean export industry, a successful strategy should focus on how fast the Korean export industry can move along the scale of quality and how smoothly it can make an intra-industry restructuring. Given the degree of competition and market pressures, there is an ample justification, or need, for the resources spent in Canada by the Korean firms and government on various marketing endeavors. In a sense, marketing seems to be a lot more of an important factor than the unit cost when it comes to Korean exports to Canada.

Additionally, I have also tested whether NAFTA or the recent Asian financial crisis has affected Canadian imports from Korea in any significant manner. We have constructed and included the dummy variables representing NAFTA and the Asian financial crisis. The test results indicate that both were factors.

However, interestingly enough, the Asian Crisis has favorably affected Canadian imports from Korea. This might be due to the special marketing efforts and export-drives launched by Korean firms and the ROK government at the onset of the international liquidity crisis.

2. Canadian Exports to Korea

The result of the estimation of the Korean demand for Canadian export goods is summarized as follow:

A 1% Increase in Explanatory Variables	leads to a change in Korea Imports from Canadian by	Short-run Elasticity	Long-run Elasticity
Korean GDP		0.35 % (+)	0.61% (+)
Canadian Commodity Prices		0.60% (-)	1.05% (-)
International Competitors' Prices		0.74 % (+)	1.30 % (+)
Value of Canadian Dollars against Korean Won		0.94% (-)	1.65% (-)

Note: The (partial) adjustment coefficient is 0.58, and is very close to that found for Korean exports to Canada.

In the short-run, Canadian exports to Korea are determined by the Korean GDP, the Canadian (Export) Commodity Price Index, international competitors' prices, and currency exchange rates. All of these variables are found to be statistically significant. However, the statistical results indicate that the Asian Crisis and NAFTA has exerted no impact on the Canadian exports to Korea.

The low income elasticity and the low base-price elasticity are more or less expected of the Canadian exports which mainly consist of primary industry outputs. The Korean import demand for Canadian products responds, to the largest extent, to the currency exchange rate among many possible factors. This means that Canadian exports to Korea are quite sensitive to the external value of the Canadian dollar. The relative strength of the Canadian exports to Korea has been largely due to a weak Canadian dollar for the last couple of years.

The next most important variable for Canadian exports to Korea is the cross-price elasticity, or the prices of international competitors who compete with the Canadian exporters. This indicates that the Canadian export industry is faced with a quite high level of competition from its international competitors, and if we ran the regression at the individual product level, it would be even higher.

IV. Conclusion

This paper attempts some macroeconomic analysis of the general features of Canadian-Korean trade. Each of the two countries claims that it is experiencing persistent and growing trade deficits. It shows that there exists some major differences in the assessment of the bilateral trade situation between Canadian and Korean perspectives. This paper shows that the differences stem from the differences in data sets that they use. The discrepancy is the largest in the Canadian imports from Korea, to which Canada and Korea apply differing data collection methodologies. Some structural changes, such as NAFTA, have compounded the long standing technical differences, and contributed to a growing gap between the data of the two countries. The growing gap also reflects Korean firms' international relocations and the resultant increase in intra-firm trades. It is left for further research to investigate whether NAFTA creates any profitable arbitrage opportunity for a circuitous export for Korean firms.

There is some convergence in the two parties' assessment of the seemingly stagnating Korean exports to Canada. This paper attempts to analyze and separate the impacts of various economic and policy factors for Canadian-Korean trade. Our regression results, based upon the partial adjustment model of exports and imports, show that the substantial part of fluctuations of the Korean exports to Canada can be explained by the Canadian business cycle. Other factors have added to the variability; a growing competition from developing countries, and the structural changes due to NAFTA. Contrary to the common expectations, the base price elasticity or the currency exchange rates has had virtually no impact on the Korean exports.

These results seem to suggest that when it comes to Korean exports to Canada, marketing may matter more than cost considerations, and that while Korean exports continue to expand due to the strong Canadian economy, their performances will show wide swings along the Canadian business cycle. Korean exports to Canada are faced with very keen competition from developing countries. Their future success depends, by and large, on the accelerated upward mobility of their products along the scales of quality and innovation.

It also show that the Asian Financial Crisis has in fact contributed to an increase of Korean exports to Canada, perhaps through enhanced marketing efforts or a renewed export-drive by the Korean firms and government during the crisis. NAFTA has led to a decrease in the Korean trade in a significant way.

The results of the regression for the Canadian exports to Korea are shown to be in line with the standard demand function for primary products; relatively low elasticities of income and base price, and a relatively high elasticity of the prices of competitors. Again, marketing efforts may bring a substantial return to the Canadian export firms in Korea. Stretching the point, we can infer that direct investment and technology transfers can lead to a substantial increase in Canadian exports to Korea. The relatively weak Canadian dollar values are shown to have contributed in the largest way to the continued expansion of Canadian exports to Korea. Institutional factors, such as the Asian Financial Crisis or NAFTA, seem to have little impact on Canadian exports to Korea.

Figure 1. Korean Trade with Canada: Korean View

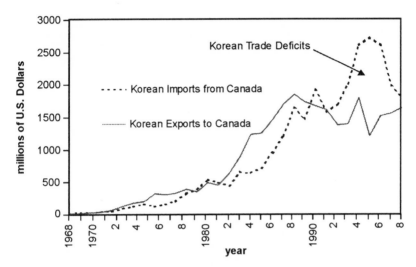

Source: IMF, Directions of Interntional Trade, various years.

Note: Canadian imports are in fact Korean exports based upon CIF statistics
      by the Korean government.

Figure 2. Canadian Shares in Korean Trade: Korean Data

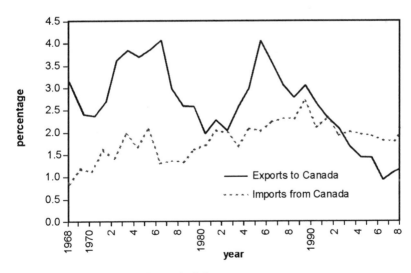

Source: IMF Data based upon Korean Statistics

Figure 3. Canadian Trade with Korea: Canadian View

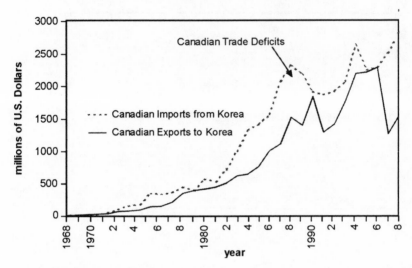

Sources: IMF, and Statistics Canada
Note: The imports from Korea is based upon FOB, or the Country of Origin.

Figure 4. Growing Gap between Canadian and Korean Statistics: Korean Exports to Canada

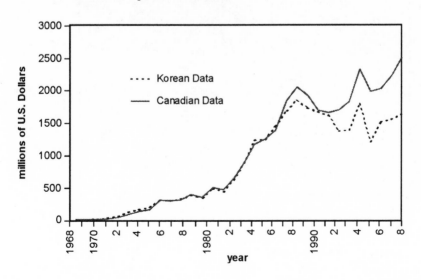

Figure 5. Canadian Imports from World: U.S. and East Asia

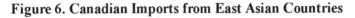

Figure 6. Canadian Imports from East Asian Countries

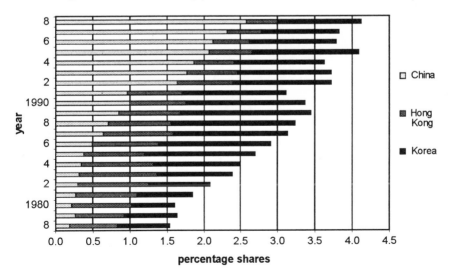

Appendix 1: Technical Notes for the Economics Model of Trade with a Partial Adjustment, and Regression

In a two-country model, one country's exports are the other country's demand for the former's output. Demand is a function of the importing country's income level, and the relative price level between the two countries. The relative prices level is the ratio of the importing country's price level to the exporting country's price level. To make the two statistics comparable, currency exchange rates should be used.

Therefore, at any time (say, time point at t) the imports of one country (M_t) are the exports of the other country (X^*_t), which are a function of the importing country's national income (GDP_t), the price level of the exporting country (P^*_t), the price level of the importing country (P_t), and currency exchange rates (S_t):

$$M_t = X^*_t = a + b\ GDP_t + c\ P_t + d\ P^*_t + e\ S_t, \quad\text{———(1)}$$

where *a, b, c, d*, and *e* are all coefficients to be estimated. In the log data, these are the elasticities of imports with respect to income, foreign price level, domestic price level, and foreign exchange rates. In this paper, the variables with the asteroid sign are of Korea, and those without it are of Canada. In the same manner, the export of one country can be specified as

$$X_t = M^*_t = e + f\ GDP_t + g\ P_t + h\ P^*_t + i\ S_t, \quad\text{———(2)}$$

The above equation should be regarded as being held at the long-run equilibrium state. In other words, the above M_t and X_t are at all desired levels. For instance,

$$\textbf{\textit{Desired }} M_t = a + b\ GDP_t + c\ P_t + d\ P^*_t + e\ S_t. \quad\text{———(1')}$$

However, in reality, it takes time for the imports (or exports) on the left-hand side of the above equation to adjust to the changes in their determinants on the right-hand side. In reality, the actual change in imports that one country can make within a unit period or from one period to another is only a portion of the desired change. This leads to a so-called 'Partial Adjustment Model', such as

$$\textbf{\textit{Actual }} M_t - M_{t-1} = k\ (\textbf{\textit{Desired }} M_t - M_{t-1}), \quad\text{———(3)}$$

where k is the adjustment coefficient, and the lagged value M_{t-1} denotes the imports of the previous period at which the desired level is equal to the actual level for simplicity.

The above equation can be rewritten as

$$\textbf{\textit{Actual }} M_t = k\ \textbf{\textit{Desired }} M_t + (1-k)\ M_{t-1}. \quad\text{———(3')}$$

Substituting (1') into equation (3') leads to

$$\textbf{\textit{Actual }} M_t = k\ \{\ a + b\ GDP_t + c\ P_t + d\ P^*_t + e\ S_t\ \} + (1-k)\ M_{t-1} \quad\text{———(4);}$$

$$\textbf{\textit{Actual }} M_t = k\ a + k\ b\ GDP_t + k\ c\ P_t + k\ d\ P^*_t + k\ e\ S_t + (1-k)\ M_{t-1} \quad\text{———(4').}$$

Equation (4) is fitted with the actual data in our paper. The so-called multi variate regression results will be given in the form of:

$$M_t = A + B\ GDP_t + C\ P_t + D\ P^*_t + E\ S_t + F\ M_{t-1} \text{——}(5).$$

Because the theoretical equation (4') should be equal to the empirical equation (5),

$$k = F;\ a = A/F;\ b = B/F;\ c = C/F;\ d = D/F;\ e = E/F.$$

Economic interpretations are as follows:

When the importing country's GDP or national income rises by 1%, the imports from the other country increases by B% in this period. But in the next period the imports will rise again with a time lag by B times F %.

Appendix 2: Data

Frequency: Quarterly
Data Period: 1980, First Quarter - 1999, Fourth Quarter

Variables	Sources
Canadian GDP	CANSIM, Statistics Canada
Canadian Imports	CANSIM
Canadian Exports	CANSIM
Canadian Imports(annual; for Figures)	IMF, Directions of International Trade
Canadian Exports(annual; for Figures)	IMF, Directions of International Trade
Canadian Implicit Price Index of Imports	CANSIM, DS15610
Canadian Commodity Price Index	Bank of Canada, CANSIM
Korean GDP	Bank of Korea
Korean Export	Bank of Korea
Korean Import	Bank of Korea
Korean Import Price Index	Bank of Korea
Korean-U.S. Exchange Rates	DRI Database
U.S.-Canadian Exchange Rates	CANSIM

Appendix 3: Regression 1

Dependent Variable: Canadian Imports from Korea (the Canadian statistical data of Korean Exports to Canada)
Explanatory Variables:

variables	estimated values	T-value	Statistal Significance
Canadian GDP	1.23	4.75	Yes
Canadian Import Price Index	2.15	3.45	Yes
Korean Producers' Price Index	-0.74	-1.58	No
Currency Exchange Rates	0.22	0.91	No
Asian Crisis Dummy	0.23	2.12	Yes
NAFTA Dummy*	-0.02*	-3.22	Yes
Lagged Dependent Variable	0.42	4.04	No

R-squares = 0.95; DW = 2.28; Number of Observations (Sample Size) = 80

Regression 2:

Dependent Variable: Korean Imports from Canada
Explanatory Variables:

variables	estimated values	T-value	Statistal Significance
Korean GDP	0.35	4.34	Yes
Canadian Commodity Price Index	-0.060	-2.36	Yes
Korean Import Price Index	0.74	2.11	Yes
Currency Exchange Rates	-0.94	-2.76	Yes
Asian Crisis Dummy	-0.01	-0.68	No
Lagged Dependent Variable	0.42	4.34	Yes

R-squares = 0.92; DW = 2.21; Number of Observations = 80

References

Integration and Trade in the America, Inter-American Development Bank, October 1999.

Hejazi, W., and Safarian, A.E., "Modeling Links between Canadian Trade and Foreign Direct Investment," *Industry Canada Paper.* November 1998.

Hejazi, W., and Trefler, D., *Canada and the Asia Pacific: Views from the Gravity, Monopolistic Competition, and Heckscher-Ohlin Model,* University of Toronto Press, 1999.

Chen, S., and Sharma, P., "Accounting for Canadian Export Growth: 1983 to 1997," *Trade and Economic Policy Paper*, Department of Foreign Affairs and International Trade, December 1998.

IMF, Directions of International Trade Statistics, various years.

CANSIM

Bank of Korea Database

DR
I Database

Korea-Canada Economic Relations: Korean Perspectives

Joung-Yong Lee
Inha University, Incheon, Korea

Introduction

Historically, Korea and Canada began their contacts as Canadian missionaries arrived in Korea in the late 1880s. (Yoo, 1987) In 1947, Canada participated in the United Nations Commission supervising free elections, and Canada was among the first countries who recognized the Republic of Korea (South Korea) in 1949. Canada sent combat soldiers during the 1950-1953 Korean War under the UN Command and suffered 516 fatalities. The Korean Embassy was established in 1954 in Ottawa, while the Canadian Embassy in Seoul opened in 1973.

This paper is about Korea-Canada economic relations. Among many different dimensions in economic relations, it focuses on the Korea-Canada trade relations. It is the author's belief that only after having understood some special features and situations of the Korean economy, can prospects of economic relations with any other country be discussed.

In order to understand the pattern and challenges of Korea's trade, this paper looks back on the historical patterns in trade during the 1980s and 1990s, and then it overviews the trade between Korea and Canada. The recent Korean economic problems will not be touched because firstly, they are somewhat irrelevant in long-term perspectives, and secondly, every indication seems to show that the Korean economy is recuperating rapidly.

The paper concludes with a few speculations on the future economic relations between Korea and Canada.

The Korean Trade

The Korean economy heavily depends on its foreign trade.[1] <Table 1 and Figure 1> The U.S. and Japan comprise the lion's share of Korean trade. On the exports side, Korea's exports to the U.S. took 28.3 percent of Korea's

---

[1] In 1996 the Korean trade dependency weight (exports plus imports in GNP) was 58 percent.

total exports ($6.1 billion) in 1982, and the year of the 1988 Seoul Olympics marked the highest peak at 35.3 percent ($21.4 billion). Since the Olympics, the U.S. importance has somewhat decreased. For example, the U.S. market took 16.7 percent ($21.7 billion) of Korea's exports in 1996.

Japan shows a similar pattern. 15.3 percent ($3.3 billion) of Korea's total exports went to Japan in 1982 and reached the peak of 21.6 percent ($13.5 billion) in 1989. The share decreased to 12.2 percent ($15.8 billion) in 1996.

The U.S. and Japan together, comprised 56.6 percent ($16.7 billion) of Korea's total exports - the highest point to these two advanced countries in 1987, followed by a decrease to 28.9 percent ($36.4 billion), almost half, in 1996.

The share of imports from the U.S. and Japan also show a similar pattern. In 1982, Korea imported 46.4 percent ($11.3 billion) of its total imports from these two countries. The share reached its highest point in 1988 at 55.4 percent ($28.7 billion), then gradually decreased. The 1996 figure, the year previous to Korea's financial crisis was 43.1 percent ($64.8 billion).

<Table 2> shows detailed trade data and [Figure 2] depicts Korea's balance of trade with the U.S.A., Japan, and the whole world. The following is a summary of the basic facts concerning Korean trade in recent years:

Exports
(1) Exports had been increasing up to the 1988 Olympics year (US) or 1989 (Japan).
(2) Since then, exports to the U.S. and Japan have decreased.
(3) During the late 1990s, exports to the U.S. somewhat stagnated while exports to Japan continuously decreased.
(4) Exports to the world, however, including the U.S. and Japan, increased for the entire period (except for the years of financial downturn since 1997).

Imports
(5) Korea's imports have been consistently increasing.
(6) Korea's trade balance with the U.S. was in favor of Korea throughout the 1980s then turned the other way around in the 1990s.
(7) Korea has never had a trade surplus balance with Japan and the deficit has grown in the 1990s.

In sum, Korea's exports to the two most important advanced countries have decreased since the 1988 Olympics while total exports kept increasing. Thus, compensation must have come from the rest of the world market, and in fact, it came from newly developing countries in Asia, and other countries whose economies were in transition. Thailand, the Philippines, China, Russia, and several socialist countries in Eastern Europe are some of those economies. This was due to Korea's so-called 'Northern Diplomacy'.

What do all of these facts imply? There is no hard evidence on how much of each of the following explanations have contributed, but these are some factors:

(1) Korea could not satisfy the demands of the advanced countries with sophisticated and high quality products. Instead, Korea was satisfied with diversifying its export markets into Asian and formerly socialist countries.

(2) Korea neglected to increase investment in R&D during its trade surplus years in the 1980s.

(3) As a result, the Korean economy has become a so-called 'sandwich economy', meaning that it had been overtaken by less developing countries while it could not overtake the advanced countries.

Of course there are many other explanations. For example, the later 1980s was marked by 'democratization' in Korea. Workers were out on the streets to strike for higher wages and better working conditions. Nominal wages grew at over 10 percent yearly for almost five years. Korea became no longer a low-wage country.

Korea's Trade with Canada

Although some people say Korea is one of Canada's more important markets, or vice versa, both countries are relatively minor trading partners. It is fair to say, however, that the two countries are becoming more important partners than before.

In 1981, eight years after the establishment of the Canadian Embassy in Seoul, the two-way trade between Korea and Canada exceeded the $1 billion mark for the first time, with Korea's exports to Canada of $484 million and imports of $531 million. <Table 3> Canadians suddenly became aware that Korea was an automobile producing country, with the arrival of the first shipments of the Hyundai Pony in 1984. In the following year, Korean exports to Canada topped the $1 billion mark with over $660 million worth of Ponies. Korea was becoming known to Canadians as no longer a producer of small electronic goods, footwear and clothing, but also as an industrial power.

Almost every Canadian newspaper, mission report, and speech related to Korea at this time was concerned with Canada's trade deficit with Korea. Some mildly threatened Korea by GPT (General Preferential Tariff) graduation and anti-dumping exercises. In response, Korean delegates, businessmen and researchers were hasty to explain how much and how soon the Korean markets were liberalizing and so, how good it would be for Canadians to invest in Korea.

The most distinctive pattern in [Figure 3] is that throughout the 1990s (again before the crisis in late 1997), Canada has enjoyed a trade surplus - totally an opposite picture of the 1980s. Korean imports from Canada kept increasing but exports to Canada decreased since 1990. This pattern can be confirmed in terms of Canada's rank among Korea's trading partners. <Table 4> In 1980, Canada was Korea's ninth-largest export market and eighth-largest import market. The rank of both exports and imports did not change much until the early 1990s. However, in the late 1990s, the relative importance of Canada changed with Korea's export market significantly decreasing while Canada as an import source remained basically the same. In 1996, the export rank decreased to 18th while the import rank was 11th. Canada's share as a Korean export market was surpassed by the markets of Taiwan, Singapore, Malaysia, Philippines, Indonesia, Thailand, Panama, Brazil, Russia and Switzerland.

In short, Canada became less important to Korea as an export market while Korea's imports from Canada grew with Korea's economic growth. Naturally, the trade balance was in favour of Canada, and were there no financial crisis in Korea, Canadian surpluses would have been much greater.

The reason for Canada's stability as a source of Korea's imports is that Korea's main imports from Canada are raw or semi-fabricated goods. In 1996, for example, 68 percent of Korea's imports from Canada were primary and chemical products while 96 percent of Korea's exports to Canada consisted of manufactured goods. <Tables 5 and 6> Korea's top import items from Canada are bituminous coal; pulp and paper; non-ferrous metals, organic chemicals; heavy water (for atomic energy); aluminum; wheat; iron ore; inorganic chemicals, and vegetable oil. On the other hand Korea's top export items to Canada are electronic parts and components; motor vehicles; computers and peripheral equipment; steel; clothing; tires and tubes.

In addressing this phenomenon - declining Korea exports to Canada from the late 1980s - some researchers contend that NAFTA might have exercised negative effects on Korea. (Jeong and Lee, 1998). It is a plausible explanation because, as we have seen, a similar pattern has occurred with the U.S. But this does not explain why Korea's exports to Japan decreased in the same period. Japan is not a member of NAFTA.

As mentioned earlier, it seems more likely that Korea has neglected on investing on R&D to develop high-tech, value added, quality products to meet the demands of advanced markets. Instead, Korea has chosen an easy way to expand its exports by selling the same low or middle quality products to Asian countries, China, Russia, and other European countries in transitional economic phases.

Investment between Korea and Canada

Up to June of 1999, the stock of Korean investment in Canada is US $315 million for 74 enterprises. Canada ranks fifteenth in Korea's direct investment abroad. The level of investment has fluctuated over the years but is significantly below the levels achieved in the period when Hyundai had a major investment in the Bromont auto plant.

Korea's overseas investment strategies have changed from expanding foreign markets to establishing manufacturing bases, taking advantage of cheap wages and rich natural resources. Therefore, much of the FDI recently went to Southeast Asia, China and Eastern Europe.

On the other hand, the stock of Canadian investment in Korea up to June of 1999 is US $570 million for 88 enterprises. During 1998, several major Canadian investments were undertaken. The Bell Canada International investment in Hansol PCS (Personal Communications Services) valued at US$290 million and the Abitibi Consolidated joint venture partnership with Hansol Paper (newsprint) valued at US$210 million, are good examples.

Future Challenges

We all understand that Canada is not content with its current trade mix. It is often said that Canada exports rocks and logs for cars and VCRs. In fact as <Table 6> shows, Canada's main exports are mostly simple resource-based commodities and they are competing with other resource abundant countries. For example, Canada, Australia, China, Indonesia, South Africa, the U.S.A. and Russia are competing with each other in selling bituminous coal, which is one of the main goods Canada exports to Korea. Pulp is another competing item among Canada, the U.S.A., Indonesia, Brazil, Chile, and Russia. Even heavy water, which Korea needs for operating the four CANDU nuclear power plants, faces growing competition from India.

As Korea develops closer relations with Russia, China, Mongolia, and even with North Korea, resource-based Canadian exports to Korea will be exposed to tougher competition. Therefore Canada's concern with its trade mix is legitimate. It needs to move out of simple production of commodities into more highly processed and manufactured goods to deflect competition from these countries.

In turn, Korea needs to upgrade its technology through R&D to catch up with the advanced countries while expanding its markets in Asia and the former socialist countries. The Korean economy is entering a new critical phase in its development. Korea's dependence on trade is threatened by rising regional bloc-ism in its major markets, and more importantly, Korea is facing growing competition from less developed countries in major labour-intensive exports such as textiles, footwear, and light manufactures. Korea must acquire higher technologies not only in manufacturing, but also in marketing and in developing its own brands in the world market. A consensus is forming in Korea through the recent crisis. People believe that the cheabol-based (Korean conglomerates) economic development policies will no longer work in the future. A reform and structural adjustment in industry, emphasizing the development of small and medium-size enterprises and also knowledge-intensive industries will be strongly encouraged.

To Canada, new market opportunities will open as Korea takes on social reform and structural adjustment in industry. Korea will remain as a significant market for coal, aluminum, steel, potash, and heavy water. But more importantly, if Canada wants to export more fabricated, highly processed and value-added products not just only to Korea but to China, Russia, and Asia, it should not depend on just the resource endowments but on the mix of technology, engineering, and manufacturing. Canada's telecommunications, transportation, energy and environmental technologies will provide ample opportunities both in Korea and neighbouring countries, especially in China and Russia. As China becomes a WTO member and Russia becomes more stable politically, Canada will be able to make use of Korea as a springboard to gain further access to these huge markets. Korea's manufacturing skills combined with Canada's technology can generate formidable competitiveness.[2] By the same token, as long as the U.S. remains as the most important export market for Korea, Korea will need more Canadian collaboration.

In the past, when Canada succeeded in obtaining contracts with Korea to build nuclear power plants (Canada has built four CANDU power plants in Korea and is seeking another contract soon), economic relations between Korea and Canada seemed to be at a peak. Also, when Hyundai decided to build its car assembly plant in Bromont, Quebec, this also seemed to be the case. But in the future, economic relations should move from the "one big deal" selling or investment type into an on-going collaborating model for developing new products and new markets together.

---

[2] Besides the technology and skill complementarity between Canada and Korea, which could be positive factor in advancing into the Chinese market together, a mix of the way of doing business could also be a big help. Canadians are known to be relatively weak in understanding the Asian business culture.

References

Choo, Myung-Gun and Whan-ho Lee, 1999. "The Economic Cooperation between Korea and Canada through Free Trade Agreement," Paper presented at the 8th Canada-Korea Conference, Institute of East and West Studies, Yonsei University, Seoul, Korea.

Jeong, Kap-Young and Yeon-ho Lee, 1998. "Post NAFTA Changes in Trade Structure of Korea," *Korean Review of Canadian Studies,* 4, 1997/1998.

Liou, To-hai, 1999, A Comparative Study of Canada's Economic Interactions with the ROC and the ROK in the 1990s, Paper presented at the 1999 Korea Association for Canadian Studies, Yonsei University, Seoul, Korea.

Okazaki, Abraham, 1988. "Canada-Korea Economic Relations: A Canadian Perspective," *Korea-Canada in Emerging Asia-Pacific Community,* ed. By Dalchoong Kim and Myungsoon Shin, Institute of East and West Studies, Yonsei University, Seoul, Korea.

Ursacki, Terry and Ilan Vertinsky, 1994, "Changing Patterns of Comparative Advantage and Strategy in Canada and Korea: Implications for Trade," *Canada-Korea Economic Relations,* ed. by Myungsoon Shin and Kap-Young Jeong, Institute of East and West Studies, Yonsei University.

Yoo, Young Sik, 1987. *Earlier Canadian Missionaries in Korea,* Westward Graphics, Ontario, Canada.

<Table 1>   **Korea's Trade with U.S.A. and Japan.**

(% of each year's total exports or imports)

Year	Exports to U.S.	Imports from U.S.	Exports to Japan	Imports from Japan	Exports to US+Japan	Imports from US+Japan
1982	28.3	24.6	15.3	21.9	43.6	46.4
1983	33.6	24.0	14.7	23.8	48.2	47.8
1984	35.8	22.4	15.7	24.9	51.6	47.4
1985	35.5	20.8	15.0	24.3	50.5	45.1
1986	40.0	20.7	15.6	34.4	55.6	55.1
1987	38.7	21.4	17.8	33.3	56.6	54.6
1988	35.3	24.6	19.8	30.7	55.0	55.4
1989	33.1	25.9	21.6	28.4	54.7	54.3
1990	29.8	24.3	19.4	26.6	49.2	50. 9
1991	25.8	23.2	17.2	25.9	43.0	49.1
1992	23.6	22.4	15.1	23.8	38.7	46.2
1993	22.1	21.4	14.1	23.9	36.1	45.3
1994	21.4	21.1	14.1	24.8	35.5	45.9
1995	19.3	22.5	13.6	24.1	32.9	46.6
1996	16.7	22.2	12.2	20.9	28.9	43.1
1997	15.9	20.8	10.8	19.3	26.7	40.1
1998	17.2	21.9	9.2	18.1	26.5	39.9
1999	20.5	20.8	11.0	20.2	31.6	41.0

Source: KOTIS Database, Korea International Trade Association

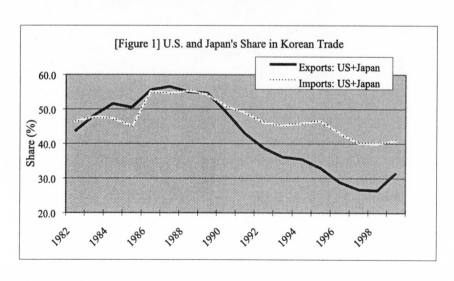

[Figure 1] U.S. and Japan's Share in Korean Trade

<Table 2>   Korea's Trade with U.S.A. and Japan

Source: KOTIS Database, Korea International Trade Association

million US$

	Vis-à-vis USA			Vis-à-vis Japan			Vis-à-vis World		
	Exports	Imports	Balance	Exports	Imports	Balance	Exports	Imports	Balance
1982	6119	5956	163	3314	5305	-1991	21616	24251	-2635
1983	8128	6274	1854	3558	6238	-2680	24223	26192	-1969
1984	10479	6875	3604	4602	7640	-3038	29245	30631	-1386
1985	10754	6489	4265	4543	7560	-3017	30283	31136	-853
1986	13880	6545	7335	5426	10869	-5443	34714	31584	3130
1987	18311	8758	9553	8437	13657	-5220	47281	41020	6261
1988	21404	12757	8647	12004	15929	-3925	60696	51811	8885
1989	20639	15911	4728	13457	17449	-3992	62377	61465	912
1990	19360	16942	2418	12638	18574	-5936	65016	69844	-4828
1991	18559	18894	-335	12356	21120	-8764	71870	81525	-9655
1992	18090	18287	-197	11599	19458	-7859	76632	81775	-5143
1993	18183	17928	255	11564	20016	-8452	82236	83800	-1564
1994	20553	21579	-1026	13523	25390	-11867	96013	102348	-6335
1995	24132	30404	-6272	17049	32606	-15557	125058	135119	-10061
1996	21671	33305	-11634 .	15767	31449	-15682	129715	150339	-20624
1997	21625	30122	-8497	14771	27907	-13136	136164	144616	-8452
1998	22805	20403	2402	12238	16840	-4602	132313	93281	39032
1999	29475	24922	4553	15862	24142	-8280	143685	119752	23933

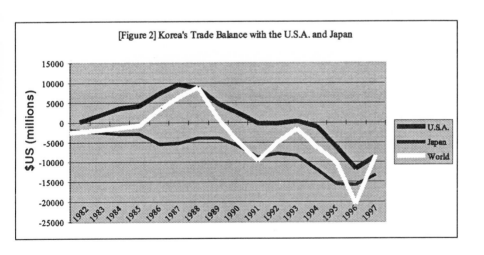

[Figure 2] Korea's Trade Balance with the U.S.A. and Japan

<Table 3>   Korea's Trade with Canada

	Vis-à-vis the World		Vis-à-vis the Canada				
	US $million		Exports		Imports		Exports + Imports
Year	Exports	Imports	Amount	Share (%)	Amount	Share (%)	Amount
1980	17,505	22,292	343	2.0	378	1.7	722
1981	21,254	26,131	484	2.3	531	2.0	1,014
1982	21,853	24,251	443	2.0	485	2.0	928
1983	24,445	26,192	629	2.6	444	1.7	1,074
1984	29,245	30,631	879	3.0	637	2.1	1,516
1985	30,283	31,136	1,229	4.1	630	2.0	1,859
1986	34,714	31,584	1,248	3.6	709	2.2	1,957
1987	47,281	41,020	1,451	3.1	947	2.3	2,398
1988	60,696	51,811	1,692	2.8	1,197	2.3	2,889
1989	62,377	61,465	1,882	3.0	1,680	2.7	3,562
1990	65,016	69,844	1,731	2.7	1,465	2.1	3,196
1991	71,870	81,525	1,673	2.3	1,907	2.3	3,580
1992	76,632	81,775	1,608	2.1	1,574	1.9	3,182
1993	82,236	83,800	1,374	1.7	1,695	2.0	3,069
1994	96,013	102,348	1,390	1.4	2,005	2.0	3,395
1995	125,058	135,119	1,790	1.4	2,604	1.9	4,395
1996	129,715	150,339	1,203	0.9	2,724	1.8	3,927
1997	136,164	144,616	1,514	1.1	2,599	1.8	4,113
1998	132,313	93,282	1,551	1.2	1,975	2.1	3,526
1999	143,685	119,752	1,638	1.1	1,793	1.5	3,431

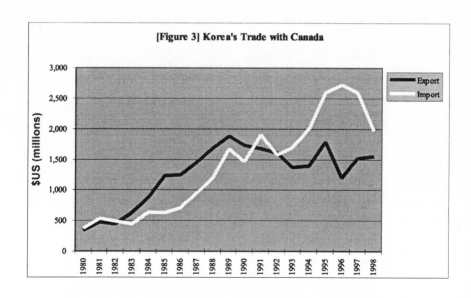

[Figure 3] Korea's Trade with Canada

<Table 4>   **Canada's Rank in Korea's Exports and Imports**

Year	Exports	Imports
1980	9	8
1985	4	6
1990	7	8
1991	7	7
1992	10	9
1993	13	8
1994	12	7
1995	13	7
1996	18	11
1997	17	11
1998	19	10
1999	20	14

<Table 5>   **Korea's Imports from Canada by Product Group**

Unit: %

	1	2	3	4	5	6	7	8	Total
1988	9.9	33.0	35.8	2.4	13.0	2.1	3.4	0.4	100.0
1989	9.0	32.1	31.9	2.4	18.4	2.9	2.8	0.5	100.0
1990	12.1	31.5	28.7	3.0	16.2	5.4	2.8	0.3	100.0
1991	11.9	31.6	25.8	2.3	19.4	5.3	3.4	0.3	100.0
1992	13.3	29.1	28.3	2.4	15.0	6.9	4.5	0.4	100.0
1993	24.1	23.8	23.4	1.9	11.5	10.0	4.8	0.4	100.0
1994	25.7	17.5	29.4	1.2	11.4	9.1	5.4	0.4	100.0
1995	10.9	21.5	36.2	1.3	9.8	13.4	6.5	0.5	100.0
1996	14.1	22.6	30.9	2.0	9.7	14.5	5.7	0.7	100.0
1997	15.6	23.3	28.2	1.6	9.4	14.4	7.0	0.5	100.0
1998	7.7	41.5	25.9	1.4	8.6	9.0	5.7	0.3	100.0

1: Agricultural & Fisheries   5: Steel, Metalic Products
2: Mining Products   6: Machinery & Transportation Machinery
3: Chemical Products   7: Electric & Electronics Products
4: Textiles   8: Others

\<Table 6\>   **Korea's Exports to Canada by Items**

Unit: %

	0	1	2	3	4	5	6	7	8	Total
1988	1.6	0.9	6.6	1.1	28.5	10.7	7.1	27.6	15.9	100.0
1989	1.6	1.0	5.8	1.5	29.2	10.2	5.2	27.0	18.4	100.0
1990	1.3	1.4	6.4	1.4	28.9	11.1	4.3	22.0	23.2	100.0
1991	1.4	1.3	5.9	1.4	24.7	9.9	3.9	27.6	23.8	100.0
1992	1.5	1.2	5.7	0.7	21.9	7.6	4.5	27.7	29.1	100.0
1993	2.4	1.2	7.0	0.6	23.5	6.9	4.8	33.5	19.9	100.0
1994	1.7	1.5	7.5	0.6	21.1	5.2	4.6	35.5	22.3	100.0
1995	1.3	1.2	5.5	0.4	14.3	3.4	28.4	31.5	14.0	100.0
1996	1.6	2.3	7.7	0.5	17.3	3.3	5.6	37.2	24.4	100.0
1997	1.5	2.4	5.5	1.5	16.4	2.5	5.9	30.5	33.8	100.0
1998	3.0	2.8	5.3	2.2	17.5	2.4	13.2	23.6	30.1	100.0

0: Primary Goods

1: Chemical Products

2: Plastic, Rubber, Leather Products

3: Non-ferrous Metalic Products

4: Textiles

5: Appliances

6: Steel, Metalic Products

7: Electronics & Electrical Products

8: Machinery & Transportation Machinery

Source: KOTIS Database.

\<Table 7\>   Canada's Main Exports to Korea and Its Competitors

COAL						PULP					
1999			1996			1999			1996		
Rank	Total	1,866,479	Rank		2,250,757	Rank	total	876,319	Rank	total	1,096,148
1	Australia	832,660	1	Australia	992,152	1	Canada	253,778	1	U.S.A	389,928
2	China	413,323	2	China	363,545	2	U.S.A	237,460	2	Canada	248,335
3	Canada	230,340	3	Canada	328,004	3	Indonesia	130,348	3	Indonesia	143,903
4	Indonesia	132,625	4	S. Africa	210,888	4	Brazil	85,643	4	Brazil	107,661
5	S. Africa	132,209	5	U.S.A	204,784	5	Chile	58,810	5	Chile	76,703
6	U.S.A	90,974	6	Indonesia	107,198	6	Russia	20,438	6	Russia	54,400
7	Russia	30536	7	Russia	41,343	7	New Zealand	25,646	7	New Zealand	20,564

ALUMINUM						HEAVY WATER					
1999			1996			1999			1996		
Rank	Total	220,136	Rank		294,650	Rank		65,000	Rank		77,142
1	Arab Emirate	69,045	1	Arab Emirate	67,204	1	Canada	28,695	1	Canada	71,284
2	Canada	31,485	2	Canada	58,861	2	India	22,778	2	Argentina	5,857
3	Australia	22,650	3	U.S.A	41,634	3	Argentina	9,939	3	China	3996.6
4	New Zealand	17,524	4	Bahrain	28,136						
5	Bahrain	15,370	5	New Zealand	22,022						
6	Russia	11,859	6	Russia	20,799						
7	Taiwan	8,256	7	Australia	24,149						

ARBITRATION SYSTEMS:
A COMPARATIVE STUDY OF CANADA AND KOREA

MOONCHUL CHANG
NATIONAL POLICE UNIVERSITY, KOREA

I. Introduction

In recent years, arbitration has become increasingly popular in settling commercial disputes both in Canada and Korea. At the end of 1999, Korea introduced new arbitration law to promote the arbitration practice, which is mainly modeled after the UNCITRAL Model Arbitration Law. On the other hand in 1986 Canada became the first country to adopt the UNCITRAL Model Law and the last advanced country to adopt the 1958 New York Convention.

Although both Canada and Korea adopted the UNCITRAL Model arbitration law, its legal background and implementation are somewhat different. The previous Korean arbitration law of 1966 was based on the old German arbitration law. As a result, the new law significantly deviated from Korean legal tradition on this field. On the other hand, Canadian arbitration law was previously based on the English and French legal traditions. More than a decade after adopting the Model Law, Canada has experienced various kinds of legal issues in utilizing new arbitration law. Now, Canadian courts have established the new case law on international arbitration by interpreting and applying the new legislation. The Canadian experience in implementing the new arbitration law could provide significant lessons to potential countries in adopting UNCITRAL Model Law.

In context, this paper highlights the comparative analysis of arbitration legal systems between Canada and Korea.

II. The New Framework of Arbitration Law in Korea and Canada

The new Korean arbitration law entered into force on December 31, 1999. Since it is mainly modeled after the UNCITRAL model law, the adoption of the new law implies a significant divorce from Korean legal tradition in this field. The previous Korean arbitration law in 1966 was modeled after old German arbitration law in the tenth book of the German Civil Code 1877; the German legal system has heavily influenced Korean law in general. On the other hand, Korean arbitration practices have been more influenced by major international arbitration centers such as AAA in New York, ICC in Paris and LCIA in London, etc. As a result there was a large gap between arbitration law and practice, which was temporarily filled by the revision of arbitration law in 1973. This revision authorized that the Rules of Korean Commercial Arbitration Board (KCAB) should regulate any disputes arising out of commercial transaction unless the parties to the arbitration have not agreed otherwise. Eventually, the new Korean arbitration law now attempts to meet the need of internationalizing the Korean arbitration system by adopting the UNCITRAL model law.

Now, all Canadian provinces and territories have enacted legislation that implements the New York Convention and the UNCITRAL Model Arbitration law, which applies to international commercial arbitration. As a result they have two sets of arbitration legislation: one is for international arbitration and the other for domestic arbitration. The federal arbitration law consists of the Commercial Arbitration Law and United Nations Foreign Arbitral Awards Convention Act, which apply only in relation to matters where at least one of the parties to the arbitration is a department of government or a Crown corporation or in relation to maritime or admiralty matters. The fashion of the legislation of the arbitration law is diverse depending on the province. In 11 Canadian jurisdictions the model law has been adopted in the form of a schedule at the end of a short enactment. Two provinces enacted statutes that incorporate the Model Law into the wording of the Act itself (B.C and Quebec). Quebec modified provisions in its Civil Code and Code of Civil Procedure that relate to arbitration.

Prior to the adoption of the new law, Canada had not been interested in commercial arbitration; the development of commercial arbitration had been slow. The arbitration laws of the Canadian common law provinces followed the English arbitration tradition while the province of Quebec followed the French tradition. However, due to the pressure from commercial communities and the desire to help case-overloaded courts, Canada changed its attitude toward commercial arbitration. It promoted the establishment of international commercial and maritime arbitration institutions in Vancouver and Quebec City. The Canadian courts have also supported this change by favoring arbitration practices.

1. The Scope of Application of Arbitration Law
In Korea, just as the previous law did, new arbitration law applies to both domestic and foreign arbitration practices. Firstly, as far as international arbitration is concerned, the two conventions would prevail over the arbitration law to which Korea is a contracting party. In 1976, Korea adopted the New York Convention on the Recognition and Enforcement of foreign

Arbitral Awards in 1958 (New York Convention) and in 1967 the Convention on the Settlement of Investment Disputes between States and Nationals of Other States in 1965 (Washington Convention). Secondly, the new law applies the basis of whether the place of arbitration is situated in Korea (so called territorial criteria). This is identical to the provision of UNCITRAL model law. (art. 2.1) Thirdly, the new law also applies to arbitration cases whether it is arising out of commercial transaction or not if it is involved in legal relationship in private law. Finally, the new law would not affect any other Korean law by virtue of which certain disputes may be submitted to arbitration only according to provisions other than those of the new law such as patent law, antitrust law, trademark law and bankruptcy law. (art. 2.2)

In Canada, all the common law provinces have separate laws for domestic and international arbitration. As far as the scope of application is concerned Canadian international arbitration legislation is identical to the provisions of the UNCITRAL model law. However, the Quebec law and Federal Act apply to both domestic and international arbitration. Several provinces also took the opportunity of the arbitration along the lines of the introduction of the Model Law to amend their laws relating to domestic arbitration along the lines of the Model Law. (B.C, N.B, Alberta, Sask, Ont) Other provinces still retain a domestic arbitration statute based on the 1889 English Act.

2. Arbitration Agreement

(1) Arbitrability

Both Canada and Korea have taken a liberal attitude on the issue of arbitrability. The new Korean law stipulates that the parties may submit to arbitration all or certain disputes which have arisen or which may arise between them in respect of a defined legal relationship whether contractual or not. (Art.3.para.2) This is identical to the provision of the Model Law but with slight modification of phrasing and order of provisions. Canadian law strictly follows the Model Law.

(2) Form of the Arbitration Agreement

In this regard both Canadian and Korean arbitration law adopted the Model Law. New Korean law maintains the position of previous law by stipulating that arbitration agreements must be made in writing. (art. 8.2) Oral agreements are excluded here. Agreement by telex, fax, email or other communication instruments shall be considered as effective arbitration agreements if only properly documented.

(3) Separation of Arbitration Agreement from the Main Contract

Although both Korean and B.C arbitration law are silent on this issue, in practice, the effect of an arbitration agreement must be separated from the main contract. Thus a defect in the formation of the main contract does not affect the validity of the arbitration agreement.

3. Court Jurisdiction for Arbitration practice

New Korean arbitration law provides, in some details for the concentration of District or Regional Court in the first instance to perform certain functions of arbitration related matters. It includes issues such as appointment of arbitrators, challenge proceedings, jurisdiction of arbitral tribunal, the deposit of original arbitral awards, recourse against arbitral awards and the enforcement of awards, etc. Local jurisdiction lies with District or Regional Court named in the arbitration agreement or, failing this, the court in whose area of jurisdiction the place of the arbitration is located. These provisions are not much different from those of the previous law.

On the other hand, BC international arbitration law is silent on this issue.

4. Arbitral Tribunal

(1) Appointment of Arbitrators

Both Canadian and Koran arbitration law follow the Model on this issue. B.C law and new Korean arbitration law provide that parties are free to agree on the number of arbitrators and, failing this, the arbitral tribunal shall consist of three arbitrators. Two arbitrators, of which each party appoints one, shall appoint the third arbitrator. If the two arbitrators fail to agree on the third arbitrator, the appointment shall be made upon request of a party, by the court. These provisions are basically identical to that of Model Law but are a significant departure from the previous Korean law. Under the previous law if the parties have not determined otherwise, each party may appoint an arbitrator and no chairman will be appointed. The result can be stalemate between the two arbitrators, which could in turn terminate the arbitration agreement. The new law abolishes this unreasonable doctrine.

On the other hand Quebec arbitration rules (QNICAC rules) provide for a unique way of determining the number of arbitrators. The number of arbitrators depends on the amount of money involved in a dispute. In the case of a dispute involving less than $500,000 a sole arbitrator is designated, and in a case involving $500,000 or more, three arbitrators are designated.

(2) Challenge to Arbitrators

Parties may challenge an arbitrator when his independence, impartiality or qualification is doubtful. The previous Korean arbitration law provided a list of grounds for challenging an arbitrator which function in the same way as the Code of Civil Procedure does. However, in practice, the test of the grounds has been whether the arbitrator in question is able to exercise impartial and independent judgment in the given circumstances. Both new Korean and B.C. law have accommodated this practice by adopting the same provision as that of the Model Law.

5. Arbitral Procedure

The previous Korean law left issues of arbitration procedure almost entirely to party autonomy except for an important proviso saying that when parties fail to agree on it in commercial disputes, Korean Commercial Arbitration Board Rules (KCAB rules) apply to them. (art.7) Since ad hoc arbitration is rare in Korea and KCAB has administered most of the commercial arbitration cases, this proviso could greatly affect domestic arbitration practice. However, considering the growth of ad hoc arbitration practice in the future there has been criticism of the proviso. In addition, in practice, parties who were uncertain which rules of procedure to apply sought to solve their problem by referring to the provisions on court procedure contained in the civil procedural law, only to lose the flexibility of arbitration procedure. In this context, the new Korean law, which adopts the Model Law almost verbatim in the majority of provisions, contains numerous procedural rules to be observed. The justification is the concern for clarity and predictability. For example, in the absence of an agreement by the parties to the contrary, the arbitral tribunal should hold a hearing if either party so requests. It is expected that the basic framework of procedural rules provided by the new law could facilitate the arbitral tribunal's task of conducting the proceedings.

Canadian law also adopted the position of the Model Law. It does not give details regarding the power of arbitrators in conducting arbitral proceedings. This may reflect the efforts of drafters of the Model Law to avoid conflicts between procedural rules of civil and common laws. Canadian law obliges parties to submit statements of claim and defenses in writing. However, it is silent as to whether the arbitrator has the power to require parties to clarify issues before the hearing or at the beginning of it. Under the common law court system parties may clarify or supplement claims or defenses during the hearings and it is not necessary to clarify issues before the hearing. Interestingly, the rule of the BC arbitration center allow parties to set up a pre-arbitration meeting to determine a number of administrative and procedural matters. In addition, it is silent as to whether or not arbitrators may directly examine parties, witnesses or experts. In contrast, Quebec law stipulates that arbitrators have all the necessary powers for the exercise of their jurisdiction, including the power to appoint experts.

6. Choice of Substantive Law

Parties have the power to determine for themselves the applicable substantive law to govern their international contract. When the parties do not agree on which law is applicable, an arbitrator will select it. However, the arbitrator faces the question of how to select applicable substantive law.

Although previous Korean law was silent about the question of applicable substantive law, in practice, parties had the power to determine it for themselves. When the parties do not agree on it, an arbitrator selects it. In this situation, the arbitrator faces the question of how to select the applicable law. The new Korean law provides that the arbitral tribunal should apply the rules of the law of the country which has the closest connection with the subject matter without referring to the domestic conflict of laws rules. This is a slight deviation from the Model Law, similar to the modifications made by many other countries. In addition, unless the parties agree, an arbitrator may not decide ex aequo et bono. B.C arbitration takes the same approach on the applicable substantive law as the new Korean law.

7. Arbitral Award

Regarding arbitral awards, the new Korean law essentially follows the provisions of the Model Law but maintains some provisions of the previous law. For example, the new Korean law maintains the provision stating that the original arbitral award should be forwarded to and deposited with the competent court. (art. 32.4) It was suggested that the award should be deposited with the competent court for recognition and enforcement purposes. It was also suggested that this stipulation is workable especially in ad hoc arbitration when the authenticity of its award is in dispute between the parties but fails to find the whereabouts of the arbitrator who moved abroad after having rendering the award.

Both new and previous arbitration law require arbitral awards to be rendered with the reasons in writing unless the parties agree otherwise. However, under the previous law, parties may challenge the arbitral award when the award is rendered without written reasons. In this respect the new law excludes the possibility of challenging the award by adopting the Model Law. (art. 36)

Canadian law also follows the position of the Model Law on this issue.

8. Grounds for Challenging Arbitral Awards (Art. 36)

In principle, judicial review of arbitral awards should be limited only to the fundamental notion of procedural justice. The idea behind this principle is that a trial de novo on the merits is not considered a desirable way to guarantee the autonomy of arbitration practice. Now a question arises as to on what grounds the party may challenge the arbitral award. Under the previous Korean law a losing party might file a lawsuit for challenging an arbitral award on exhaustively listed grounds. Among them were such controversial grounds as: (i) when arbitral awards had been rendered without written reasons unless otherwise agreed (art.13.1d); (ii) when the arbitral award did not deal with material issues which might significantly affect the result of award. (art 13.1c)

The new Korean law, which follows provisions of the Model Law, eliminates these controversial grounds for challenging awards. In fact Korean courts had narrowly interpreted the grounds under the previous law and restricted its judicial review of arbitral awards. Courts have often recognized as valid, awards which stated insufficient reason in writing or did not contain details of reasoning.

Under the new Korean law the list of the grounds for setting aside awards is essentially the same as that of Article V of the 1958 New York Convention for refusal of recognition and enforcement. This exclusive list of grounds also applies for refusing the enforcement of domestic arbitral awards. (art.38) The only difference is that article 36 of the new law does not contain the ground provided in article V(1)(e) of the 1958 New York Convention, which stipulates that the arbitral award may be refused when the award has been set aside or suspended by the competent authority in the country in which, or under the law of which, that award was made.

However, as an explanatory note by the UNCITRAL secretariat points out, although the grounds for setting aside are identical to those for refusing enforcement, there might still be two practical differences in international arbitration practice. Firstly, the grounds relating to public policy may be different in substance, depending on the country where a losing party would tend to seek a setting aside of the same award in that country, where a winning party would insist on enforcement by that country. Secondly, the grounds for refusal of enforcement are effective only in the country where the winning party seeks enforcement. According to article V(1)(e) of the 1958 New York Convention, the setting aside of an award at the place of origin prevents enforcement of the award in all other countries

Canadian arbitration law is identical to the Model Law in this issue.

III. Recognition and Enforcement of Arbitral Awards: Law and Practice

1. General Rules: Res Judicata (Art. 37)

The new Korean law stipulates that arbitral awards are in effect res judicata, or "matter adjudged". As a result, arbitral awards are binding on the parties as final court's judgments are. However, upon the application of a party the awards could be only enforced by virtue of the judgment made by the competent court. This approach is identical with that of the previous law. On the other hand, some legislation provides that arbitral awards can be enforced by virtue of the declaration made by the competent court. (e.g new

German law) It was suggested in drafting the law that the judgment of the court for enforcing arbitral awards is more persuasive to parties than the declaration of the court, though the latter might be more simple and convenient to a party. Regarding the enforcement of arbitral awards the new law contains two separate provisions: one for domestic awards and the other for foreign awards.

Under the arbitration laws of Canadian common law, in all provinces the arbitral award has the same effect between parties as a final judgment of a court. In Schreter v. Gasmac Inc. (1992) the Ontario court held that the previous decision in the Stolp (1930) case denying direct enforcement of a foreign award and requiring a foreign judgment confirming the award, is directly contrary to the Model Law. It continued to state that there is no basis or reason to give further effect to part of the underlying rationale for that decision, the doctrine of merger of the award in a confirmatory judgment. In Murmansk Trawl Fleet v. Bismman Realty Inc. (1994) the court also reinforced that conclusion by declaring that it is not necessary that the award be confirmed in order to be enforceable in Ontario.

However, Quebec law provides that, although an award binds the parties, it cannot be put into compulsory execution until it has been "homologated".

2. Enforcement of Domestic Arbitral Awards (Art. 38)

Under article 38 of the new law the criterion for a domestic award is that the award should be rendered in the territory of Korea. This is a deviation from the position of Model Law and the New York Convention. Irrespective of where the arbitral awards were made, both the Model Law and the New York Convention draw a demarcation line between "international (or foreign)" and "non-international (or domestic)". In consideration of this demarcation line, the definition of domestic arbitration in new Korean law might look outdated. However, there is no substantive difference in practice with whatever demarcation line they have chosen. This is because under the new law both domestic and foreign arbitral awards should be enforced on the same grounds used for refusing the enforcement.

3. Enforcement of Foreign Arbitral Awards (Art.39)

(1) Korea is a contracting party to the New York Convention on the Recognition and Enforcement of Foreign Arbitral Awards. In acceding to the Convention in 1973, Korea made two reservations: it recognizes and enforces only foreign awards made in the territory of other contracting states (reciprocity reservation) and limits the application of the convention to arbitral awards in disputes considered commercial in nature under Korean law (commercial reservation). The new law differentiates between the foreign arbitral awards to which the New York Convention applies and foreign awards to which the convention does not. While a limited number of countries

have not yet ratified the New York Conventions, foreign awards made in the territory of non-contracting countries would be enforced in Korea subject not to the New York Convention but to article 203, 476, and 477 of the Code of Civil Procedure.

As mentioned above, Canada is also a contracting party to the 1958 New York Convention without any reservation on the specific provisions.

(2) The New York Convention reduces the grounds for refusing the recognition and the enforcement of the arbitral award as much as possible and at the same time maintains the effectiveness of arbitration practice. The most intriguing question to foreign practitioners would be how courts interpret the grounds for refusing the enforcement of article V of the New York Convention. Both Canadian and Korean courts are in a position to resist all but the most strongly based arguments against recognition and enforcement of arbitral awards.

There remain two controversial issues in the Korean courts which are briefly examined here.

A. Public Policy of Article V(2) of the New York Convention

Korean courts abide by the spirit of the New York Convention by interpreting the concept of public policy in a very strict manner. Regarding the enforcement of a foreign arbitral award, the Supreme Court of Korea held in the Judgment of 10 April 1990, 89 Daka20252, that the court should take into account the need for the stability of international trade as well as domestic trade in determining whether or not to enforce foreign awards. In this case an arbitral tribunal applied the US prime interest rates which is higher than the English commercial rate. This was against the English law which parties had agreed to apply. It is generally accepted that Korean courts would interpret the notion of public policy by referring to international pubic policy rather than to domestic policy.

Furthermore, the Supreme Court of Korea also held in the Judgment of 14 February 1995, 93Da53054, that even if the rule of foreign law applied in the foreign award is against the domestic mandatory law, the enforcement of the award should be granted unless its enforcement would result in the breach of fundamental social moral conviction. In this case the application of the rule on limitation of period in the Dutch contract law had contravened mandatory rules in Korean contract law.

In a judgment of the Seoul Civil District Court, 30 December 1983, 82 Gahap5372, the court rejected the respondent's argument of the lack of oral hearings on public policy grounds, stating in dictum that public policy grounds for vacating awards should be confined to violation of a nation's constitutional order or fundamental economic regulations. The above-mentioned cases show that courts are reluctant in refusing foreign arbitral awards in any but extreme cases. Therefore, foreign practitioners need probably not concern themselves about the enforceability of foreign arbitral awards in Korea.

B. Procedural Fairness of Article V (1)(b) and (d) of the New York Convention

Under the New York Convention, the enforcement of the foreign arbitral award may be refused if the party against whom the award is invoked was not given proper notice of the arbitral proceedings or was otherwise unable to present the case. This provision allows the forum room to apply its municipal procedural law for the enforcement of foreign arbitral awards. However, Korean courts have also restricted it to fundamental justice rather than applying mandatory rules of domestic procedural law as has been with public policy grounds. In the above-mentioned Judgment of the Supreme Court, 10 April 1990, 89 Daka20252, it was held that the test of fundamental procedural injustice is whether or not the party was seriously deprived of the opportunity to defend himself in arbitral proceedings. In this case, one party argued against enforcing the foreign arbitral award on the grounds of the lack of proper notice of arbitral proceedings.

The Seoul High Court, in the Judgment of 15 March 1995, 94 Nal 1868, also rejected the argument that, since a party did not satisfy the requirement of the discovery procedure under Californian law in which the arbitral award was rendered, the enforcement should be refused on the procedural fairness ground of V(1)(d) of the New York Convention. The court concluded that the breach of discovery procedure does not result in violating fundamental procedural fairness from an international point of view

IV. Conclusion

Both Canada and Korea have now introduced the new arbitration law, which is essentially based on the UNCITRAL Model Arbitration Law, to promote international arbitration practices. They are also in favor of the new arbitration practice and greatly restrict judicial reviews of the arbitral awards. Especially regarding foreign arbitral awards, Korean courts abide by the sprit of the New York Convention by granting the recognition and enforcement in so favorable a manner that foreign practitioners need probably not concern themselves about the enforceability of arbitral awards. However, due to the different legal backgrounds and traditions, the management of the arbitration process and the implementation of the arbitration law might be different. This issue requires further study on the arbitration practice and the courts' position. At present these recent developments in the Korean and Canadian arbitration systems are expected to make both a more attractive place of arbitration for the international community.

IMPLICATIONS OF CANADIAN FILM POLICY FOR THE KOREAN FILM INDUSTRY

SIMON YOUNG-SUK MOON
KANGNAM UNIVERSITY

I. Introduction

Culture is the heart of a nation. Culture provides cohesiveness to a society as well as a sense of national pride and identity. And so, a nation's identity is inseparable from its cultural identity, because the cultural expression of a nation is to maintain sovereignty and a sense of national identity. However, discussions concerning the cultural identity of Canada have been particularly problematic due to the geographical and historical influences of the United States.

Canada's giant neighbor, the United States, has pervaded Canada in many ways, but its greater influence is in the cultural sector. In film particularly, Canada's situation is similar to that of Korea, because the products of Hollywood have also dominated the Korean film industry. However, the trends to open markets and a free trading world are creating both opportunities and challenges for both countries' cultural industries.

How should Canada and Korea respond to the allure of Hollywood and the global markets of keen competition? Under those pressures, how might both countries promote and preserve their own cultural industries? A survey of Canadian film policy might provide a benchmark to guide the Korean film industry into the future.

II. Basic Tenets of Canadian Cultural Policy

Culture is more than a commodity, and in this sense provides Canada with a critical tool in the task of nation building. Canadian culture represents the values that make the country unique from other nations. In this domain, cultural policies emphasize the need to preserve or to invigorate cultural identity, or at least to create an environment in which a distinctive culture can emerge. Such policies are often developed as an antidote to external pressures, and in the case of Canada, these pressures traditionally come from the overwhelming presence of the United States.

Canada has long been played a leading role in cultural policies and has been a strong and persuasive voice in the international community, especially regarding cultural sovereignty. Since the beginning of the twentieth century, Canada was one of the first modern states to recognize that the nation itself could play a significant role in the production of motion-picture images to promote immigration and industrial development.[1] Thus, Canada has a relatively long experience with cultural industries. In the face of American encroachments, Canada was the first North American State to establish a national broadcasting system, modeled on the British Broadcasting Corporation. Michael Roland observes that:

In the Second World War, the National Film Board of Canada grew into one of the major film propaganda factories serving the Allied war effort, its newsreels appearing on thousands of theatre screens across North America (Morris, 1986). The development of Canadian television in the 1950s, particularly in the French language, remains a triumph of technical innovation on a continental scale, as well as an extraordinarily creative use of limited dramatic resources for nation building (See Deutsche, [1961], Laurence [1982], Miller [1987], Rutherford [1990]). Canada would extend its television-signal delivery infrastructure to become one of the most heavily cabled countries in the world (Babe, 1975). Whether one talks about film animation, community radio, educational television, telecommunications development, northern broadcasting, the development of new communications technologies or computer software, the role played by Canadian institutions and firms has been pioneering and consistently innovative, earning a well-deserved and worldwide reputation for technical excellence and high-quality standards.[2]

The goal of the Canadian government's cultural policy is to develop Canadian cultural content and to ensure that Canadian cultural content is available to all Canadians without limiting their access to foreign cultural products. As a result of these policy objectives, Canada has one of the most open markets for foreign cultural goods in the world. While an open market clearly has its advantages, it also creates pressure on local cultural industries, since Canada is a ready market for their cultural goods. While the government does not want to limit access to foreign cultural goods, it wants to ensure that

---

[1] Liss Jeffrey, "The Impact of Globalization and Technological Change on Culture and National Identity: A Call for Visionary Pragmatism," *The Culture/Trade Quandary: Canada's Policy Options*, ed. Dennis Browne (Ottawa: Centre for Trade Policy and Law, Carleton University, 1998), p. 180.

[2] Michael Dorland, "Cultural Industries and the Canadian Experience: Reflections on the Emergence of a Field," *The Cultural Industries in Canada: Problems, Policies and Prospects*, ed. Michael Dorland (Toronto: James Lorimer & Company, 1996), pp. 347-348.

Canadians can experience their own cultural products and that there is a place for them in the Canadian market. Canada ranks among the world's largest per capita consumers of cultural goods, both domestic and foreign, but has been able to make a place for Canadian products in their market without limiting access to cultural products from around the world. Canada supports worldwide trends toward more trade and greater liberalization.[3]

Since the World Trade Organization (WTO) was established in 1995, Canada has been an active participant in international and regional trade negotiations and agreements, such as the North American Free Trade Agreement (NAFTA). Since 1948, when 23 countries first signed the General Agreement on Tariffs and Trade (GATT) instituting the most comprehensive round of multilateral trade negotiations ever undertaken—to be known as the Uruguay Round, markets are becoming more open. Trade barriers have fallen, and under international trade agreements, countries generally agree to grant their trading partners "most favored nation"(MFN) status and treat all of them equally. It means that once trading partners' goods or services have entered their market, members of the agreement must treat them the same as their own national goods and services.

In the General Agreement on Trade in Services (GATS) negotiated during the Uruguay Round of multinational trade talks (1986 to 1994), members did not agree to exempt culture from the agreement but they did allow countries to opt out of MFN obligations and to opt into national treatment obligations. As a result, Canada took a MFN exemption for its film and television co-productions and did not include any commitments for national treatment in the cultural sector. In other words, Canada effectively withheld its cultural policies from the GATS disciplines and maintained its right to promote Canadian cultural services and suppliers. This is consistent with Canadian cultural policy objectives and the view of Canadians that cultural products are not commodities. Under NAFTA, Canada can still continue to support and foster its cultural industries as long as the measures it uses are otherwise consistent with the pre-existing Canada/USA Free Trade Agreement.[4]

Despite shifting mandates and jurisdictional disputes, the federal and provincial governments of Canada have been increasingly involved in cultural matters. Canadian content regulations somewhat limit the play of foreign programs on television, and Canadian stations are permitted to substitute their own signals on cable stations when showing the same

---

[3] See "Canadian Culture in a Global World," in the Cultural Industries Sectoral Advisory Group on International Trade (February 1999). This publication is available on-line at http://www.infoexport.gc.ca.

[4] Ibid.

program as an American station. Only Canadians are allowed to own cable systems or radio or television stations. Canada has developed a policy and regulatory environment that gives Canadians a worldwide choice of cultural products, and still allows Canadians to maintain their cultural identity.

To promote and foster Canadian cultural products, the Canadian government has developed an approach to create and produce domestic content to compete with foreign products. According to this regulation on broadcasting, "all national and regional broadcasters must air a minimum of 50% Canadian content in prime time and 60% overall." [5] Thus, Canada's current policies, which are intended to encourage the creation, production and distribution of Canadian cultural products in the Canadian marketplace, can be grouped into the following "tools."

1. Financial and program incentives
2. Canadian content requirements and other regulatory support mechanisms
3. Tax measures
4. Foreign investment and ownership
5. Measures to protect intellectual property

Such tools to promote or to protect activities in areas defined as Canadian culture have been able to provide policy and regulatory measures that ensure that Canadians have access to the best the world has to offer while preserving a space for Canadian culture.[6]

III. Canadian Film policy

The United States is the world's most successful cultural exporter. Geographical and cultural proximity to the United States and the sharing of a common language makes it very easy for English-speaking Canada to become an extension of the American market and for American cultural products to spill over the border. With regard to cinema, the Massey-Levesque Report pointed out that "most Canadians saw no films except those shown in commercial theatres where little else but Hollywood material was available." [7]

Canada is the largest foreign market for US films. In film and video distribution, an industry with revenues of $1.5 billion, foreign distributors generated 84% of the distribution revenues from the theatrical market from 1990 to 1994, leaving only 16% for Canadian-owned firms. And between 94 and 97% of screen time in Canadian theatres is given over to foreign products

---

[5] *The Guide '98: The Practical Guide to Canada's Film and Television Industry* (Scarborough: Canadian Film and Television Production Association, 1998), p. 57.
[6] See "Canadian Culture in a Global World."
[7] Quoted in *The Culture/Trade Quandary*, p. 28.

in the 1990s.[8] In any given year, the number of foreign films in Canada outnumbers Canadian films 10 to 1.

In fact, such is the Hollywood domination in the Canadian film market, that Telefilm Canada was established as the Canadian Film Development Corporation (CFDC) by an Act of Parliament in 1967 to foster and promote Canadian film industry because "the Canadian market for feature films is small, linguistically divided and film distribution systems in Canada have been controlled for decades in Hollywood."[9] Telefilm Canada, whose purpose is to assist the financing of feature films, has played a vital role in developing a feature film and television industry in Canada. The Canadian Film or Video Production Tax Credit program is designed to encourage a more stable financing environment and longer-term corporate development for production companies.

In 1974, a 100% tax deduction for investment in Canadian film produced a boom in production, but resulted in numerous "tax-shelter films" of dubious worth. It was replaced with a refundable federal tax credit for eligible films and videos in 1995. Telefilm Canada's Feature Film Fund and Feature Film Distribution Fund provided $22 million and $10.3 million respectively to support the film industry in 1996-97. Telefilm also provides a Loan Guarantee Program and a Production Revenue Sharing Program that support television and film production.

Telefilm Canada also invests in the distribution, marketing and subtitling of films produced with its support. It co-ordinates Canada's participation in international film festivals, and administers a program of grants to Canadian festivals. Over the years Canada has signed 39 co-production treaties, in effect in 47 countries. Recognition as a treaty co-production entitles a production to domestic status in each jurisdiction.[10] As a result, the Canadian film and television industry, or so its proponents claim, has grown to over "a-billion-dollar-a-year business".[11] Canada ranks second in the world after the United States in the production of film and television programming.[12]

Considering the size and openness of Canadian market, Canada has developed a relatively strong cultural sector. The success that Canadians have managed to achieve in the competitive Canadian market is due to:

a) The dedication, talent and skills of Canadian artists, creators, producers and distributors, and;

---

[8] See "Canadian Culture in a Global World,"

[9] Quoted in *The Culture/Trade Quandary*, p. 31.

[10] *The Guide '98*, p. 15.

[11] Enchin, Harvey. 1995. "Film Industry Sweeter Than Maple Syrup." *The Globe and Mail*, August 18, B2.

[12] Michael Dorland, "Introduction," *The Cultural Industries in Canada* (Toronto: James Lorimer & Company, 1996), x-xi.

b) The sector's ability to adapt to new technologies which increase its capacity and improve the quality of its products.[13]

If Canadian cinema has always been a marginal cinema-as are all national cinemas in comparison with the Hollywood entertainment machine-it has become an international cinema. By becoming more diversified, Canadian margins are now of greater interest to other nations-especially in Europe.

The Canadian government recognizes that the cultural industry is a important source of employment, revenue and tourism. Alongside the emergence of production companies, Canada has also become an important site for the production of American television programs and feature films. American companies come to Canada to take advantage of a cheap dollar and to use Canadian crews now well trained in their crafts. Especially in the late 1980s and the 1990s, foreign film and television producers, particularly Americans, have used Canada as a production base for many projects. Cities such as Toronto, Vancouver and Montreal actively promote foreign productions, and the federal government and some provinces offer tax credits for on-location production in Canada. British Columbia where, for example, the X-Files was shot, is second only to Ontario as a site for this activity. In 1995, US productions accounted for at least $200 of the $400 million spent in film and television production in the province. The Canadian Film and Television Producer's Association estimates that in an industry worth a total of $2 billion, $700 million comes directly from outside, mostly American sources. The Canadian film industry is now driven by its links to foreign markets: either in the form of "runaway" American productions shot in Canada, or the few Canadian companies that recoup most of their revenue in markets other than Canada.

IV. Korea and the Screen Quota System

South Korea is in a rapid transition as it moves from a government-controlled economic development which was mainly defensive against external pressures, to an open-market economy. Since the Korean economic crisis led to a rescue package from the International Monetary Fund (IMF) in late 1997, Korea has been experiencing a myriad of complex processes of globalization and restructuring of the economy. Under the demands and pressures of the United States and Japan, Korea is rapidly opening its markets in most sectors.

In light of the Korea-U.S. Bilateral Investment Treaty (BIT), the American Film Industry is pressuring the Korean government to abolish the existing screen quota system, which requires all theatres to screen domestic movies for a minimum of 106 days a year. This pressure provoked Korean

---

[13] Ibid.

filmmakers and actors to take to the streets to protest the government's move to reduce the quota requirement. They were worried that their industry would be swept away by foreign films mainly from the United States and Japan. They feel that the Korean film industry is really at a crossroads at this moment.

Korea is a country with one of the most active film industries in Asia. Even though Hollywood films have been dominant for decades on Korean screens, Korea still maintains 25.5% of the overall domestic market share with the remaining 74.5 % going to imported films, of which U.S. films occupied 55% in 1997.[14] However, a series of recently successful Korean films rapidly increased their share of the domestic market. For example, when *Shiri* topped the all-time local box office record (with 2.43 million viewers in Seoul compared to 1.97 million for *Titanic*), in the summer of 1998, the success of Korean films leaped from a 46.5% domestic share to 53% of Hollywood products.

The Korean film industry has survived under a special umbrella of protection offered by the government, but many problems remain:

1. Production: poor finance, concentration of commercialization
2. Distribution Network: lack of screens, poor computerized system
3. Infrastructure: lack of expertise and technical infrastructure
4. International Relations: lack of marketing system
5. Film Education: poor educational facilities and lack of cooperation between production and research
6. Research: lack of research on the promotion and development of domestic film.[15]

There are ongoing arguments over whether Korea's screen quota system should be reduced or not. Supporters for free trade may argue that the screen quota system is a stumbling block of excessive protectionism, and Korean films should able to compete with foreign films in the long run.[16] Opponents warn that "abolition or reduction of the screen quota is tantamount to a death knell for Korea's film industry." [17] Many critics are concerned that the majority of moviegoers, especially young people, will flock to foreign films if the screen quota is reduced.

[14] Joung-Yong Lee, "Canadian Policies on Cultural Industries," *Korean Review of Canadian Studies*, vol. 5 (1999), p. 13.

[15] "Film Development Policy in the Age of Image Culture of 21st Century," The Ministry of Cultural Affairs of Korea and Korean Film Commission jointly held a press conference on March 30, 2000.

[16] Kim Jin-kyoon, "Need to Block 'Monopolization' of Local Movie Market," in *Korea Focus*, vol. 7, no. 1 (1999), p. 144.

V. Conclusion

For decades, the Canadian and Korean film industries were dominated by Hollywood megaton projects with huge budgets and backed by strong distribution networks. But the recent emergence of fresh, young talented artists has produced the invigorating nature of both countries' film industries today and its hopeful possibilities for the future. In today's global market, countries are struggling to sell products that are unique or that have distinct images. Those countries which now dominate the global market not only express various cultural images, but are also continuously creating new ones.

It is time to determine how Canada and Korea should find the balance between cultural policy objectives and open market obligations. As nations, both expect the benefits of an open market, but are concerned about the effect the globalization of trade, combined with rapid technological change, may have on identity as a nation and the sense of cultural community. These concerns are putting pressure on both countries' cultural policies and raising questions. How does a nation continue to nurture its own culture and identity, and still be an active participant in an era of open competition? Over the next few years, Canada and Korea will be involved in major trade and investment negotiations. Protectionism is contrary to the spirit of both GATT and the WTO, and both countries will have to develop a negotiating strategy with the most powerful cultural empire, namely the United States. Hollywood products control some 80 percent of the world film market, which is tantamount to a virtual monopoly.[18] It is in this context that international solidarity should be pursued to prevent an even greater monopoly by the Hollywood Empire. Canada's cultural policies have been constantly revised to adapt to global challenges in meeting rapid technological change, and securing competitive global market shares, and has always been at the forefront of international efforts to liberalize global markets. At the same time, Canada has been a champion of cultural sovereignty and cultural diversity. Once again, Canada has an opportunity to lead the debate.

---

[17] Ibid., p. 143.
[18] Ibid., p. 144.

The Theme of Mutability in Korean and Canadian Poetry: A Comparative Essay

Sung-Il Lee
Yonsei University

I have often wondered why I, a Korean, should be spending so much time and energy reading and writing about English literature. Now, as I have reached my mid-fifties, I have finally come to realize the validity of a non-native speaker of English coping with the difficulties involved in trying to understand a literary tradition which may look alien to anyone whose native tongue is not English. It has taken years of self-denial, as well as self-assertion, for me to come to terms with the apparently unfair ordeal of studying a foreign tongue and the literature in it. But, at long last, I have come to feel, in the deepest core of my heart, that the hardship and pain one must go through in order to understand a foreign literature is none other than an effort to understand fully and relish one's own literary heritage. Only those who have wandered away from home can really appreciate the beauty of their native land. Pain is the sole prerequisite for pleasure, in that sense. And I feel sorry for those who, in the so-called "age of globalization," are willing to forget their own cultural identity and indulge in the self-negating act of underestimating their cultural legacy in favor of whatever is Western and therefore more "advanced," as they see it.

But I am not a specimen of cultural chauvinism. What I aim to achieve in this brief paper is to prove that the East and the West, more specifically Korean literature and Canadian literature, share a common ground in dealing with the perennial subject of time and change. You may call it a comparative study, but only in the sense that I shall try to see the convergence of thoughts and sentiments contained therein, rather than the differences.

Among species blessed with life, only humans are designated with the appellation "mortals." This word indicates that only humans are subject to the occasional onslaught of the thought of mortality. Indeed, the theme of time and change is a universal element in all literature, both of the West and of the East. Life's transitoriness and the transience of worldly glory and pomp have been repeatedly emphasized in innumerable poems. But the poets' goal is not to negate the meaning of the present or the fleeting life. By putting the present in the context of the flow of time, the poets reassert the permanence of the life force and the unchanging cosmic spirit pervading phenomenal nature.

The principle of mutability, observable in human history and its legacy, may lead to a notion leaning toward *contemptus mundi*. But paradoxically it reaffirms the preciousness of the present. Korean poets, of the classical period and of modern times, have left many works containing their thoughts on the vicissitudes of kingdoms and the precariousness of human affairs. What reasserts itself, however, is the realization that life goes on, and phenomenal nature, despite its apparent changes, still retains an unchanging spirit. Several Canadian poets also have perused on the principle of time and change, a principle that pervades not only human life but nature, the milieu of human existence. My essay will reflect an attempt to compare the two nations' poets' views on the mutability of life and nature.

Let me first introduce to you a few Korean poems containing thoughts on mutability:

> The frosty moon shines cold on Swallow Pavilion.
> My friend is gone in a long, weary dream.
> Those who remain have ceased to grumble on growing old;
> Beauties who would entertain them now wear white hair.
> ("The Swallow Pavilion" by Chang Il (1207-1276); my translation)

The poet has returned, after many years, to the pavilion, the seat of pleasure in his youthful days. Although the same moon shines bright, his dear friend is no more around: "My friend is gone in a long, weary dream." Those who are still alive used to grumble on growing old, but not any more: they are resigned to the truth of time and change, and calmly accept it, for even the once beautiful women, who would entertain them, they know, are now wearing white hair. The same message is found in the following poem:

> Thirty springs have passed since I first came here;
> Visiting the site of my first pleasure only grieves my heart.
> In the yard, the pear tree still blossoms,
> But those who sang and danced are gone.
> ("The Pear-Blossom Pavilion" by Shin Cham (1491-1554); my translation)

The above poems are simple statements on the transitoriness of life. They flatly state the irreversibility of the flow of time. In the following poem, however, we find a man who, in spite of his having grown old, still retains a youthful heart and exults in the return of the spring:

> After last night's fog soaked my thatched roof,
> Peach blossoms near the bamboo are suddenly in full bloom.
> Drunk with wine, I forget the white streaks of my hair--
> I stand in the spring breeze, wearing a flowery crown.
> ("On a Spring Day" by Wang Paek (1277-1350); my translation)

Although the poet wrote, "I forget the snowy streaks of my hair," the fact that he wrote the words indicates that he is fully aware of his old age. But he feels exultant, drunk with the vernal spirit, not only with wine. The image of the petals blown onto his white hair explains the poet's being conscious of the apparent incongruity of his feeling stirred up by the advent of spring.

The theme of time and change is applicable not only to an individual's growing old, but, more extensively, to the vicissitudes of kingdoms. A prominent scholar toward the end of the Koryo Dynasty, Yi Saek left the following poem:

> Passing by Yongmyong Temple the other day,
> I ascended to Pu-byok Pavilion.
> The moon was floating above the castle ruin,
> Clouds encircled the moss-grown steps.
> The legendary stallion is gone for ever.
> Where are the successive monarchs loitering now?
> I sigh, standing on the windswept stair--
> The mountains are still green, and the river continues to flow.
> ("At Pu-byok Pavilion" by Yi Saek (1328-1396); my translation)

The poet wrote the work while visiting an old pavilion, where he could see the ruins of a castle built in the ancient Koguryo Kingdom. The moon and the clouds are there, as they have been for countless ages; only "the legendary stallion," the emblem of the ancient dynasty, is gone for ever, never to return. The poet, asking the question *Ubi sunt qui ante nos fuerunt* ("Where are the successive monarchs loitering now?"), contemplates the vicissitudes of fortune, the rise and fall of kingdoms. Only the green mountains and the river remain the same as they were ages ago.

Yi Saek's poem looks back on the prosperity of a dynasty that had preceded the one he lived in. As the flow of time is irreversible, and as time takes its toll as the ultimate equalizer, the Koryo Dynasty had to fall to give rise to a new kingdom, the Choson Dynasty. A poet of the Choson Dynasty, Yi Kyong-min, visited in his turn the site of the once prosperous royal town of the former dynasty, and composed the following lines:

> Now five hundred years of kingly glory is gone,
> Its pomp has left no trace but exuberant pines.
> Upon ruins where flowers have wilted, sadness reigns.
> The nightingale's song deepens pathos over castle grounds.
> Plowed fields encroach the palace stairs;
> Spring grass, undeterred, grows over the railings.
> Though it grieves my heart to watch it,
> Kingdoms rise and fall like a flowing stream.
> ("The Full-Moon Hill" by Yi Kyong-min (1814-1883); my translation)

The time interval between Yi Saek and Yi Kyong-min was about five centuries. But didn't they write poems containing practically the same thoughts and revealing the same sentiments? Time may flow; but the theme of mutability remains immutable.

Noteworthy is the fact that many women writers appeared during the Choson Dynasty. Among them, Hwang Jini (1506-1544), a *kisaeng* (Korean equivalent to Japanese *geisha*), merits special attention for her unusual poetic genius. She left a poem with the same title as the above poem by Yi Kyong-min, "The Full Moon Hill":

> Silence reigns over an old temple by the ruined palace;
> A tall tree in the setting sun makes an onlooker sad.
> Chilly fog spreads--the lingering dreams of the monks;
> On the broken pagoda, time-stacked layers of dust.
> Where a royal bird would soar, nameless birds fly;
> Where azaleas bloom no more, sheep and cattle graze.
> The overlooking mountain may recall pomp and glory.
> Did it know spring would turn quickly into autumn?
> ("The Full-Moon Hill" by Hwang Jini (1506-1544); my translation)

The poem is all the more poignant for the awareness that she is able to express about the transitoriness of life and the ephemerality of her physical beauty. Just as spring turns into autumn, so, she realizes, her life as a *kisaeng* will end when her youth is gone. The poem allows the reader to envision a scene: a young, beautiful woman is standing on the ruins of a palace of the bygone kingdom. With the bleak landscape as a background, there stands a woman in full bloom of her youth, seeing in her mind's eye the pomp and grandeur of the palace that must have stood there. But as she throws the question in the last line-- "Did [the overlooking mountain] know spring would turn quickly into autumn?"--the dreariness of the scene suddenly becomes applicable to herself, for, if a five-hundred-year-old kingdom did fall eventually, the spring of her life would certainly turn quickly into autumn.

Having introduced a few Korean poems originally composed in classical Chinese, I now would like to examine a few Canadian poems that deal with the theme of mutability.

Canada is a relatively young nation. For that reason, one cannot expect to find a Canadian poem on the vicissitudes of kingdoms. However, "the collective consciousness of man," in the term used by Elizabeth Drew, has led Canadian poets to writing on the changes that the flow of time inevitably brings.

The Roman appellation of a poet was *vates* ("the seer"). One who sees the future is also one who has seen the panoramic view of the human drama buried in the past. One who can prophesy is one who has taken the whole picture of human existence into his poetic vision. And at the moments of contemplating the transience of terrestrial existence a poet is granted a comprehensive soul that enables him to see through the meaning of the timeless truth of mortality. Here is a Canadian poem which I have always thought is tangible evidence that a poet is one who, despite the temporal nature of his corporeal existence, can hear the sounds of the past, see those who are no more, and even envision the "pastness" of the present in his mind's eye:

> Underfoot rotten boards, forest rubble, bones. . .
> Animals were here after the plague,
> after smallpox to make another ending:
> for the tutelary gods of decay
> acknowledge aid from any quarter. . .
>
> Here the charging cotyledons of spring
> press green forefingers
> on femurs, vertebrae, and delicate
> belled skulls of children;
> the moon's waylaid light does not shrink
> from bone relics and other beauties of nature. . .
>
> Death is certainly absent now,
> at least in the overwhelming sense

that it once walked at night in the village
and howled thru the mouths of dogs--
But everything fades
and wavers into something else,
the seasonal cycle and the planet's rhythm
vary imperceptibly into the other;
spirits of the dead are vanished,
only great trees remain,
and the birth certificate of cedars
specifies no memory of a village. . .

(And I have seen myself fade
from a woman's eyes
while I was standing there,
and the earth was aware of
me no longer--)
But I come here as part of the process
in the pale morning light,
thinking what has been thought by no one
for years of their absence,
in some way continuing them--
And I observe the children's shadows
running in this green light from
                    a distant star
into the near forest--
wood violets and trilliums of
a hundred years ago
blooming and vanishing--
the villages of the brown people
toppling and returning--
What moves and lives
          occupying the same space,
what touches what touched them
                    owes them. . .
Standing knee-deep in the joined earth
of their weightless bones,
in the archeological sunlight,
the trembling voltage of summer,
in the sunken reservoirs of rain,
standing waist-deep in the criss-cross

> rivers of shadows
> in the village of nightfall,
> the hunters silent and women
> bending over dark fires,
> I hear their broken consonants. . .
> ("Remains of an Indian Village" by Al Purdy, 1962)

I have quoted the poem in its entirety, for, in my judgment, it is a powerful and sublime evocation of the past converging on the present. The sense of guilt that the white men have inherited through generations is there; but the thought which compelled the poet to make these poetic utterances embraces an insight far deeper than the white men's guilt over the brown people's fate. What throws a touch of grandeur upon these lines is the poet's blessed moment of having a glimpse of the timeless truth that nothing remains the same as it is now. Time is the ultimate conqueror, and, no matter what may have happened, the past cannot be revoked. The solemn truth, however, is that the past dictates the present: the remains of an Indian village makes the poet, who lives today, write these lines, and while doing so he can envision the eventual annihilation of his own being, which the poet knows is inevitable "as part of the process" of time:

> (And I have seen myself fade
> from a woman's eyes
> while I was standing there,
> and the earth was aware of
> me no longer--)

What gives the poem such powerful reverberation in the reader's heart is not the time-honored motif of *ubi sunt*, but the acceptance of the past as the past, and the spiritual insight into the timeless truth that life continues, which is evidenced by the fact that the poet, who is mortal, is temporarily granted the privilege to witness the ruins of time, though he himself in due course of time will become its prey. Standing on the ruins of time, while visiting the remains of an Indian village, the poet contemplates on the transience of earthly existence.

While Al Purdy's poem depicts a scene of havoc observable in the ruins of a human community, the following poem by Charles Roberts, a Confederation poet, emphatically stresses the destruction of nature that it inflicts on itself. The picture is that of a wasteland:

On other fields and other scenes the morn
Laughs from her blue,--but not such fields are these,
Where comes no cheer or summer leaves and bees,
And no shade mitigates the day's white scorn.
These serious acres vast no groves adorn;
But giant trunks, bleak shapes that once were trees,
Tower naked, unassuaged of rain or breeze,
Their stern grey isolation grimly borne.

The months roll over them, and mark no change.
But when spring stirs, or autumn stills, the year,
Perchance some phantom leafage rustles faint
Through their parched dreams,--some old-time notes ring strange,
When in his slender treble, far and clear,
Reiterates the rain-bird his complaint.
("Burnt Lands" by Charles G. D. Roberts, 1893)

One may read this poem side by side with Hwang Jini's "The Full-Moon Hill." Both poems present scenery of the devastation that time has brought; but while Hwang Jini's poem is about the destruction of a man-made building, Charles Roberts' poem is about the destruction that perpetuates itself in nature. As in Hwang Jini's poem, the poet, while looking at the bleak landscape, can see in his mind's eye the exuberance of a forest that must have existed before the present devastation occurred. Therefore, he can even hear "some phantom leafage [rustling] faint/ Through their parched dreams," and "some old-time notes [ringing] strange" in the slender treble of the rain-bird. When nature proves herself capable of self-destruction, mutability becomes part of the attributes of all phenomenal nature.

In "Burnt Lands", Charles Roberts saw change at the heart of things. But for some poets, change exists only in the superficialities of appearance. Archibald Lampman, another Confederation poet, thus sought the vision of the true and unchanging reality that lies beneath the surface. In his poetry there are moments of intense experience with nature that provide glimpses of eternal truth:

We have not heard the music of the spheres,
The song of star to star, but there are sounds
More deep than human joy and human tears,
That nature uses in her common rounds;
The fall of streams, the cry of winds that strain

The oak, the roaring of the sea's surge, might
Of thunder breaking afar off, or rain
That falls by minutes in the summer night.
These are the voices of earth's secret soul,
Uttering the mystery from which she came.
To him who hears them grief beyond control,
Or joy inscrutable without a name,
Wakes in his heart thoughts bedded there, impearled,
Before the birth and making of the world.
("Voices of Earth" by Archibald Lampman, 1899)

Here the poet conceives of all the sounds coming from phenomenal nature as manifestations of "earth's secret soul." And whenever he hears them, they reawaken in him the dormant spirit that was embedded in his soul at the moment of his birth, and lead to communion between his soul and the cosmic spirit pervading phenomenal nature. They are moments of sudden revelation and complete fusion of his poetic soul with the *anima mundi*. Certainly, the poet himself is an ephemeral being, an infinitesimal part of the creation; but when there comes a moment of communion between the poet's microcosm and the macrocosm, his soul becomes fully awake. Eternity melts into the soul of a transitory being, a fleeting shadow.

Yu Chi-hwan, whom I consider as the greatest of all twentieth-century Korean poets, shared a similar poetic experience:

Standing on the road where dusk falls,
I feel my eyes being glazed with tears;
But I know my tears are not for sadness.

Looking at the distant mountain fading into dark,
The crescent moon throwing its beams on the road,
And the sunset clouds melting away traceless,
I feel a sudden gush of happiness--
For my being able to see them
And tell what they all mean;
Therefore, I weep for joy and gratitude.

Standing in the dusk gradually spreading,
I feel my eyes being glazed with tears;
But I know my tears are not for grief.

As the glow of the setting sun lingers above the hill
And the sound of the evening bell is spreading far,
I weep for joy and gratitude--
For being blessed with life prostrate in prayer.
("Standing in the Dusk" by Yu Chi-hwan (1908-1967); my translation)

Mutability is a cosmic law. Not only human existence but nature herself is subject to it. But in spite of the demise of an individual, the withering of a plant, the species live on, while the grand cosmos remains immutable, unfolding only a small portion of its secrets to all transitory earthly beings. Yu Chi-hwan's tears of gratitude for being blessed with life, no matter how transitory it may be, come from the realization that a moment in one's life is linked to eternity, that the present stands for the perpetuity of lifeforces which transcends the phenomenal manifestation of time and change.

In an attempt to prove that poetry reveals a universal paradigm of the collective consciousness of man, I have read with you a few poems by Korean and Canadian poets which treat the theme of mutability. There are three stages of the poets' coming to terms with the truth of time and change: expressing personal grief over loss of dear ones and lamenting the swift flow of time; expanding the theme of mutability to the whole of creation, as well as human affairs in general, and embracing it as a cosmic principle; and finally, attaining spiritual awakening to the truth of the perpetuity of life and the immutability of the cosmic scheme. Perhaps it is a futile attempt to compare two apparently heterogeneous literary traditions, such as Korean and Canadian literature. But the few poems I have examined are enough to prove that, despite differences in culture and verbal media, poets have sung the same songs--in different notes and keys, but on the same theme.

NOTE; The Korean poems quoted in this essay are from:
   The Moonlit Pond: Korean Classical Poems in Chinese. Translated and introduced by Sung-Il Lee. Port Townsend: Copper Canyon Press, 1998.
   The Wind and the Waves: Four Modern Korean Poets. Translated and introduced by Sung-Il Lee. Berkeley: Asian Humanities Press, 1989.

AFTERWORD

WHITHER NORTH KOREA? SOME REFLECTIONS ON THE DEMOCRATIC PEOPLE'S REPUBLIC OF KOREA

DONALD S. RICKERD
YORK UNIVERSITY-UNIVERSITY OF TORONTO
JOINT CENTRE FOR ASIA PACIFIC STUDIES

Almost a century before the Cold War extended its tentacles to so many locations around the world, a small, mountainous peninsula in North East Asia had, for a number of geopolitical reasons, become a focal point for Great Power rivalry. Korea's complex early history is one of perseverance and, ultimately, survival in the face of so many confrontations with Mongols, Chinese, and Japanese over the centuries. In more modern times, and partly as a result of better transportation and communications, it was once again involved in the competitive struggles of imperial powers such as Russia, Japan, Britain, France, Germany, and the United States. And then, after agonizing decades of occupation by Japan, and at a time when so many other countries were experiencing the exhilaration of liberation at long last, Korea found itself in the throes of a sad fate for any people, that of being divided internally into two states, two states united by history, family ties, language, customs, and geography, yet two states separated by conflicting national philosophies, a fortified border, hostile superpowers, and, most tragically of all, family divisions.

While it is tempting to delve deeply into the origins of the present unfortunate situation, time limitations are such that I will confine my remarks today mainly to the current situation in North Korea, with some limited reference to the few decades which lead up to this new Millennium.

An English schoolboy was once asked to delineate the differences between geography and history, and, after careful thought, he summed it up nicely by saying, "Geography is about maps; history is about chaps!" Nowhere in the world are geography and history melded together more completely than in Korea. With such powerful neighbours on its doorstep such as China, Russia, and Japan, and with the United States playing a crucial role in its projection of military power across the Pacific, the Korean Peninsula is buffeted from all sides, just as if it were an island. Truly, its geography has been, in many ways, its history. (I should note, in passing, that a powerful Korea itself has had very expansive periods, at times controlling what are now adjacent areas of China and south along the coast, possibly with a presence as far as some Indonesian islands, according to recent archaeological finds.)

In 1945, the Soviet Union turned its attention to the War in the Pacific only after its titanic struggle with Germany had ended in victory. While there is speculation as to how much Stalin knew about the atomic bomb, he did decide to attack Japan in the last few days of the Second World War and thus secured very considerable Soviet gains in the resulting series of settlements in Asia after the Japanese surrender.

Not the least of these gains was the ability to play a role in the complex activities on the Korean Peninsula where the 38th Parallel formed a dividing line for occupying forces from the USSR and the US, prior to what was expected to be an early reunification of the country. Soon the US withdrew most of its military forces, as did the USSR from the North.

On January 12, 1950, Dean Acheson, in a famous speech to the National Press Club in Washington, did not include Korea within the so-called U.S. defence perimeter or area of concern and there was much speculation as to the implications of this omission. On June 25, the Korean War broke out. Most of us are familiar with the outbreak of that war, although the Democratic People's Republic of Korea (DPRK) today stoutly maintains that it was caused by an attack from the South, while it is our Western belief that it was a well-prepared, well thought out attack from the North. The role of the UN forces under General Douglas MacArthur, the see-saw nature of the conflict, plus China's intervention, eventually led to the sad stalemate that persists today, almost fifty years later.

As a student in England, I participated in a seminar given by Capt. Basil Liddell Hart, the brilliant military strategist whose ideas on tank warfare led, perversely, to the amazing successes of the German panzer divisions. Recently my son gave me a copy of the new biography of Liddell Hart by Danchev. As I opened it, my eye fell on a photograph of Liddell Hart in 1948 with a globe of the world on his desk. He had just been asked what he thought the most likely location was for the start of another World War. His index finger is clearly pointing to the Korean peninsula!

Well, what is happening on the Korean Peninsula today, especially in the DPRK, and why are the stakes so high?

I believe that we are seeing a fascinating process unfolding, a process whose elements are only now becoming clear.

We are seeing interwoven factors coming together in a way that can be either:

a) the ultimate laying to rest of one of the last relics of the debilitating Cold War, or,

b) a flashpoint for an explosion which could have consequences too tragic to contemplate.

From the perspective of Pyongyang, what are the current factors that have come into play?

1. a tiny peninsula with a total population of about 68 million people crowded into a mountainous land, 22 million in the DPRK and 46 million in the Republic of Korea.

2. a rift (that has now lasted over half a century) in an ethnically extremely homogenous country.

3. a legacy of tensions amongst the Great Powers over Korea. (This, of course has been the fate of other countries, too, and one has only to think of the tragic history of Poland, of Turkey and the Dardanelles, and of Belgium.)

4. the withdrawal of support for the DPRK, which had come to depend economically on both China and the USSR.

5. a confidence in two Great Leaders, father and son, that borders on the absolute.

6. the continued presence of US troops in South Korea, augmenting the military forces of the Republic of Korea.

7. years of famine, resulting in what has been estimated at up to several million starvation-related deaths plus related shortages of foreign exchange, oil, electricity, and productive capacity.

8. surprising advances in North Korea in both the nuclear and missile fields.

9. changing concepts of sovereignty which differ from those held in most of the rest of the world.

Of these, I will argue, the changing concepts of sovereignty issue may well be an extremely important one and I would like to come back to it shortly.

Most of the other factors are self-explanatory although I propose to comment briefly on several.

The rift in such a small country has produced sad results quite apart from the Korean War. Even up to a few decades ago, North Korea was more prosperous that the South, possessing as it does remarkable natural resources and heavy industry. Precise statistics are lacking, but now its production is a tiny fraction of that of the South. But the greatest human tragedy is that of divided families, which, for decades, have been unable to communicate with each other. Now, they don't know whether their relatives are alive or dead. The border, or DMZ, is almost impenetrable.

North Korea, like Cuba, became very dependent over the years, on many forms of assistance from the USSR. It also had support from China. The collapse of the USSR was a severe jolt and then came the shock of the PRC's recognition diplomatically of South Korea, the archenemy. The North's economy, already almost stagnant, began to crumble at an alarming rate.

The fanaticism in North Korea I spoke of focuses on the deceased Great Leader, Kim Il-sung, and now on his son-successor, Kim Jong-il. This succession from father to son marks the first such succession in the communist world. The reverence and adulation for the two is, to a foreigner, quite amazing as an example of the personality cult writ large. Statues, memorials, and tributes of all kinds, testify to the worship of the founder of the country. Every aspect of life is related to the Great Leader-his inspiration, his advice, his wisdom, all form the basis of education, the arts, sports, music, sculpture, and national destiny. An unquestioning loyalty is drummed into people at every turn. Coupled with an almost complete blackout of information from outside North Korea, the result has been a near hypnosis of the entire population.

Whether a stabilizing influence or a destabilizing one, the presence of 37,000 US troops in South Korea is a potent factor in the complex mix of issues in Korea today. The force is an easy target for North Korean invective, but it does signal a solid US commitment to the integrity of the Republic of Korea. The latter is aware of its vulnerability to a surprise attack from the North, especially as Seoul, a huge city of about 10 million people, is so close to the DMZ that most of it is within range of the North's long range artillery. Recently the argument has been made in some quarters that, with a population double that of the North and an economy many, many times larger, the South should be able to cover its own defence needs. But to do so might require a major expansion of its military from about 625,000 to 1.25 million, if it were to match the North in numbers. That comparison may be very misleading, however, since much of the North's air force, navy, and command systems is well out of date and badly hampered by fuel shortages. The transportation infrastructure is decades out of date as is the communications system. Not surprisingly, the DPRK has made the withdrawal of US troops one of its main foreign policy objectives in negotiations, even while apparently arguing that their presence brings means of stability to an otherwise very volatile area. It is only very recently that South Korean analysts have started to speculate about the implications of an American withdrawal.

The famine in North Korea has been devastating. Floods, followed by unusual droughts, have been catastrophic for crops. But the rigidly planned economy, inefficient transportation system, lack of refrigeration, and many other factors have exacerbated the deadly situation. The loss of up to 2.5 million people and the malnutrition of millions more have combined to cause the whole economy to plummet into a disastrous spiral and an embarrassing dependence on foreign aid. This is especially important in a country whose cornerstone philosophy is "juche", or self-reliance, a country which dropped Soviet-style Marxism-Leninism from its constitution only a couple of years ago.

But despite everything, despite disasters which for a time convinced many in the US and the ROK that the DPRK regime was in danger of imminent collapse, some positive steps have been taken and I must confess I am increasingly impressed by how skillfully North Korea has played an unbelievably weak hand. What has been accomplished?

There are three major defence concerns that confront countries today:

i)   nuclear weapons.
ii)   biological and chemical weapons of mass destruction.
iii) missiles which can carry nuclear and other weapons of mass destruction.

In 1994, the US became extremely alarmed about reports that the DPRK was actively developing a nuclear capability. Indeed there are some unconfirmed reports that, as discussions were scarcely advancing at all with the North, the US was actively planning to take unilateral steps, the details of which have never been revealed, to counter the developments in the North.

After intense bargaining in Geneva, negotiations did ultimately lead, however, to a settlement, the so-called Agreed Framework of 1994. In return for a pledge to halt its nuclear work, the DPRK obtained a commitment to the construction by KEDO, the Korean Energy Development Organization, of two light water nuclear reactors, 500,000 tons of oil p.a., a lifting of sanctions and the reciprocal opening of liaison offices in Pyongyang and Washington. The agreement is an interesting one as the reactors will cost an estimated $4.5-$5.1 billion (US) to construct, and South Korea, in order to play the major role, undertook, prior to the Asian financial crisis, to provide the lion's share of the huge cost.

Halting nuclear activity was a great accomplishment and no proof has been given of any violation of the Agreement by the North, although monitoring has been somewhat difficult. Unfortunately, the oil deliveries have lagged as a recalcitrant US Congress has not provided adequate funds for oil purchases and shipments, thus forcing the US administration to seek foreign financial support for the oil. The critical path plan for the light water reactors has fallen far behind schedule, and the US has not eased economic sanctions nor have liaison offices been opened.

The overall result has been a DPRK belief that the Framework has not been adhered to although it stopped its nuclear work. The feeling of being surrounded by hostile forces, of being victimized, of being unfairly dealt with, has been greatly increased.

The DPRK then skillfully played on American fears that it had broken the Agreed Framework by constructing a major underground facility north of Pyongyang. The North Koreans are expert tunnellers and, according to Western experts, have an enormous number of underground sites throughout the country, safe from the eyes of satellite photography. Meeting American demands to inspect the new facility with skillful negotiating, the DPRK watched the issue spiral almost out of control before demanding a large payment (some have suggested food aid in the equivalent of $300-million) for the right to inspect. The anti-climax was that no nuclear evidence was found by the US inspection teams and the DPRK pocketed the proceeds and proceeded on its unique way.

Secondly, in August 1998, the DPRK launched a rocket whose trajectory took it over Japan. It was either a missile test, according to most sources, or a communications satellite, according to the DPRK. It clearly caught the US and Japan by surprise as their sophisticated tracking equipment did not reveal clear data on the event. The DRPK claimed it was a success, though Western devices could not locate it in orbit. No matter what it was, the launch produced an incredible response, a response that was in many ways an indicator of how faulty the North's reasoning was and how counter-productive its actions were. The Japanese immediately took countermeasures-halting charter flights, threatening to block transfer of funds, reconsidering light water reactor funding, and re-examining Constitutional provisions limiting Japanese rearmament.

The US, too, saw a firestorm in Congress where threats were made to break the Agreed Framework which, by the way, had said nothing about banning missile tests. A stoppage of food aid was advocated, new equipment was air-lifted to the US forces in South Korea, and tensions mounted, fueled by several Republican Congressmen who made policy on North Korea their special focus.

President Clinton, wishing to maintain the Agreed Framework and thereby to continue the halt to nuclear programmes in North Korea, appointed a former Secretary of Defence, William Perry, to conduct a review of US policy towards North Korea.

The Perry Report has been made public, but only in part. It is a thoughtful document, calling for a dual track policy-a carrot and stick approach. It focuses on the nuclear freeze, advocating gradual sanction lifting, and the opening of liaison offices in both capitals. It goes on to call for a very firm response if cooperation is not forthcoming, a response closely coordinated with Japan and South Korea. The details of that line of response are still secret. Rather interestingly, the US appears to have consulted closely with China, seeking the latter's efforts to reason with North Korea. China seeks stability on the Korean Peninsula, too, but it is very dubious how much real influence the PRC has on North Korea at this time.

Thirdly, with the PRK having in a sense done so well on each of the nuclear and missile issues, is it at all unlikely that the next round of tensions will involve the issue of chemical and biological weapons of mass destruction? Surely this is a card that the DPRK, beset with so many problems, is likely to play in the future.

But one factor I feel is underlying much tension is that of changing concepts of sovereignty.

Even within living memory, the concept of sovereignty was one of a virtually absolute series of rights. Occasional international treaties were signed which may have infringed on a nation's sovereignty to a limited extent, but, more recently, national sovereignty in many countries has been "eroded" to a remarkable extent. Nowhere is this more evident than in the United Nations framework and in the European Union. Canada, too, has entered into many agreements which limit our own national sovereignty and you can all think of examples. The United States has been somewhat more reluctant to limit its national sovereignty, sometimes for constitutional reasons, sometimes out of distrust of international organizations.

Professor Josef Joffe of Stanford has said "in international politics, no concept is less understood and more misused than sovereignty." Joffe concurs with Stephen Krasner's new book "Sovereignty: Organized Hypocrisy" in distinguishing carefully between domestic and international legal sovereignty. This issue of sovereignty is a complex one and I am of the opinion that what we are seeing in Korea is a classical, dysfunctional confrontation, pitting two time-related definitions of sovereignty against each other. Leaving aside for the moment the "rights" and "wrongs" of the situation, it is revealing to analyze the position of the two protagonists. We are all familiar with the ancient doctrine which holds that sovereignty involves the fullest rights, extending, classically, from the center of the earth to the furthest heavens. While that has been greatly modified over the years, mostly by international agreements, the DPRK's position is very similar to commonly shared definitions of sovereignty from decades ago. Many other countries, including the ROK, Japan, the US, and Canada, have adopted evolving definitions of sovereignty, based on more modern international legal principles, UN discussions, etc. Thus, in a sense, the DPRK, which lives a uniquely isolated existence, is caught in a legal time warp, professing a doctrine which has been relegated to history by much of the rest of the world.

The US, Japan, and South Korea were extremely distressed by the firing of the North Korean missile, while the North Koreans see it as an act their sovereignty fully justifies. Any retreat, they say, would be an infringement on their sacred, sovereign rights. This is a very deep-seated belief, a fundamental in North Korean policy, are for which the population is willing to make extreme sacrifices. Intense negotiations have been taking place in an effort to halt the DPRK tests. Interestingly, during the course of the negotiations, the DPRK reportedly said it would halt testing if the U.S. would do the same. Agreement was finally reached a few months ago in Berlin that no further DPRK tests would take place, at least while negotiations were continuing for a permanent halt.

Many issues bedevil attempts to reach agreements concerning the Korean Peninsula. The US continues to label the DPRK as a terrorist or rogue state and the DPRK continues to utilize very shrill language. Elections in both Japan and the United States have had outcomes which have altered Japanese and American policies towards the DPRK.

Well, what are Canadians to make of this complex, volatile situation? How can one best analyze a situation that has defied some of the world's most dedicated internationalists for decades? Is there any role that Canada could, or should, play?

I'd like to look at a limited number of issues that bear directly on those questions.

1.   The plight of North Korea Today

The DPRK is in dire straits, to put it mildly. Its problems go a long way to explaining its stance on so many issues. In today's world, it is the ultimate closed society. Joachim Gauck, Germany's federal commissioner for the Stasi files, has said: "Under totalitarianism people don't want to know the facts, because it's more important to know the opinions of the rulers than to know reality, so step by step the importance of factual truth is eroded and lost." This observation certainly applies in the DPRK today. The DPRK's inability to feed its people may well be a permanent phenomenon, partly because of the limited availability of arable land in such a mountainous country. Only through food donated from, or purchased from, abroad can the DPRK bridge the gap of several million tons of grain per year. The UN and the World Food Program note that "donor fatigue" is setting in and almost no foreign exchange is available. The DPRK appears to be in default on about $12-billion of foreign debt. Almost no foreign exchange can be earned as there is so little to export. Many factories are closed, severe drought has cut hydroelectric generating capacity, many trains are not running, little heat or light is available, and people in the countryside are frantically foraging for food and firewood. A terrible tragedy has overtaken a talented people who have been committed to a regime, many of whose principles are totally out of step with the rest of the world in the year 2000.

2.   What effect is this tragedy having?

Imagine for a moment that we are trying to advise North Korea on what to do to extricate itself from its present dilemmas. Because of the rigidity of the system it is impossible for a public, or even a private, non-official, debate to take place on what courses of action are possible. Whatever solution there is must emanate from Kim Jong-il and his close advisors and this, of course, limits the possibility of innovative solutions emerging from a wide ranging debate.

Food shortage, power shortage, little light, almost no heat, foreign debt, closed factories, a huge military, hostile neighbours, the list goes on.

The tragedy has taken its toll on a proud Korean people who have had to launch:

- Appeals for food aid from abroad to save the lives of the starving
- Appeals for medicines and supplies for the sick and especially for infants and children

3.   Are there any hopeful signs, and, if so, what can Canada do to assist?

There are a number of hopeful signs and I am relatively optimistic about some of them, although, to alleviate human suffering, time is of the essence.

i)   President Kim Dae-jung of South Korea will undoubtedly press ahead with his **"sunshine policy"** or opening to the North. He has warned of the likelihood of many rebuffs along the way, but pledges to stay the course. The first North-South Summit took place in Pyongyang, a surprisingly modern city, and, one might assume, a reciprocal visit to Seoul may well have been pledged. The DPRK approached the Summit with much inflammatory language, thus justifying some observers' speculation that Korean history has been noted for the rapid escalation of crises rather than the utilization of confidence - building measures, Track Two diplomacy, and a general desire to lower tensions. Pyongyang stated that "at the request of President Kim Dae-jung he will visit Pyongyang" for the Summit, and North Korea "will demonstrate the superiority of the DPRK in the eyes of all Koreans living in the South and abroad. ... The side that is morally weaker and that committed so many crimes against its own nation must kowtow before the real and only leader of all Koreans."

ii)   The Republic of Korea has substantially modified its views and policies on reunification, now being fully aware of the unbelievable costs the Federal Republic of Germany has incurred in absorbing the former German Democratic Republic. In practice its current goal is coexistence rather than reunification as before.

iii) TMost European Union countries, Canada, Australia and others have opened diplomatic ties with the DPRK. Canada has had a very low-key exchange of officials with the DPRK, a first step in re-building a relationship.

iv)   International food aid is arriving and this has brought several hundred foreigners into the DPRK, where none were permitted before. Some, especially the World Food Program officials, have indicated that they are now permitted to monitor food distribution in most, but not all, of the country.

v)   The Hyundai Chair and founder, Mr. Chung, who was born in the North, has developed the popular tours to sacred Mount Kumgang, negotiated for factories in the North, sent sports teams to play, and donated many head of cattle to the DPRK.

vi)   Some small initiatives are proving successful. The Nautilus Institute of California has set up demonstration wind power generators in the DPRK and a Canadian company is building a small number of prefabricated houses. A Canadian basketball team has visited. Roger Clinton, the President's half-brother, was in Pyongyang with a rock group while I was there.

vii) William Perry visited the DPRK in preparing his Report and a Vice Foreign Minister from the DPRK negotiated to visit Washington.

viii) Four Power Talks involving the two Koreas, the PRC and the US are under way.

I am a strong advocate of Canada moving forward, step by careful step, in its recognition of the DPRK and of the establishment of normal diplomatic relations. My reasoning centres on several considerations:

Firstly, as long as we remain isolated from the DPRK, Canada can have little or no influence on that country and its involvement in the North Pacific security situation.

Secondly, Canada now has the assurance of President Kim of South Korea that his country's policy is to encourage other countries to engage the DPRK in constructive dialogue.

Thirdly, we have the opportunity to play at least a continuing humanitarian role with a country that appears to harbour no negative feelings towards Canada and its participation in the 1950-3 conflict.

Fourthly, I do not agree with those who say there are few prospects for trade with the DPRK, and therefore we should ignore that country. A review of other countries with which Canada has diplomatic ties reveals some very dubious regimes.

And finally, I believe that Canada could make a clear statement that it is fully prepared to engage in working towards a solution of one of the world's most difficult international problems. We have to remind ourselves - we Canadians are good at diplomacy, we Canadians have had successes before, we're untarnished in the eyes of both South and North. We have a role to play!

I believe Canada's whole-hearted, even-handed participation would be welcomed by Canada's substantial Korean-Canadian population. Paul Evans recently wrote a perceptive article for the Toronto *Globe and Mail*, advocating a somewhat similar point of view on recognition. The Council on Foreign Relations in New York recently published the Report of its Task Force on the Korean Peninsula, a balanced booklet, which looks at the problem from a moderate American perspective and there are several other sound publications now available on this complex subject. Gradually, the general public is becoming aware of the changing situation on the Korean Peninsula. It will soon see what, if any, progress is being made in relations between the ROK and the DPRK. If it looks carefully it will see a people, both North and South, who are positioned to play a major role in both Asia and the world, a people who have exceptional discipline and pride, extraordinary willpower, and a history of overcoming all challenges. Canada should be ready to help in the process.